A BAPTIST
TREASURY

This is a volume in the
Arno Press collection

THE BAPTIST TRADITION

Advisory Editor
Edwin S. Gaustad

See last pages of this volume
for a complete list of titles.

A BAPTIST
TREASURY

COMPILED AND EDITED BY

Sydnor L. Stealey

ARNO PRESS

A New York Times Company
New York • 1980

Editorial Supervision: Steven Bedney

———

Reprint Edition 1980 by Arno Press Inc.

Copyright © 1958 by Sydnor L. Stealey

Reprinted by permission of Mrs. Jessie Wheeler Stealey

THE BAPTIST TRADITION

ISBN for complete set: 0-405-12437-6
See last pages of this volume for titles.

Manufactured in the United States of America

———

Library of Congress Cataloging in Publication Data

Stealey, Sydnor Lorenzo, ed.
    A Baptist treasury.

    (The Baptist tradition)
    Reprint of the ed. published by Crowell, New York.
    1. Baptists--Addresses, essays, lectures.
I. Title. II. Series: Baptist tradition.
[BX6215.S76 1980]   286.1   79-52607
ISBN 0-405-12472-4

A BAPTIST TREASURY

A BAPTIST TREASURY

COMPILED AND EDITED BY

Sydnor L. Stealey

THOMAS Y. CROWELL COMPANY

Established 1834 • *New York*

ACKNOWLEDGMENTS

Sincere gratitude is hereby tendered to the following, who have kindly granted permission to reprint from their copyrighted materials:

The Broadman Press, Nashville, *What Is the Church?* edited by Duke K. McCall.

Colgate Rochester Divinity School Bulletin, December 1938 issue, "Why I Am a Baptist" by Walter Rauschenbusch.

Harper & Brothers, *Prayers for Daily Use* by Samuel H. Miller.

The Judson Press, *Baptist Confessions of Faith* by W. J. McGlothlin.

The Kingsgate Press, London, *The Life and Faith of the Baptists* by H. Wheeler Robinson and *The Mistery of Iniquity* by Thomas Helwys.

Benjamin E. Mays, "Christian Light on Human Relations."

Arnold Ohrn, Secretary of the Baptist World Alliance, addresses in the *Official Reports,* Baptist World Congresses.

Culbert G. Rutenber, "The Totalitarian State and the Individual."

The Sunday School Board of the Southern Baptist Convention and the Broadman Press, "Have Faith in God" by Baylus Benjamin McKinney.

The Virginia Baptist Board of Missions and Education, *The Baptists of Virginia* by Garnett Ryland.

The Westminster Press, *Experiments of Spiritual Life and Health* by Roger Williams, edited by Winthrop S. Hudson.

The executors of T. P. G. Whitley, the Baptist Historical Society, and the Cambridge University Press, *The Works of John Smyth,* edited by W. T. Whitley.

In a few cases, such as the selections from John Smyth, Thomas Helwys, and Roger Williams, we have presumed to modify some spelling and punctuation. Otherwise we have tried to follow the text accurately.

Preface

The hope of helping many of the almost twenty million Baptists in North America to know more about their history and their faith and practices has long challenged me. During my ten years in seminary classrooms, I worked as diligently as I could (what with all the extracurricular duties that beset the modern seminary teacher) at learning and then helping others to learn the history of all Christian people and particularly the history of Baptists. Two things especially I tried to do: first, show our deep ties with other evangelical Christians and, second, discern and evaluate our own distinctive truths. Then followed seven years of heavy responsibilities as an administrator in a new and rapidly developing seminary. Because of this I may have lost a large part of what I had learned, but certainly none of my desire to help Baptists know more about themselves.

When such a book as this was proposed by the publisher, some of my friends suggested me for the editorship. When they and others agreed to help I ventured, without proper modesty, I fear, to try it. I knew that there were others much better qualified for the work, but I *wanted* to do it, and so bade modesty be down. If this effort proves of value, perhaps better men will be induced to follow it with better collections.

The selections have been made with average Baptist pastors and church members in mind. I know that scholarly historians will not be benefited, unless the book prove worthy of their recommendation to beginning students. The chief criterion for selecting has been to try to help the average reader discourse intelligently on "Why I Am a Baptist." Therefore, the essay by Walter Rauschenbusch was the very first choice. I was delighted when I found the old pamphlet by John A. Broadus on "The Duty of Baptists to Teach. . . ." The convictions, especially that concerning believers' baptism, that motivated our founding fathers in England and America have, I believe, an unquestionable place; therefore John Smyth, Thomas Helwys, and Roger Williams. Spurgeon on believers' baptism would also probably be agreed upon by all, and most people would agree that a few confessions of faith and a catechism should be included; but after these the decisions were indeed difficult. Times of internal or external tension reveal much, so I have included a summary of the debate on the ordinances (on the Kiffen-Bunyan debate), the debate between Calvinism and Arminianism (John Gill and Andrew Fuller), and an example of the contention that develops so often between conservatives and progressives (John Clifford's "The Great Forty Years"). William R. Williams was chosen for his beauty of style and his adept handling of a phase of the Catholic question. Benjamin Mays superbly represents his race and thinks clearly on racial issues. In each selection I saw something that I believed would enlighten the average reader whom I had in mind. With some of the older sources I have taken a few liberties with the phrasing, spelling, and punctuation in order to help readers who are not acquainted with the old forms.

It is most likely that I would change some selections if I had another year to consider values. It was agony not to include something from Balthasar Hubmaier, Isaac Backus, John Jasper, J. G. Oncken, Alexander Maclaren, and at least a dozen others.

Limitations of space have required that we shorten many selections and leave out sections of others. We have tried, however, to give the essence of each—for example, of Dr. Truett's address on religious liberty. We believe the average reader will appreciate more such selections than the fewer that could otherwise have been given.

The very few selections from living writers are chosen because they deal with live questions now deserving careful Christian thought, not in order to present biased views of the editor. In the main, our purpose has been to present selections demonstrating particular Baptist principles and emphases.

I have been greatly aided by the suggestions of Winthrop S. Hudson, Robert G. Torbet, Miss Mary Christian, James E. Tull,

Pope A. Duncan, Marc A. Lovelace, John W. Eddins, and John E. Steely. Professor Steely sought out and typed many of the sources. My secretary, Mrs. Earline C. Brett, typed faithfully and urged continually. The responsibility for errors in form or judgment are mine alone. I must take responsibility also for the decision to use longer and fewer selections. My part of the work is lovingly dedicated to the millions of Baptists who give us preachers the grandest opportunity preachers have ever had to tell the deep truth about life, and to Jessie.

S. L. S.

CONTENTS

———————◆◆◆———————

ix

I

BAPTIST BEGINNINGS

———◦∽◦———

JOHN SMYTH (c. 1568-1612)

JOHN SMYTH *is generally acknowledged to be the father of modern Baptists. We know nothing of his parentage or childhood but we do know that he graduated from Cambridge University and served as Fellow until 1600. This was a restless age in England. Puritanism was striving to gain control of the state church, and Separatists and others were pushing more radical causes. Smyth was ordained in the Church of England and served her as a lecturer in Lincoln from 1600 to 1602, but his mind was deeply religious and inquisitive. By 1606 he had joined the Separatists and became their pastor in Gainsborough, near Scrooby, the home church of our American Pilgrim Fathers.*

Persecution struck under James I, and Smyth's church, including Thomas Helwys, followed other Separatists to Amsterdam in Holland. There his thought progressed until, in 1609, he became convinced of baptism for believers only. He baptized himself (by affusion) and all the others. They then formed the first English Baptist Church. Tension had already developed between Smyth's church and the other Separatists. Strong controversy now broke out. Smyth's writings reveal the strong feelings between him and protagonists of many other religious views.

Smyth soon felt that he had erred in starting a new church when his views were found to be similar to Mennonites whom he met in Amsterdam. He and about thirty others applied for membership in a Mennonite church. Thomas Helwys and ten others believed he was falling again for apostolic succession and a bad theology, and they broke with him and returned to England to establish the first Baptist church on English soil.

Smyth's mind was restless, but essentially spiritual and reasonable in spite of some bitter writing, so characteristic of the times. Our selections from among his many writings illustrate both sides of his nature. Like Roger Williams in America, he was a pathfinder. We owe him much, even if his path differs occasionally from our present Baptist highway.

Introduction to *The Character of the Beast,* entitled "The Epistle to the Reader"

To Every One That Loveth the Truth, Salutations:

It may be thought most strange that a man should oft times change his religion, and it cannot be accounted a commendable quality in any man to make many alterations and changes in such weighty matters as are the cases of conscience, but if constancy be commendable in anything, it is religion. And if inconstancy be worthy reproof in matters of inferior estimation, it is much more blamable in matters of salvation in respect whereof the wisest and most religious men have been always most constant in their profession and faith. And inconstant persons cannot escape the deserved imputation of folly or weakness of judgment therein.

This must needs be true (and we confess it) if one condition be admitted, that the religion which a man changeth be the truth. For otherwise to change a false is commendable, and to retain a false religion is damnable. For a man of a Turk to become a Jew, of a Jew to become a Papist, of a Papist to become a Protestant are all commendable changes though they all of them befall one and the same person in one year, nay if it were in one month. So that not to change religion is evil simply, and therefore that we should fall from profession of Puritanism to Brownism to true Christian baptism is not simply evil in itself, except it be proved that we have fallen from true religion. If we, therefore, being formerly deceived in the way of Pedobaptistry, now do embrace the truth in the true Christian Apostolic baptism, then let no man impute this as a fault unto us.

This, therefore, is the question: whether the baptism of infants be lawful, yea or nay; and whether persons baptized, being infants, must not renounce that false baptism and assume the true baptism of Christ, which is to be administered upon persons confessing their faith and their sins, this being the controversy now betwixt us and the Separation commonly called Brownists. For the glory of God, the manifesting of the truth to our nation and the destruction of the man of sin, we have thought good to publish this present treatise wherein the whole cause is handled. Let the indifferent reader judge of the whole and give sentence without partiality and I doubt not but he shall be constrained to give glory to God in acknowledging the error of baptizing infants to have been a chief point of Antichristianity and the very essence and constitution of the false Church, as is clearly seen in this treatise.

Now happily some man will wish that the controversy had been with the Rabbis of the Separation and not with Mr. Clifton whom they calumniate as being a weak man, unable to deal in so great a controversy. Well, let the reader take notice, that although it be Mr. Clifton's pen yet it is not Mr. Clifton's cause and defence, but his allegations and reasons are the best plea of the greatest Rabbis themselves; and if they think that they can say better they may now speak. For by publishing answers to their reasons we do challenge all the Separation in special to the combat.

Be it known therefore to all the Separation that we account them in respect of their constitution to be as very an harlot as either her Mother England or her grandmother Rome is, out of whose loins she came. And although once in our ignorance we have acknowledged her a true Church, yet now, being better informed, we revoke that, our erroneous judgment, and protest against her, as well for her false constitution as for her false ministry, worship and government. The true constitution of the Church is of a new creature, baptized unto the Father, the Son, and the Holy Ghost. The false constitution is of infants baptized.

We profess, therefore, that all those churches that baptize infants are of the same false constitution, and all those Churches that baptize the new creature, those that are made disciples by teaching, men confessing their faith and their sins, are of one true constitution. And, therefore, the Church of the Separation, being of the same constitution with England and Rome, is a most unnatural daughter to her mother England and her grandmother Rome, who, being of the selfsame genealogy and generation, . . . she dare, notwithstanding, most impudently wipe her own mouth and call her mother and her grandmother adultresses. Herein, therefore, we do acknowledge our error [Before he separated from the Pedobaptist Separatists.—Ed.] that we, retaining the baptism of England which gave us our constitution, did call our mother England a harlot and upon a false ground made our separation from her.

For, although it be necessary that we separate from England, yet no man can separate from the baptism of England, which giveth England her constitution; and whosoever doth retain the baptism of England doth withal retain the constitution of England and cannot, without sin, call England a harlot as we have done. And this we desire may be well minded of all that separate from England; for if they retain the baptism of England, viz., the baptism of infants as true baptism, they cannot separate from England as from a false Church, though they may separate for corruptions. And whosoever doth separate from England as from a false Church must needs separate from the baptism of England, as from false baptism. For the baptism of England cannot be true and to be retained and the Church of England false and to be rejected. Neither can the Church of England possibly be false except the baptism be false, unless a true constitution could be in a false Church, which is as impossible as for light to have fellowship with darkness. It is impossible that contraries should both be true and so it is impossible that a false Church should have a true constitution or a true baptism. . . .

But the Separation they say England hath a false constitution and is a false Church, to be separated from. And yet they say also: England hath a true baptism (that is, a true constitution) which is not to be separated from. For a true constitution and true baptism are one and the same thing; so is a false constitution and a false baptism; so that the speeches and actions of the Separation are contradictory in this particular.

Finally, they that defend the baptism of infants cannot with any truth or good conscience separate from England as from a false Church, though they may separate for corruptions. And they that separate from England as from a false Church must of necessity separate from the baptism of England and account the baptism of infants false baptism. Therefore, the Separation must either go back to England or go forward to true baptism; and all that shall in time to come separate from England must separate from the baptism of England, and if they will not separate from the baptism of England there is no reason why they should separate from England as from a false Church. . . .

Now concerning this point of baptizing infants, we do profess before the Lord and before all men in sincerity and truth that it seemeth unto us the most unreasonable heresy in all Antichristianity. For, considering what baptism is, an infant is no more capable of baptism than is any unreasonable or insensible creature. For baptism is not washing with water; but it is the baptism of the Spirit, the confession of the mouth, and the washing with water. How then can any man without great folly wash with water, which is the least and last of baptism, one that is not baptized with the Spirit and cannot confess with the mouth? Or how is it baptism if one be so washed? Now that an infant cannot be baptized with the Spirit is plain, I Peter 3:21, where the Apostle saith that the baptism of the Spirit is a question of good conscience unto God; and Heb. 10:22, where the baptism which is inward is called the sprinkling of the heart from an evil conscience.

Seeing, therefore, infants neither have an evil conscience, nor

the question of a good conscience nor the purging of the heart—
for all these are proper to actual sinners—hence it followeth that
infants' baptism is folly and nothing. Again, John's baptism was
the baptism of repentance. Infants have not repentance, and
therefore cannot have the baptism of repentance. That infants
cannot have repentance is evident, seeing repentance is knowledge of sin by the Law, sorrow for sin by the Gospel, mortifica-
tion of sin and new obedience, all which are as much in the basin
of water as in the infant baptized.

Now I confess the Pedobaptists have many shows of reason
for the maintenance of their heresy, and one man shapeth them
into one form, another man into an other, as every man's wit
and learning teacheth him, but indeed they are all built upon the
same sandy foundations, the wresting of some places of Scripture. . . .

Now, because men call for antiquity, and except they see antiquity they will not believe, though the Scriptures be most
ancient, I have thought good, therefore, to propound two pregnant testimonies of antiquity . . . against baptism of infants that
men may know that this truth also hath her footsteps among
the Fathers. . . .

Here follows a quotation from Tertullian's work on baptism
against Quintillian and one from Eusebius' *Ecclesiastical History*, Book 10, Chap. 15.—Ed.

And thus much for the testimonies of antiquity, which hereafter shall be produced more plentifully upon further occasion
offered if the Separation or any other dare adventure the trial of
the matter out of antiquity. . . .

Howsoever it be, we profess our time and readiness to employ
our time and cost for the manifestation of the truth and we desire the Separation that they will not in craftiness withdraw
from the combat, as hitherto they have done in the matter of
translation, worship and the Presbytery; but we require them in
the fear of the Lord that, seeing they have suffered so much for
the truth, as they profess, they would not now subtly (being
guilty in their consciences of their disability to defend their er-

rors) draw back and pretend excuses as they do; but we require them, nay we charge them, yea we challenge them to the defence of their errors.

Lo, we protest against them to be a false Church falsely constituted in the baptism of infants and their own unbaptized. We protest against them to have a false ministry of Doctors or Teachers. Finally, we protest against them that, seeing their constitution is false, therefore there is no one ordinance of the Lord true among them. These things we have published, and of these things we require an answer. For we proclaim against them as they proclaim against their own mother England [Church of England.—Ed.]: That the Separation, the youngest and fairest daughter of Rome, is an harlot; for as is the mother, so is the daughter.

Now furthermore, we desire the Separation and all them that they would not impute unto us untruths and condemn the innocent without cause. For we disclaim the errors commonly but most slanderously imputed unto us. We are indeed traduced by the world as Atheists by denying the Old Testament and the Lord's Day, as traitors to magistrates in denying magistracy, and as heretics in denying the humanity of Christ.

Be it known therefore to all men: first, that we deny not the scriptures of the Old Testament, but with the apostles acknowledge them to be inspired of God, and that we have a sure word of the prophets whereunto we ought to attend as unto a light shining in a dark place, and that whatsoever is written aforetime is written for our instruction that we through patience and comfort of the scriptures might have hope, and that we ought, as Christ counselleth, to search the scriptures of the Old Testament as the men of Berea did, because that in them we may find everlasting life, and that they do testify of Christ. This we believe according to these scriptures: John 5:39; Acts 17:11; Romans 15:4; II Timothy 3:16; II Peter 1:19. Yet, nevertheless, we affirm all the ordinances of the Old Testament, viz., the Church, Ministry, Worship and Government of the Old Testament, to be abolished, all which were types and shadows of God's things to come, but the body is in Christ. Colossians 2:14-17, 20.

Secondly, we acknowledge that according to the precedent of Christ's Disciples and the primitive churches, the saints ought upon the first day of the week, which is called the Lord's Day, Revelation 1:10, to assemble together to pray, prophesy, praise God, and break bread and perform other parts of spiritual communion for the worship of God, their own mutual edification, and the preservation of true religion and piety in the church. And that we might be better enabled to the aforesaid duties, we ought to separate ourselves from the labors of our callings which might hinder us thereto; and that according to these scriptures: John 20:19; Acts 2:1, 41, 42 and 20:7; I Corinthians 16:1.

Thirdly, concerning magistrates, we acknowledge them to be the ordinances of the Lord that every soul ought to be subject unto them; that they are the ministers of God for our wealth; that we ought to be subject unto them for conscience' sake; that they are the ministers of God to take vengeance on them that do evil; that we ought to pray for them that are in authority; that we ought not to speak evil of them that are in dignity, nor to despise government, but to pay tribute, toll, custom, etc.; and that according to these scriptures: Romans 13:1-7; I Timothy 2:2; I Peter 2:13-15; II Peter 2:10. But of magistrates converted to the faith and admitted into the church by baptism, there may many questions be made, which to answer neither will we if we could nor can we if we would. When such things fall out [come to pass.—Ed.], the Lord, we doubt not, will direct us unto the truth concerning that matter. In the meantime, we are assured according to the scripture that the kings of the earth shall at the length bring their glory and honor to the visible church, Revelation 21:24.

Finally, concerning the flesh of Christ, we do believe that Christ is the seed of Abraham, Isaac and Jacob, and of David, according to the prophecies of the scriptures, and that He is the Son of Mary, His Mother, made of her substance, the Holy Ghost overshadowing her. So have other children their bodily substance of their parents. Also (we believe) that Christ is one person in two distinct natures, the Godhead and the manhood, and we detest the contrary errors. Our grounds of scripture are these:

Genesis 22:18; 26:4 and 28:14; Psalms 132:11 compared with
Acts 2:30; Romans 1:3 and 4; Hebrews 1:8-10 and 2:11, 14, 16.

Briefly to conclude, let the Separation be advertised: That
whereas they do so confidently, through their self-love and self-
conceit, fill their mouths with heresy and heretics as if thereby
they would fear babes, that herein they tread in the steps of all
Antichristians, their predecessors. Do not the Papists call the
Protestants (Lutherans, Calvinists, Zwinglians, Church of England) heretics and call for fire and fagot? Do not the Protestants
call the Separation schismatics and heretics and judge them
worthy of the gibbet? Not the affirmation of men without proof,
but the evidence of wilful obstinacy in error maketh men heretics. And let them take heed that they, notwithstanding their
sirens' songs, prove not cages full of most ugly and deformed
Antichristian heretics.

Thus, desiring the Separation not to be wise in their own eyes
through pride, but to become fools in order that they may be
made wise through humility, and desiring the forwardest preachers and professors of the English nation well to weigh what is
the true constitution of the church, I cease, wishing the light and
love of the truth to every one that readeth.

Selections from his *Retraction and Confirmation*

(*The Last Book of John Smyth Called the Retraction of
His Errors, and the Confirmation of the Truth* is the full
title of this work.)

I am not of the number of those men which assume unto themselves such plenary knowledge and assurance of their ways, and
of the perfection and sufficiency thereof, as that they perempto-
rily censure all men except those of their own understanding,
and require that all men upon pain of damnation become subject
and captivate in their Judgment and walking to their line and
level; of which sort are those our English nation who publish in
print their proclamation against all churches except those of their
own society and fellowship. I mean the double separation Mas-

ter Hainsworth [Ainsworth] and Master Helwys, although the one more near the truth than the other.

Neither is my purpose in this writing to accuse and condemn other men, but to censure and reform myself. If I should walk with either of the double separation, I must from the persuasion of mine own alone perfect reformation reprove all other, and reject them as short of that mark whereto I were come, and I must shut my ears from hearing any instruction which others may afford me; for this is the quintessence of the separation, to assume unto themselves a prerogative to teach all men and to be taught of no man. Now I have in all my writings hitherto received instruction of others, and professed my readiness to be taught by others; and therefore have I so often times been accused of inconstancy. Well, let them think of me as they please. I profess I have changed, and shall be ready still to change for the better; and if it be their glory to be peremptory and immutable in their articles of Religion, they may enjoy that glory without my envy, though not without the grief of my heart for them.

The Articles of Religion which are the ground of my salvation are these, wherein I differ from no good Christian: That Jesus Christ, the Son of God and the Son of Mary, is the anointed King, Priest and Prophet of the Church, the only mediator of the New Testament, and that through true repentance and faith in Him Who alone is our Savior we receive remission of sins and the Holy Ghost in this life, and therewith all the redemption of our bodies and everlasting life in the resurrection of the body. And whosoever walketh according to this rule, I must needs acknowledge him as my brother; yea, although he differ from in divers other particulars.

And howsoever in the days of my blind zeal and preposterous imitation of Christ I was somewhat lavish in censuring and judging others, and namely in the way of separation called Brownism, yet, since having been instructed in the way of the Lord more perfectly, and finding my error therein, I protest against that, my former course of censuring other persons, and especially for all those hard phrases wherewith I have in any of my writings inveighed against either [the Church of] England or the separation. For England, although I cannot with any good conscience acknowledge the wicked ones mingled with the zealous professors in one congregation to be the true, outward, visible church which Christ and His Apostles at the first instituted, which consisted only of penitent persons and believers; yet therefore to say that the zealous professors themselves are Antichristians, is a censure such as I cannot justify before the Lord who is my Judge in my conscience. And therefore I utterly revoke and renounce it.

Again, howsoever I doubt not it is an error of the forward professors of the English churches to be mingled with the open wicked in the supper of the Lord, as they daily are, seeing therein they do transgress the first institution of Christ, who ate his supper only with eleven (for Judas departed so soon as he had received the sop of the Passover), yet I cannot therefor conclude the said forward professors under the same judgment, or fellowship, of sin with the wicked ones with whom they partake the supper. Yea, rather, I do also renounce that evil and perverse judgment which I have pronounced in my writings in this particular acknowledgement of my error therein. . . .

I retract not for that it [his bitter censures against individuals] is wholly false, but for that it is wholly censorious and critical, and for that therein the contention for outward matters, which are of inferior note, hath broken the rules of love and charity, which is the superior law.

Now for the Separation, I cannot, nor dare not in my conscience before the Judge of the whole world, justify my writings and dealings against them. For the truth of the matter, I doubt not but it is on my side; but the manner of writing is that alone wherein I have failed. For I should have with the spirit of meekness instructed them that are contrary minded, but my words have been stout and mingled with gall. And therefore hath the Lord repaid me home full measure into my bosom, for according to the measure wherewith I measured hath it been measured again to me, by Master Clifton, especially by Master Ainsworth and Master Bernard. The Lord lay none of our sins to the charge of any of us all, but He of His mercy pass by them. For my part, the Lord hath taught me thereby; for hereafter shall I set a watch before my mouth that I sin not again in that kind and degree.

[Smyth then treats some of the differences between himself and Thomas Helwys, who separated from him in Holland and returned to England to establish the first Baptist church there.]

———————•⟨∞⟩•———————

THOMAS HELWYS (d. 1614?)

JOHN SMYTH's *church of baptized believers, established in Holland, was the first Baptist church whose history we can now trace, but Thomas Helwys led the first Baptist church on English soil. A man of some wealth and position, he had followed Smyth's thought and travels from Anglicanism and England. When Smyth sought fellowship with the Mennonites, Helwys and about a dozen others sorrowfully separated from their leader in 1612 and returned to London and persecution. He died probably in jail, about 1614. His little book,* The Mistery of Iniquity *(Rev. 13), is not great writing nor great theology, but in it a rugged layman bares his soul as he vigorously attacks Romanism, kingly presumption in religion, Puritanism and Separatism and demands religious liberty (for the first time in England) and believers' baptism. The copy he presented to James I carries a penned inscription and is preserved at Oxford. The inscription well summarizes his views on religious liberty, and our other selection illustrates his style and his protests against pedobaptism in general.*

The inscription (uncorrected):

> Heare o King, and dispise not ye counsell of ye poore, and let their complaints come before thee.

The King is a mortall man, and not God therefore hath no power over ye immortall soules of his subjects, to make lawes and ordinances for them, and to set spiritual Lords over them.

If the King have authority to make spirituall Lords and lawes, then he is an immortall God, and not a mortall man.

O King, be not seduced by deceivers to sin so against God, whome thou oughtest to obey, nor against thy poore subjects who ought and will obey thee in all things with body life and goods, or else let their lives be taken from ye earth.

God Save ye King

Tho: Helwys.

Spillefeild
    neare London

Selections from *The Mistery of Iniquity*

The text of The Mistery of Iniquity *has been slightly amended. Note emphasis upon believers' baptism, which was the real reason Baptists withdrew from Separatists, Puritans, Anglicans, Catholics and all others. Infant baptism was an important mark of the beasts in Rev. 13, which Helwys identified as the Roman Church, and those who followed her.*

•

And now let the covenant of the lord stand firme and good against al the adversaries thereof, which Covenant is, they which believe & are baptized, shal be saved, the words whereof being spoken by him that made it, do with authority convince to the consciences of all that will hear them, that this covenant is made onely with them that are beleeve [believers] and are baptized, which is with them that [are] of the faith of Abraham. Rom. 4:12-16. And not they that are of the Flesh of Abraham: there are (saith the apostle) Children of the Flesh, and Children of the promisse, but the Children of the promisse are counted for the seed. Rom. 9:8. How ignorant and obstinate are men become,

whom no word of God can persuade, but they wil have the
Children of the Flesh to be the Children of the promisse, and
the seed: for they will have the seed of the faithful, that is, al
the Children begotten off their bodies, to bee the Children of
the promisse, and seed with whome the Covenant is made, saying: the Covenant is made with the faithful and their seed, meaning all the Children begotten of the Flesh; yet the apostle saith,
the Children of the flesh are not the seed, but the apostels testimony will not serve the turne, the Pope saith it is not so. And
the Bishops and Presbitary (having learned it of the Pope) say
it is not so. And the Brownists (having learned it of the Bishops)
say it is not so. There are manie witnesses, and they have long
and ancient custome, and the script is faire to looke upon, and
pleasant to the eie and mynd, that infants are begotten and borne
Christians. The most wicked and prophane parents that are like
this way, that they may be accounted to beget Christians and
that their children may be made members off the body of Christ
when they are new borne. The best men like this way; and
the worst like it. . . . This pleaseth al Flesh in these parts of the
world. There was never anie one doctrine of Christ, nor of the
apostles that ever was so acceptable to all men. It must needs be
acceptable, because so good a thing is so easily come by. What
a grevious thinge would it bee if one might not bee a Christian,
and a member of Christs body, before they had learned Christ,
and to believe in him. This would trouble Children if they
should bee forced to learne to knowe Christ before they could
be admitted to bee his Disciples, and to be Baptized, and this
would bee a great trouble to parents that their Children should
not be baptized before they had carefully brought them up in
the instruction and information of the Lord, and this would bee
a great burden to Bishops and Priests, if they should have none
admitted members of their Church, until by their diligent and
faithful preaching of the gospel, they were brought to knowledge, faith, and repentance, and to amend their lives and bee Baptized. If these old doctrines of Christ and his Appostles should
now be put in practice it would trouble and offend all the world,
being so contrary to custome, and Counsels, and affections off

men. O crooked and foolish generation, how long shal the Lord beare with you, how long shall he suffer you. Will you make the way broad and wide which he hath made strait and narrow? Wil you stil walke in the traditions of men after the lusts of your owne harts and treade his statutes under your feet? Shal the long evil custome, and the false testimony of men, agreable to your owne affections, overthrowe the divine and true witness of our Lord Christ and his Apostles? Doth our Saviour Christ say that those with whome he hath made the new Covenant are they in whose mynds and harts he hath written his Law, whome hee declares to be those, that believe and are baptized? And will you add unto the covenant of the Lord and say, it is made with the faithful, and their seed before they can beleeve? And doth the apostle say, that the seed to whome the promisse is made are they which are off the faith off Abraham not they that are of the flesh of Abraham and wil you say, that they that are of the flesh of the faithful, are the seed with whome the Covenant is made? Can you devise in your harts more directly to oppose the Lord and falsifie his truth then ye do herein? . . . Oh consider this and forget not God. What shal it profit you to have your infants washed with water and a few words, whereby the name of the Lord is blasphemed, and you perish for so prophaning his Ordinance? The infant is never the better, it shal not be saved thereby, and there is no such obedience required at your hands. Let the word off the Lord be your guide in these things, and not the word of man nor long custome, although it be in a thinge that is most pleasing to your carnal mynds.

ROGER WILLIAMS (c. 1603-1683)

THE FIRST LEADER *of Baptists in America can hardly be called the "father" of American Baptists because Baptists of other kinds than his Particular or Calvinistic sort appeared independently in other colonies. However, Roger Williams did first set up in America the absolute ideals of religious freedom and the separation of church and state, and these became a part of the American heritage. He was born in England and well educated there (Cambridge) before being ordained by the Church of England. However, his Puritan leanings were discovered by James I's watchdogs and he was "harried out of the land." He arrived in Massachusetts in 1631 and, finding the Separatists at Salem nearest to his mind, he settled there.*

Soon his radical ideas of fair dealing with the Indians and on the separation of church and state got him in trouble with the Boston authorities. He was banished in January 1636 and passed fourteen weeks of bitter hardships in midwinter among Indian friends. In the spring he settled at what is now Providence, R. I., attracted friends from Salem, and set up there a government claiming authority "only in civil things." *His constant concern with religious matters soon led him to the Baptist position on believers' baptism and he was baptized by Ezekiel Holliman whom he then baptized, with ten others, and formed the first Baptist church on American soil. His restless mind, ever seeking perfection, soon became dissatisfied with this church and he became a Seeker for the rest of his life—waiting for God to reveal His perfect will.*

Williams was long thought to have been primarily interested in political theory, but recent studies reveal that his ideas on government stem from his deepest interest in religion and especially in spiritual freedom. This impelled him to write many volumes protesting persecution of religious minorities. His Bloudy Tenent of Persecution for Cause of Conscience *is the most famous of these. His* Experiements of Spiritual Life and Health *shows his deep interest in spiritual matters, therefore we reproduce excerpts from it. Also famous was his* A Key into the Language of America, *the first attempt of an Englishman to produce a dictionary of an Indian dialect. All his life and writings show the unconditional character of God's claim upon his life.*

The Bloudy Tenent of Persecution for Cause of Conscience

LIST OF PROPOSITIONS DISCUSSED IN THE WORK

First, That the blood of so many hundred thousand soules of Protestants and Papists, spilt in the Wars of present and former Ages, for their respective Consciences, is not required nor accepted by Jesus Christ the Prince of Peace.

Secondly, Pregnant Scripturs and Arguments are through-out the Worke proposed against the Doctrine of persecution for cause of Conscience.

Thirdly, Satisfactorie Answers are given to Scriptures, and objections produced by Mr. Calvin, Beza, Mr. Cotton, and the Ministers of the New English Churches and others former and later, tending to prove the Doctrine of persecution for cause of Conscience.

Fourthly, The Doctrine of persecution for cause of Conscience, is proved guilty of all the blood of the Soules crying for vengeance under the Altar.

Fifthly, All Civill States with their Officers of justice in their respective constitutions and administrations are proved essentially Civill, and therefore not Judges, Governours or Defendours of the Spirituall or Christian state and Worship.

Sixthly, It is the will and command of God, that (since the coming of his Sonne the Lord Jesus) a permission of the most Paganish, Jewish, Turkish, or Antichristian consciences and worships, bee granted to all men in all Nations and Countries: and they are onely to bee fought against with that Sword which is only (in Soule matters) able to conquer, to wit, the Sword of Gods Spirit, the Word of God.

Seventhly, The state of the Land of Israel, the Kings and people thereof in Peace & War, is proved figurative and ceremoniall, and no patterne nor president for any Kingdome or civill state in the world to follow.

Eighthly, God requireth not an uniformity of Religion to be inacted and inforced in any civill state; which inforced uniformity (sooner or later) is the greatest occasion of civill Warre, ravishing of conscience, persecution of Christ Jesus in his servants, and of the hypocrisie and destruction of millions of souls.

Ninthly, In holding an inforced uniformity of Religion in a civill state, wee must necessarily disclaime our desires and hopes of the Jewes conversion to Christ.

Tenthly, An inforced uniformity of Religion throughout a Nation or civill state, confounds the Civill and Religious, denies the principles of Christianity and civility, and that Jesus Christ is come in the Flesh.

Eleventhly, The permission of other consciences and worships then a state professeth, only can (according to God) procure a firme and lasting peace, (good assurance being taken according to the wisedome of the civill state for uniformity of civill obedience from all sorts.)

Twelfthly, lastly, true civility and Christianity may both flourish in a state or Kingdome, notwithstanding the permission of divers and contrary consciences, either of Jew or Gentile.

CHAPTER XXXIX
. . . . .

. . . True it is, the Sword may make (as once the Lord complained, Isa. 10.) a whole Nation of Hypocrites: But to recover a Soule from Sathan by repentance, and to bring them from Antichristian doctrine or worship, to the doctrine or worship Christian, in the least true internall or externall submission, that only works the All-power-full God, by the sword of the Spirit in the hand of his Spirituall officers. p. 136

CHAPTER LVII
. . . . .

. . . From this perverse wresting of what is writ to the Church and the Officers thereof, as if it were written to the Civill State and the Officers thereof; all may see how since the Apostacie of Antichrist, the Christian World (so called) hath swallowed up Christianity, how the Church and civill State, that is the Church and the World are now become one flocke of Jesus Christ; Christs sheepe, and the Pastors or Shepherds of them, all one with the severall unconverted, wilde or tame Beasts and Cattell of the World and the civill and earthly governours of them: The Christian Church or Kingdome of the Saints, that stone cut out of the mountaine without hands, Daniel 2. now made all one with the mountaine or Civill State, the Roman Empire, from whence it is cut or taken: Christs lilies, garden and love, all one with the thornes, the dangers and wildernesse of the World, out of which the Spouse or Church of Christ is called, and amongst whom in civill things for a while here below, she must necessarily be mingled and have converse, unlesse she will goe out of the World (before Christ Jesus her Lord and Husband send for her home into the Heavens, I Cor. 5:10.) p. 175

CHAPTER XCII
. . . . .

. . . a People may erect and establish what forme of Government seemes to them most meete for their civill condition: It is evident that such Governments as are by them erected and established, have no more power, nor for no longer time, than the civill power of people consenting and agreeing shall betrust them with. This is cleere not only in Reason, but in the experience of all commonweales, where the people are not deprived of their naturall freedome by the power of Tyrants. pp. 249 f.

Marks of Spiritual Life and Health

> (Williams followed each Mark with a few paragraphs of comments)

I. MARKS OF SPIRITUAL LIFE

THE FIRST MARK: God's Children cry unto God as to a Father.
A SECOND MARK: God's Children Long for More and More Knowledge of God.

A THIRD MARK: God's Children Hunger and Thirst after God's Word.

A FOURTH MARK: God's Children Have a True Desire to Know and to Do God's Will.

A FIFTH MARK: God's Children Cannot Live in Known Sin without Struggling and Mourning.

A SIXTH MARK: A True Child of God Is Tender of God's Name.

A SEVENTH MARK: A True Child of God Is Patient Under the Rod of His Heavenly Father.

AN EIGHTH MARK: God's People Long After God's True Worship.

A NINTH MARK: God's Children Have No Peace in Sin Unrepented of.

A TENTH MARK: Another Sort of God's People Long for the Grace They See in Others, Though Wanting in Themselves.

II. MARKS OF SPIRITUAL HEALTH

THE FIRST MARK: God's Children Ought to Walk in Constant Amazedness of Spirit as to God, His Nature, and Works.

A SECOND MARK: The Glorifying of God is the Great Work of God's Children.

A THIRD MARK: Delightful Privacy with God Argues Strong Affection.

A FOURTH MARK: Frequent Prayer an Argument of Much of God's Spirit. True Prayer Is the Pouring Out of the Heart to God. God's Children Are Most in Private with God. The Prayers of God's People Most Respect Spiritual mercies. God's People Wait for and Rest in God's Answer.

A FIFTH MARK: God's People Are Sensible of Their Unworthiness.

A SIXTH MARK: God Himself Regarded as the Portion of His People. . . . "as the hart panteth after the water brooks. . . . Ps. 42:1 . . .

A SEVENTH MARK: Ready Obedience to God.

AN EIGHTH MARK: The Patience of God's Children Under God's Hand.

A NINTH MARK: The Mournful Confession of God's People.

A TENTH MARK: God's People Long After God in an Open Profession of His Ordinances.

AN ELEVENTH MARK: Their Hearts Are Ready and Prepared.

A TWELFTH MARK: God's People's Sense of Their Own Insufficiencies.

MATTERS CONCERNING OURSELVES

THE FIRST MARK: Brokenness of Spirit.

A SECOND MARK: Spiritual Battles.

A THIRD MARK: Godly Loathing for Sin.

A FOURTH MARK: True Self-denial.

A FIFTH MARK: Willingness to Stay in Hard and Difficult Service.

A SIXTH MARK: Spiritual Contentment in God's Will.

A SEVENTH MARK: Joy in Sorrow.

AN EIGHTH MARK: Christian Weaned from This World's Comforts.

A NINTH MARK: God Glorified in All Earthly Business.

A TENTH MARK: The True Watch of God's People Over Their Tongue.

AN ELEVENTH MARK: God's Children Shun the Appearance of Sin.

A Ship at Sea—Liberty of Conscience

There goes many a ship at sea with many hundred souls in one ship, whose weal and woe is common and is a true picture of a commonwealth, or human combination of society. It hath fallen ₂out some times that both Papists and Protestants, Jews and Turks may be embarked in one ship; upon which supposal I affirm, that all the liberty of conscience that ever I pleaded for, turns upon these two hinges—that none of the Papists, Protestants, Jews or Turks be forced to come to the ship's prayers or worship nor compelled from their own particular prayers or worship, if they have any. I further add that I never denied, that notwithstanding this liberty, the commander of this ship ought to command the ship's course, yea, and also command that justice, peace, and sobriety, be kept and practiced, both among the seamen and all the passengers. If any of the seamen refuse to perform their services, or passengers to pay their freight; if any refuse to help in person or purse toward the common charges or defense; if any refuse to obey the common laws and orders of the ship concerning their common peace or preservation; if any shall mutiny and rise up against their commanders and officers; if any should preach that there ought to be no commander or officers, no laws, nor orders, nor corrections, nor punishments;—I say, I never denied but in such cases, whatever is pretended, the commander, or commanders may judge, resist, compel and punish such transgressors, according to their deserts and merits.

WILLIAM CAREY (1761-1834)

WILLIAM CAREY, *"the father of the modern mission movement," needs little introduction to Baptists. Shoemaker, humble pastor, self-taught scholar, pioneer missionary, extraordinary linguist, benefactor of India, he exemplifies Christian vision, consecration and achievement. With Andrew Fuller, who "held the rope" in England while Carey labored in India, he contributed immeasurably to the break-up of the rigid Calvinism of the John Gill school. The pamphlet we present was first published in 1792 and, along with his famous sermon of May 31, 1792, on Isaiah 54:2-3, brought about the formation of the Baptist Missionary Society at Kettering on October 2, 1792. He led in establishing Serampore College (India) in 1810. It is still one of Asia's great schools. He died in Serampore.*

From *An Enquiry*

An
ENQUIRY
into the
OBLIGATIONS OF CHRISTIANS,
to use means for the
CONVERSION
of the
HEATHENS
in which the
Religious state of the different nations
of the world, the success of former
undertakings, and the practicability
of further undertakings, are considered.
By William Carey

For there is no difference between the Jew and the Greek; for the same Lord over all, is rich unto all that call upon him. For whosoever shall call upon the name of the Lord shall be saved. How then shall they call on him, in whom they have not believed? and how shall they believe in him of whom they have not heard? and how shall they hear without a Preacher? and how shall they preach except they be sent?

PAUL

LEICESTER:

Printed and sold by Ann Ireland, and the
other Booksellers in Leicester; J. Johnson,
St. Paul's Church yard; T. Knott, Lombard
Street; R. Dilly, in the Poultry, London,
and Smith, at Sheffield.
(Price One Shilling and Six-pence)
MDCCXCII

INTRODUCTION

As our blessed Lord has required us to pray that his kingdom may come, and his will be done on earth as it is in heaven, it becomes us not only to express our desires of that event by words, but to use every lawful method to spread the knowledge of his name. In order to this, it is necessary that we should become, in some measure, acquainted with the religious state of the world; and as this is an object we should be prompted to pursue, not only the gospel of our Redeemer, but even by the feelings of humanity, so an inclination to conscientious activity therein would form one of the strongest proofs that we are the subjects of grace, and partakers of that spirit of universal benevolence and genuine philanthropy, which appear so eminent in the character of God himself.

Sin was introduced amongst the children of men by the fall of Adam, and has ever since been spreading its baneful influence. By changing its appearances to suit the circumstances of the times, it has grown up in ten thousand forms, and constantly counteracted the will and designs of God. One would have supposed that the remembrance of the deluge would have been transmitted from father to son, and have perpetually deterred mankind from transgressing the will of their Maker; but so blinded were they, that in the time of Abraham, gross wickedness prevailed wherever colonies were planted, and the iniquity of the Amorites was great, though not yet full.

After this, idolatry spread more and more, till the seven devoted nations were cut off with the most signal marks of divine displeasure. Still, however, the progress of evil was not stopped, but the Israelites themselves too often joined with the rest of mankind against the God of Israel. In one period the grossest ignorance and barbarism prevailed in the world; and afterwards, in a more enlightened age, the most daring infidelity, and contempt of God; so that the world which was once overrun with ignorance, now by wisdom knew not God, but changed the glory of the incorruptible God as much as in the most barbarous ages, into an image made like to corruptible man, and to birds,

and four-footed beasts, and creeping things. Nay, as they increased in science and politeness, they ran into more abundant
and extravagant idolatries.

Yet God repeatedly made known his intention to prevail finally over all the power of the Devil, and to destroy all his
works, and set up his own kingdom and interest among men, and
extend it as universally as Satan had extended his. It was for this
purpose that the Messiah came and died, that God might be just,
and the justifier of all that should believe in him. When he had
laid down his life, and taken it up again, he sent forth his disciples to preach the good tidings to every creature, and to endeavor by all possible methods to bring over a lost world to God.
They went forth according to their divine commission, and wonderful success attended their labors; the civilized Greeks, and
uncivilized barbarians, each yielded to the cross of Christ, and
embraced it as the only way of salvation.

Since the apostolic age many other attempts to spread the gospel have been made, which have been considerably successful,
notwithstanding which a very considerable part of mankind are
still involved in all the darkness of heathenism. Some attempts
are still making, but they are inconsiderable in comparison of
what might be done if the whole body of Christians entered
heartily into the spirit of the divine command on this subject.
Some think little about it, others are unacquainted with the state
of the world, and others love their wealth better than the souls
of their fellow creatures.

In order that the subject may be taken into more serious consideration, I shall enquire, whether the commission given by our
Lord to his disciples be not still binding on us,—take a short view
of former undertakings,—give some account of the present state
of the world,—consider the practicability of doing something
more than is done,—and the duty of Christians in general in this
matter.

SECTION I

AN ENQUIRY WHETHER THE COMMISSION GIVEN
BY OUR LORD TO HIS DISCIPLES BE NOT
STILL BINDING ON US

Our Lord Jesus Christ, a little before his departure, commissioned
his apostles to "Go, and teach all nations"; or, as another evangelist expresses it, "Go into all the world, and preach the gospel
to every creature." This commission was as extensive as possible, and laid them under obligation to disperse themselves into
every country of the habitable globe, and preach to all the inhabitants, without exception or limitation. They accordingly
went forth in obedience to the command, and the power of God
evidently wrought with them.

Many attempts of the same kind have been attended with various success; but the work has not been taken up, or prosecuted
of late years (except by a few individuals) with that zeal and
perseverance with which the primitive Christians went about it.
It seems as if many thought the commission was sufficiently put
in execution by what the apostles and others have done; that we
have enough to do to attend to the salvation of our own countrymen; and that, if God intends the salvation of the heathen,
he will some way or other bring them to the gospel, or the gospel to them. It is thus that multitudes sit at ease, and give themselves no concern about the far greater part of their fellow sinners, who to this day are lost in ignorance and idolatry. There
seems also to be an opinion existing in the minds of some, that
because the apostles were extraordinary officers and have no
proper successors, and because many things which were right for
them to do would be utterly unwarrantable for us, therefore it
may not be immediately binding on us to execute the commission, though it was so upon them. To the consideration of such
persons I would offer the following observations.

First, If the command of Christ to teach all nations be restricted
to the apostles, or those under the immediate inspiration of the
Holy Ghost, then that of baptizing should be so too; and every

denomination of Christians, except the Quakers, do wrong in baptizing with water at all.

Secondly, If the command of Christ to teach all nations be confined to the apostles, then all such ordinary ministers who have endeavored to carry the gospel to the heathens, have acted without a warrant, and run before they were sent. Yea, and though God has promised the most glorious things to the heathen world by sending his gospel to them, yet whoever goes first, or indeed at all, with that message, unless he have a new and special commission from heaven, must go without any authority for so doing.

Thirdly, If the command of Christ to teach all nations extend only to the apostles, then, doubtless, the promise of the divine preference in this work must be so limited; but this is worded in such a manner as expressly precludes such an idea. Lo, I am with you always, to the end of the world.

That there are cases in which even a divine command may cease to be binding is admitted. As for instance, if it be repealed, as the ceremonial commandments of the Jewish law; or if there be no subjects in the world for the commanded act to be exercised upon, as in the law of septennial release, which might be dispensed with when there should be no poor in the land to have their debts forgiven (Deut. 15:4); or if, in any particular instance, we can produce a counter-revelation, of equal authority with the original command, as when Paul and Silas were forbidden of the Holy Ghost to preach the word in Bithynia (Acts 16:6, 7); or if, in any case, there be a natural impossibility of putting it in execution.

It was not the duty of Paul to preach Christ to the inhabitants of Otaheite, because no such place was then discovered, nor had he any means of coming at them. But none of these things can be alleged by us in behalf of the neglect of the commission given by Christ. We cannot say that it is repealed, like the commands of the ceremonial law; nor can we plead that there are no objects for the command to be exercised upon. Alas! the far greater part of the world, as we shall see presently, are still covered with heathen darkness! Nor can we produce a counter-revelation, concerning any particular nation, like that to Paul and Silas, concerning Bithynia; and, if we could, it would not warrant our sitting still and neglecting all the other parts of the world; for Paul and Silas, when forbidden to preach to those heathens, went elsewhere, and preached to others. Neither can we allege a natural impossibility in the case.

It has been said that we ought not to force our way, but to wait for the openings, and leadings of Providence; but it might with equal propriety be answered in this case, neither ought we to neglect embracing those openings in Providence which daily present themselves to us. What openings of Providence do we wait for? We can neither expect to be transported into the heathen world without ordinary means, nor to be endowed with the gift of tongues, etc., when we arrive there. These would not be providential interpositions, but miraculous ones. Where a command exists nothing can be necessary to render it binding but a removal of those obstacles which render obedience impossible, and these are removed already. Natural impossibility can never be pleaded so long as facts exist to prove the contrary.

Have not the popish missionaries surmounted all those difficulties which we have generally thought to be insuperable? Have not the missionaries of the Unitas Fratrum, or Moravian Brethren, encountered the scorching heat of Abyssinia, and the frozen climes of Greenland, and Labrador, their difficult languages, and savage manners? Or have not English traders, for the sake of gain, surmounted all those things which have generally been counted insurmountable obstacles in the way of preaching the gospel? Witness the trade to Persia, the East Indies, China, and Greenland, yea even the accursed slave trade on the coasts of Africa. Men can insinuate themselves into the savor of the most barbarous clans, and uncultivated tribes, for the sake of gain; and how different soever the circumstances of trading and preaching are, yet this will prove the possibility of ministers being introduced there; and if this is but thought a sufficient reason to make the experiment, my point is gained.

It has been said that some learned divines have proved from Scripture that the time is not yet come that the heathen should be converted; and that first the witnesses must be slain, and many other prophecies fulfilled. But admitting this to be the case (which I much doubt) yet if any objection is made from this against preaching to them immediately, it must be founded on one of these things; either that the secret purpose of God is the rule of our duty, and then it must be as bad to pray for them as to preach to them; or else that none shall be converted in the heathen world till the universal downpouring of the Spirit in the last days. But this objection comes too late; for the success of the gospel has been very considerable in many places already.

It has been objected that there are multitudes in our own nation, and within our immediate spheres of action, who are as ignorant as the South Sea savages, and that therefore we have work enough at home, without going into other countries. That there are thousands in our own land as far from God as possible, I readily grant, and that this ought to excite us to tenfold diligence in our work, and in attempts to spread divine knowledge amongst them is a certain fact; but that it ought to supersede all attempts to spread the gospel in foreign parts seems to want proof. Our own countrymen have the means of grace, and may attend on the Word preached if they choose it. They have the means of knowing the truth, and faithful ministers are placed in almost every part of the land, whose spheres of action might be much extended if their congregations were but more hearty and active in the cause; but with them the case is widely different, who have no Bible, no written language, (which many of them have not) no ministers, no good civil government, nor any of those advantages which we have. Pity therefore, humanity, and much more Christianity, call loudly for every possible exertion to introduce the gospel amongst them.

SECTION II

CONTAINING A SHORT REVIEW OF FORMER UNDERTAKINGS FOR THE CONVERSION OF THE HEATHEN

[*The story of missions in the book of Acts is omitted.*]

Thus far the history of the Acts of the Apostles informs us of the success of the Word in the primitive times; and history informs us of its being preached about this time in many other places. Peter speaks of a church in Babylon; Paul proposed a journey to Spain, and it is generally believed he went there, and likewise came to France and Britain. Andrew preached to the Scythians, north of the Black Sea. John is said to have preached in India, and we know that he was at the Isle of Patmos, in the Archipelago. Philip is reported to have preached in upper Asia, Scythia, and Phrygia; Bartholomew in India, on this side the Ganges, Phrygia, and Armenia; Matthew in Arabia, or Asiatic Ethiopia, and Parthia; Thomas in India, as far as the coast of Coromandel, and some say in the island of Ceylon; Simon, the Canaanite, in Egypt, Cyrene, Mauritania, Libya, and other parts of Africa, and from thence to have come to Britain; and Jude is said to have been principally engaged in the lesser Asia, and Greece.

Their labors were evidently very extensive, and very successful; so that Pliny the Younger, who lived soon after the death of the apostles, in a letter to the emperor Trajan, observed that Christianity had spread, not only through towns and cities, but also through whole countries. Indeed before this, in the time of Nero, it was so prevalent that it was thought necessary to oppose it by an Imperial Edict, and accordingly the proconsuls, and other governors, were commissioned to destroy it.

Justin Martyr, who lived about the middle of the second century, in his dialogue with Trypho, observed that there was no part of mankind, whether Greeks or barbarians, or any others, by what name soever they were called, whether the Sarmatians, or the Nomades, who had no houses, or the Scenites of Arabia

Petraea, who lived in tents among their cattle, where supplications and thanksgivings are not offered up to the Father, and maker of all things, through the name of Jesus Christ. Irenaeus, who lived about the year 170, speaks of churches that were founded in Germany, Spain, France, the eastern countries, Egypt, Libya, and the middle of the world. Tertullian, who lived and wrote at Carthage in Africa, about twenty years afterwards, enumerating the countries where Christianity had penetrated, makes mention of the Parthians, Medes, Elamites, Mesopotamians, Armenians, Phrygians, Cappadocians, the inhabitants of Pontus, Asia, Pamphylia, Egypt, and the regions of Africa beyond Cyrene, the Romans, and Jews, formerly of Jerusalem, many of the Getuli, many borders of the Mauri, or Moors, in Mauritania; now Barbary, Morocco, etc., all the borders of Spain, many nations of the Gauls, and the places in Britain which were inaccessible to the Romans; the Dacians, Sarmatians, Germans, Scythians, and the inhabitants of many hidden nations and provinces, and of many islands unknown to him, and which he could not enumerate.

The labors of the ministers of the gospel, in this early period, were so remarkably blessed of God, that the last-mentioned writer observed, in a letter to Scapula, that if he began a persecution the city of Carthage itself must be decimated thereby. Yea, and so abundant were they in the first three centuries, that ten years constant and almost universal persecution under Dioclesian could neither root out the Christians, nor prejudice their cause.

After this they had great encouragement under several emperors, particularly Constantine and Theodosius, and a very great work of God was carried on, but the ease and affluence which in these times attended the church, served to introduce a flood of corruption, which by degrees brought on the whole system of popery, by means of which all appeared to be lost again; and Satan set up his kingdom of darkness, deceit, and human authority over conscience, through all the Christian world.

In the time of Constantine, one Frumentius was sent to preach to the Indians, and met with great success. A young woman who was a Christian, being taken captive by the Iberians, or Georgians, near the Caspian Sea, informed them of the truths of Christianity, and was so much regarded that they sent to Constantine for ministers to come and preach the Word to them. About the same time some barbarous nations having made irruptions into Thrace, carried away several Christians captive, who preached the gospel; by which means the inhabitants upon the Rhine, and the Danube, the Celtae, and some other parts of Gaul, were brought to embrace Christianity. About this time also James of Nisbia, went into Persia to strengthen the Christians, and preach to the heathens; and his success was so great that Adiabene was almost entirely Christian. About the year 372, one Moses, a monk, went to preach to the Saracens, who then lived in Arabia, where he had great success; and at this time the Goths, and other northern nations, had the kingdom of Christ further extended amongst them, but which was very soon corrupted with Arianism.

Soon after this the kingdom of Christ was further extended among the Scythian Nomades, beyond the Danube, and about the year 430, a people called the Burgundians, received the gospel. Four years after that Palladius was sent to preach in Scotland, and the next year Patrick was sent from Scotland to preach to the Irish, who before his time were totally uncivilized, and some say, cannibals; he, however, was useful, and laid the foundations of several churches in Ireland. Presently after this, truth spread further among the Saracens, and in 522, Zathus, king of the Colchians encouraged it, and many of that nation were converted to Christianity. About this time also the work was extended in Ireland, and Finian, and in Scotland by Constantine and Columba; the latter of whom preached also to the Picts, and Brudaeus, their king, with several others, were converted. About 541, Adad, the king of Ethiopia, was converted by the preaching of Mansionarius; the Heruli beyond the Danube, were now made obedient to the faith, and the Abasgi, near the Caucasian Mountains.

But now popery, especially the compulsive part of it, was risen to such a height, that the usual method of propagating the gospel, or rather what was so called, was to conquer pagan nations by force of arms, and then oblige them to submit to Christianity, after which bishoprics were erected, and persons then sent to instruct the people. I shall just mention some of those who are said to have labored thus.

In 596, Austin, the monk, Melitus, Justus, Paulinus, and Ruffinian, labored in England, and in their way were very successful. Paulinus, who appears to have been one of the best of them, had great success in Northumberland; Birinnius preached to the West Saxons, and Felix to the East Angles. In 589, Amandus Gallus labored in Ghent, Chelenus in Artois, and Gallus and Columbanus in Suabia. In 648, Egidius Gallus in Flanders, and the two Evaldi, in Westphalia. In 684, Willifred, in the Isle of Wight. In 688, Chilianus, in upper Franconia. In 698, Boniface, or Winifred, among the Thuringians, near Erford, in Saxony, and Willibroad in West Friesland.

Charlemagne conquered Hungary in the year 800, and obliged the inhabitants to profess Christianity when Modestus likewise preached to the Venedi, at the source of the Save and Drave. In 833, Ansgarius preached in Denmark, Gaudibert in Sweden, and about 861, Methodius and Cyril, in Bohemia.

About the year 500, the Scythians overran Bulgaria, and Christianity was extirpated; but about 870 they were reconverted. Poland began to be brought over about the same time, and afterwards, about 960 or 990, the work was further extended amongst the Poles and Prussians. The work was begun in Norway in 960, and in Muscovy in 989; the Swedes propagated Christianity in Finland, in 1168; Lithuania became Christian in 1386, and Samogitia in 1439.

The Spaniards forced popery upon the inhabitants of South America, and the Portuguese in Asia. The Jesuits were sent into China in 1552. Xavier, whom they call the apostle of the Indians, labored in the East Indies and Japan, from 1541 to 1552, and several missions of Capuchins were sent to Africa in the seventeenth century. But blind zeal, gross superstition, and infamous cruelties, so marked the appearances of religion all this time, the professors of Christianity needed conversion, as much as the heathen world.

A few pious people had fled from the general corruption, and lived obscurely in the valleys of Piedmont and Savoy, who were like the seed of the church. Some of them were now and then necessitated to travel into other parts, where they faithfully testified against the corruptions of the times. About 1369 Wickliffe began to preach the faith in England, and his preaching and writings were the means of the conversion of great numbers, many of whom became excellent preachers; and a work was begun which afterwards spread in England, Hungary, Bohemia, Germany, Switzerland, and many other places. John Huss and Jerome of Prague, preached boldly and successfully in Bohemia and the adjacent parts. In the following century Luther, Calvin, Melanchthon, Bucer, Martyr, and many others, stood up against all the rest of the world; they preached, and prayed, and wrote; and nations agreed one after another to cast off the yoke of popery, and to embrace the doctrine of the gospel.

In England, episcopal tyranny succeeded to popish cruelty, which, in the year 1620, obliged many pious people to leave their native land and settle in America; these were followed by others in 1629, who laid the foundations of several gospel churches, which have increased amazingly since that time, and the Redeemer has fixed his throne in that country, where but a little time ago, Satan had universal dominion.

In 1632, Mr. Elliot, of New England, a very pious and zealous minister, began to preach to the Indians, among whom he had great success; several churches of Indians were planted, and some preachers and schoolmasters raised up amongst them; since which time others have labored amongst them with some good encouragement. About the year 1743, Mr. David Brainerd was sent a missionary to some more Indians, where he preached, and prayed, and after some time an extraordinary work of conversion was wrought, and wonderful success attended his ministry. And at this present time, Mr. Kirkland and Mr. Sergeant are employed in the same good work, and God has considerably blessed their labors.

In 1706, the king of Denmark sent a Mr. Ziegenbalg, and some others, to Tranquebar, on the Coromandel coast in the East Indies, who were useful to the natives, so that many of the heathens were turned to the Lord. The Dutch East India Company likewise having extended their commerce, built the city of Batavia, and a church was opened there; and the Lord's Supper was administered for the first time, on the third of January, 1621, by their minister James Hulzibos; from hence some ministers were sent to Amboyna, who were very successful. A seminary of learning was erected at Leyden, in which ministers and assistants were educated, under the renowned Walaeus, and some years a great number were sent to the East, at the Company's expense, so that in a little time many thousands at Formosa, Malabar, Ternate, Jaffanapatnam, in the town of Columba, at Amboyna, Java, Banda, Macassar, and Malabar, embraced the religion of our Lord Jesus Christ. The work has decayed in some places, but they now have churches in Ceylon, Sumatra, Java, Amboyna, and some other of the spice islands, and at the Cape of Good Hope, in Africa.

But none of the moderns have equaled the Moravian Brethren in this good work; they have sent missions to Greenland, Labrador, and several of the West Indian Islands, which have been blessed for good. They have likewise sent to Abyssinia, in Africa, but what success they have had I cannot tell.

The late Mr. Wesley lately made an effort in the West Indies, and some of their ministers are now laboring amongst the Caribs and Negroes, and I have seen pleasing accounts of their success.

SECTION IV

THE PRACTICABILITY OF SOMETHING BEING DONE, MORE THAN WHAT IS DONE, FOR THE CONVERSION OF THE HEATHEN

The impediments in the way of carrying the gospel among the heathen must arise, I think, from one or other of the following things;—either their distance from us, their barbarous and savage manner of living, the danger of being killed by them, the difficulty of procuring the necessaries of life, or the unintelligibleness of their languages.

First, As to their distance from us, whatever objections might
have been made on that account before the invention of the
mariner's compass, nothing can be alleged for it, with any color
of plausibility in the present age. Men can now sail with as much
certainty through the Great South Sea, as they can through the
Mediterranean, or any lesser Sea. Yea, and providence seems in a
manner to invite us to the trial, as there are to our knowledge
trading companies, whose commerce lies in many of the places
where these barbarians dwell.

At one time or other ships are sent to visit places of more
recent discovery, and to explore parts the most unknown; and
every fresh account of their ignorance, or cruelty, should call
forth our pity, and excite us to concur with providence in seeking their eternal good. Scripture likewise seems to point out this
method. "Surely the isles shall wait for me; the ships of Tarshish
first, to bring thy sons from far, their silver and their gold with
them unto the name of the Lord thy God" (Isa. 60:9). This
seems to imply that in the time of the glorious increase of the
church, in the latter days, (of which the whole chapter is undoubtedly a prophecy,) commerce shall subserve the spread of
the gospel. The ships of Tarshish were trading vessels, which
made voyages for traffic to various parts; thus much therefore
must be meant by it, that navigation, especially that which is
commercial, shall be one great mean of carrying on the work of
God; and perhaps it may imply that there shall be a very considerable appropriation of wealth to that purpose.

Secondly, As to their uncivilized, and barbarous way of living,
this can be no objection to any, except those whose love of ease
renders them unwilling to expose themselves to inconveniences
for the good of others.

It was no objection to the apostles and their successors, who
went among the barbarous Germans and Gauls, and still more
barbarous Britons! They did not wait for the ancient inhabitants
of these countries to be civilized before they could be Christian-
ized, but went simply with the doctrine of the cross; and Tertullian could boast that "those parts of Britain which were proof

against the Roman armies, were conquered by the gospel of Christ."

It was no objection to an Elliot, or a Brainerd, in later times. They went forth, and encountered every difficulty of the kind, and found that a cordial reception of the gospel produced those happy effects which the longest intercourse with Europeans, without it, could never accomplish. It is no objection to commercial men. It only requires that we should have as much love to the souls of our fellow creatures, and fellow sinners, as they have for the profits arising from a few otter-skins, and all these difficulties would be easily surmounted.

After all, the uncivilized state of the heathen, instead of affording an objection against preaching the gospel to them, ought to furnish an argument for it. Can we as men, or as Christians, hear that a great part of our fellow creatures, whose souls are as immortal as ours, and who are as capable as ourselves, of adorning the gospel, and contributing by their preaching, writings, or practices to the glory of our Redeemer's name, and the good of his church, are enveloped in ignorance and barbarism? Can we hear that they are without the gospel, without government, without laws, and without arts and sciences, and not exert ourselves to introduce amongst them the sentiments of men, and of Christians? Would not the spread of the gospel be the most effectual mean of their civilization? Would not that make them useful members of society?

We know that such effects did in a measure follow the aforementioned efforts of Elliot, Brainerd, and others amongst the American Indians; and if similar attempts were made in other parts of the world, and succeeded with a divine blessing (which we have every reason to think they would) might we not expect to see able divines, or read well-conducted treatises in defense of the truth, even amongst those who at present seem to be scarcely human?

Thirdly, In respect to the danger of being killed by them, it is true that whoever does go must put his life in his hand, and not consult with flesh and blood; but do not the goodness of the cause, the duties incumbent on us as the creatures of God, and

Christians, and the perishing state of our fellow men, loudly call upon us to venture all and use every warrantable exertion for their benefit?

Paul and Barnabas, who hazarded their lives for the name of our Lord Jesus Christ, were not blamed as being rash, but commended for so doing, while John Mark who through timidity of mind deserted them in their perilous undertaking, was branded with censure. After all, as has been already observed, I greatly question whether most of the barbarities practiced by the savages upon those who have visited them, have not originated in some real or supposed affront, and were therefore, more properly, acts of self-defense, than proofs of ferocious dispositions. No wonder if the imprudence of sailors should prompt them to offend the simple savage, and the offense be resented; but Elliot, Brainerd, and the Moravian missionaries, have been very seldom molested. Nay, in general the heathen have shewed a willingness to hear the word; and have principally expressed their hatred of Christianity on account of the vices of nominal Christians.

Fourthly, As to the difficulty of procuring the necessaries of life, this would not be so great as may appear at first sight; for though we could not procure European food, yet we might procure such as the natives of those countries which we visit, subsist upon themselves. And this would only be passing through what we have virtually engaged in by entering on the ministerial office. A Christian minister is a person who in a peculiar sense is not his own; he is the servant of God, and therefore ought to be wholly devoted to him. By entering on that sacred office he solemnly undertakes to be always engaged, as much as possible, in the Lord's work, and not to choose his own pleasure, or employment, or pursue the ministry as something that is to subserve his own ends, or interests, or as a kind of bye-work. He engages to go where God pleases, and to do, or endure what he sees fit to command, or call him to, in the exercise of his function. He virtually bids farewell to friends, pleasures, and comforts, and stands in readiness to endure the greatest sufferings in the work of his Lord and Master.

It is inconsistent for ministers to please themselves with

thoughts of a numerous auditory, cordial friends, a civilized country, legal protection, affluence, splendor, or even a competency. The slights, and hatred of men, and even pretended friends, gloomy prisons, and tortures, the society of barbarians of uncouth speech, miserable accommodations in wretched wildernesses, hunger and thirst, nakedness, weariness, and painfulness, hard work, but little worldly encouragement, should rather be the objects of their expectation. Thus the apostles acted, in the primitive times, and endured hardness, as good soldiers of Jesus Christ; and though we, living in a civilized country where Christianity is protected by law, are not called to suffer these things while we continue here, yet I question whether all are justified in staying here, while so many are perishing without means of grace in other lands.

Sure I am that it is entirely contrary to the spirit of the gospel, for its ministers to enter upon it from interested motives, or with great worldly expectations. On the contrary the commission is a sufficient call to them to venture all, and, like the primitive Christians, go everywhere preaching the gospel.

It might be necessary, however, for two, at least, to go together, and in general I should think it best that they should be married men, and to prevent their time from being employed in procuring necessaries, two, or more, other persons, with their wives and families, might also accompany them, who should be wholly employed in providing for them.

In most countries it would be necessary for them to cultivate a little spot of ground just for their support, which would be a resource to them, whenever their supplies failed. Not to mention the advantages they would reap from each other's company, it would take off the enormous expense which has always attended undertakings of this kind, the first expense being the whole; for though a large colony needs support for a considerable time, yet so small a number would, upon receiving the first crop, maintain themselves. They would have the advantage of choosing their situation, their wants would be few; the women, and even the children, would be necessary for domestic purposes; and a few articles of stock, as a cow or two, and a bull, and a few other cattle of both sexes, a very few utensils of husbandry, and some corn to sow their land, would be sufficient.

Those who attend the missionaries should understand husbandry, fishing, fowling, etc., and be provided with the necessary implements for these purposes. Indeed a variety of methods may be thought of, and when once the work is undertaken, many things will suggest themselves to us, of which we at present can form no idea.

Fifthly, As to learning their languages, the same means would be found necessary here as in trade between different nations. In some cases interpreters might be obtained, who might be employed for a time; and where these were not to be found, the missionaries must have patience, and mingle with the people, till they have learned so much of their language as to be able to communicate their ideas to them in it. It is well known to require no very extraordinary talents to learn, in the space of a year, or two at most, the language of any people upon earth, so much of it at least, as to be able to convey any sentiments we wish to their understandings.

The missionaries must be men of great piety, prudence, courage, and forbearance; of undoubted orthodoxy in their sentiments, and must enter with all their hearts into the spirit of their mission; they must be willing to leave all the comforts of the life behind them, and to encounter all the hardships of a torrid, or a frigid climate, an uncomfortable manner of living, and every other inconvenience that can attend this undertaking. Clothing, a few knives, powder and shot, fishing-tackle, and the articles of husbandry above-mentioned, must be provided for them; and when arrived at the place of their destination, their first business must be to gain some acquaintance with the language of the natives, (for which purpose two would be better than one,) and by all lawful means to endeavor to cultivate a friendship with them, and as soon as possible let them know the errand for which they were sent.

They must endeavor to convince them that it was their good alone which induced them to forsake their friends and all the comforts of their native country. They must be very careful not to resent injuries which may be offered to them, nor to think highly of themselves, so as to despise the poor heathens, and by those means lay a foundation for their resentment, or rejection of the gospel. They must take every opportunity of doing them good, and laboring, and traveling, night and day, they must instruct, exhort, and rebuke, with all long suffering, and anxious desire for them, and, above all, must be instant in prayer for the effusion of the Holy Spirit upon the people of their charge. Let but missionaries of the above description engage in the work, and we shall see that it is not impracticable.

It might likewise be of importance, if God should bless their labors, for them to encourage any appearances of gifts amongst the people of their charge; if such should be raised up many advantages would be derived from their knowledge of the language and customs of their countrymen; and their change of conduct would give great weight to their ministrations.

SECTION V

AN ENQUIRY INTO THE DUTY OF CHRISTIANS IN GENERAL, AND WHAT MEANS OUGHT TO BE USED, IN ORDER TO PROMOTE THIS WORK

If the prophecies concerning the increase of Christ's kingdom be true, and if what has been advanced, concerning the commission given by him to his disciples being obligatory on us, be just, it must be inferred that all Christians ought heartily to concur with God in promoting his glorious designs, for he that is joined to the Lord is one Spirit.

One of the first, and most important of those duties which are incumbent upon us, is fervent and united prayer. However, the influence of the Holy Spirit may be set at nought, and run down by many, it will be found upon trial, that all means which we can use, without it, will be ineffectual. If a temple is raised for God in the heathen world, it will not be by might, nor by power, nor by the authority of the magistrate, or the eloquence of the orator; but by my Spirit, saith the Lord of Hosts. We must therefore be in real earnest in supplicating his blessings upon our labors.

It is represented in the prophets, that when there shall be a great mourning in the land, as the mourning of Hadad-rimmon in the valley of Megiddon, and every family shall mourn apart, and their wives apart, it shall all follow upon a spirit of grace, and supplication. And when these things shall take place, it is promised that there shall be a fountain opened for the house of David, and for the inhabitants of Jerusalem, for sin, and for uncleanness,—and that the idols shall be destroyed, and the false prophets ashamed of their profession (Zech. 12:10-14; 13:1-6). This prophecy seems to teach that when there shall be a universal conjunction in fervent prayer, and all shall esteem Zion's welfare as their own, then copious influences of the Spirit shall be shed upon the churches, which like a purifying fountain shall cleanse the servants of the Lord. Nor shall this cleansing influence stop here; all old idolatrous prejudices shall be rooted out, and truth prevail so gloriously that false teachers shall be so ashamed as rather to wish to be classed with obscure herdsmen, or the meanest peasants, than bear the ignominy attendant on their detection.

The most glorious works of grace that have ever took place, have been in answer to prayer; and it is in this way, we have the greatest reason to suppose, that the glorious outpouring of the Spirit, which we expect at last, will be bestowed.

With respect to our own immediate connections, we have within these few years been favored with some tokens for good, granted in answer to prayer which should encourage us to persist, and increase in that important duty. I trust our monthly prayer-meetings for the success of the gospel have not been in vain. It is true a want of importunity too generally attends our prayers; yet unimportunate, and feeble as they have been, it is to be believed that God has heard, and in a measure answered them. The churches that have engaged in the practice have in general since that time been evidently on the increase; some controversies which have long perplexed and divided the church, are more clearly stated than ever; there are calls to preach the gospel in many places where it has not been usually published;

yea, a glorious door is opened, and is likely to be opened wider and wider, by the spread of civil and religious liberty, accompanied also by a diminution of the spirit of popery; a noble effort has been made to abolish the inhuman slave trade, and though at present it has not been so successful as might be wished, yet it is to be hoped it will be persevered in, till it is accomplished. In the meantime it is a satisfaction to consider that the late defeat of the abolition of the slave trade has proved the occasion of a praiseworthy effort to introduce a free settlement, at Sierra Leona, on the coast of Africa; an effort which, if succeeded with a divine blessing, not only promises to open a way for honorable commerce with that extensive country, and for the civilization of its inhabitants, but may prove the happy mean of introducing amongst them the gospel of our Lord Jesus Christ.

These are events that ought not to be overlooked; they are not to be reckoned small things; and yet perhaps they are small compared with what might have been expected, if all had cordially entered into the spirit of the proposal, so as to have made the cause of Christ their own, or in other words to have been so solicitous about it, as if their own advantage depended upon its success. If a holy solicitude had prevailed in all the assemblies of Christians in behalf of their Redeemer's kingdom, we might probably have seen before now, not only an open door for the gospel, but many running to and fro, and knowledge increased; or a diligent use of those means which providence has put in our power, accompanied with a greater blessing than ordinary from heaven.

Many can do nothing but pray, and prayer is perhaps the only thing in which Christians of all denominations can cordially and unreservedly unite; but in this we may all be one, and in this the strictest unanimity ought to prevail. Were the whole body thus animated by one soul, with what pleasure would Christians attend on all the duties of religion, and with what delight would their ministers attend on all the business of their calling.

We must not be contented however with praying, without exerting ourselves in the use of means for the obtaining of those things we pray for. Were the children of light, but as wise in their generation as the children of this world, they would stretch every nerve to gain so glorious a prize, nor ever imagine that it was to be obtained in any other way.

When a trading company have obtained their charter they usually go to its utmost limits; and their stocks, their ships, their officers, and men are so chosen, and regulated, as to be likely to answer their purpose; but they do not stop here, for encouraged by the prospect of success, they use every effort, cast their bread upon the waters, cultivate friendship with every one from whose information they expect the least advantage. They cross the widest and most tempestuous seas, and encounter the most unfavorable climates; they introduce themselves into the most barbarous nations, and sometimes undergo the most affecting hardships; their minds continue in a state of anxiety and suspense, and a longer delay than usual in the arrival of their vessels agitates them with a thousand changeful thoughts, and foreboding apprehensions, which continue till the rich returns are safe arrived in port.

But why these fears? Whence all these disquietudes, and this labor? Is it not because their souls enter into the spirit of the project and their happiness in a manner depends on its success? Christians are a body whose truest interest lies in the exaltation of the Messiah's kingdom. Their charter is very extensive, their encouragements exceeding great, and the returns promised infinitely superior to all the gains of the most lucrative fellowship. Let then every one in his station consider himself as bound to act with all his might, and in every possible way for God.

Suppose a company of serious Christians, ministers and private persons, were to form themselves into a society, and make a number of rules respecting the regulation of the plan, and the persons who are to be employed as missionaries, the means of defraying the expense, etc. This society must consist of persons whose hearts are in the work, men of serious religion, and possessing a spirit of perseverance; there must be a determination not to admit any person who is not of this description, or to retain him longer than he answers to it.

From such a society a committee might be appointed whose

business it should be to procure all the information they could upon the subject, to receive contributions, to enquire into the characters, tempers, abilities and religious views of the missionaries, and also to provide them with necessaries for their undertakings.

They must also pay a great attention to the views of those who undertake this work; for want of this the missions to the Spice Islands, sent by the Dutch East India Company, were soon corrupted, many going more for the sake of settling in a place where temporal gain invited them, than of preaching to the poor Indians. This soon introduced a number of indolent, or profligate persons, whose lives were a scandal to the doctrines which they preached; and by means of whom the gospel was ejected from Ternate, in 1694, and Christianity fell into great disrepute in other places.

If there is any reason for me to hope that I shall have any influence upon any of my brethren, and fellow Christians, probably it may be more especially amongst them of my own denomination. I would therefore propose that such a society and committee should be formed amongst the particular Baptist denomination.

I do not mean by this, in any wise to confine it to one denomination of Christians. I wish with all my heart, that every one who loves our Lord Jesus Christ in sincerity, would in some way or other engage in it. But in the present divided state of Christendom, it would be more likely for good to be done by each denomination engaging separately in the work, than if they were to embark in it conjointly. There is room enough for us all, without interfering with each other; and if no unfriendly interference took place, each denomination would bear good will to the other, and wish, and pray for its success, considering it as upon the whole friendly to the great cause of true religion; but if all were intermingled, it is likely their private discords might throw a damp upon their spirits, and much retard their public usefulness.

In respect to contributions for defraying the expenses, money will doubtless be wanting; and suppose the rich were to embark a portion of that wealth over which God has made them stewards, in this important undertaking, perhaps there are few ways that would turn to a better account at last.

Nor ought it to be confined to the rich; if persons in more moderate circumstances were to devote a portion, suppose a tenth, of their annual increase to the Lord, it would not only correspond with the practice of the Israelites, who lived under the Mosaic economy, but of the patriarchs Abraham, Isaac, and Jacob, before that dispensation commenced. Many of our most eminent forefathers amongst the Puritans followed that practice; and if that were but attended to now, there would not only be enough to support the ministry of the gospel at home, and to encourage village preaching in our respective neighborhoods, but to defray the expenses of carrying the gospel into the heathen world.

If congregations were to open subscriptions of one penny, or more per week, according to their circumstances, and deposit it as a fund for the propagation of the gospel, much might be raised in this way. By such simple means they might soon have it in their power to introduce the preaching of the gospel into most of the villages in England; where, though men are placed whose business it should be to give light to those who sit in darkness, it is well known that they have it not. Where there was no person to open his house for the reception of the gospel, some other building might be procured for a small sum, and even then something considerable might be spared for the Baptist, or other committees, for propagating the gospel amongst the heathen.

Many persons have of late left off the use of West India sugar on account of the iniquitous manner in which it is obtained. Those families who have done so, and have not substituted anything else in its place, have not only cleansed their hands of blood, but have made a saving to their families, some of sixpence, and some of a shilling a week. If this, or a part of this were appropriated to the uses before-mentioned, it would abundantly suffice. We have only to keep the end in view, and have our hearts thoroughly engaged in the pursuit of it, and means will not be very difficult.

We are exhorted to lay up treasure in heaven, where neither moth nor rust doth corrupt, nor thieves break through and steal. It is also declared that whatsoever a man soweth, that shall he also reap. These Scriptures teach us that the enjoyments of the life to come, bear a near relation to that which now is; a relation similar to that of the harvest, and the seed. It is true all the reward is of mere grace, but it is nevertheless encouraging; what a treasure, what a harvest must await such characters as Paul, and Elliot, and Brainerd, and others, who have given themselves wholly to the work of the Lord. What a heaven will it be to see the many myriads of poor heathens, of Britons amongst the rest, who by their labors have been brought to the knowledge of God. Surely a crown of rejoicing like this is worth aspiring to. Surely it is worth while to lay ourselves out with all our might, in promoting the cause, and the kingdom of Christ.

II

CONFESSIONS, A CATECHISM, CHURCH COVENANTS

———••◆••———

BAPTIST CONFESSIONS OF FAITH

Baptists have ever repudiated authoritative creeds and confessions but they have recognized the value of statements of faith as expressions before the world of our common beliefs and as suggestive helps to local churches. The two confessions of widest influence in America have been the so-called Philadelphia Confession and the New Hampshire Confession. Many others have been made by individuals and by groups, as for example, A Treatise on the Faith of the Freewill Baptists *(1834), but they have had very limited circulation. W. J.* McGlothlin's Baptist Confessions of Faith *(a new edition is forthcoming) contains all the better known ones.*

The "Philadelphia Confession" is really a slightly enlarged edition of the Second London Confession of the Particular Baptists, adopted in 1689. It was an expression of the desire of Baptists of that period to show their relationship to other bodies of Christians and was, therefore, based firmly upon the Presbyterians' Westminster Confession of 1648, modified as to the doctrine of the church by the words taken from the Congregational-

48

ists' (Independents) Savoy Confession of 1658. The Baptists added their own statements on the ordinances. The Philadelphia Association adopted this Confession, with the addition of an article calling for "the laying on of hands" and another approving the singing of psalms. The whole Confession, with scripture references, is in McGlothlin and, without scriptures, in Cathcart's Baptist Encyclopedia (the appendix). The Philadelphia Confession is strong on Calvinism and on the general or invisible church. The articles we reprint show these emphases.

The New Hampshire Confession is only moderately Calvinistic and it stresses visible or particular churches. It was approved to the churches by the Board of the Baptist State Convention of New Hampshire in 1833. It has had wide circulation in all parts of the country except the southeastern area, where the Philadelphia had strong prior hold. J. M. Pendleton included it in his Church Manual and it has been used by "Landmark" Baptists ever since.

The Philadelphia Confession of Faith

. . . . .

III. OF GOD'S DECREE.—1. God hath decreed in himself from all eternity, by the most wise and holy counsel of his own will, freely and unchangeably, all things whatsoever comes to pass; yet so as thereby is God neither the author of sin, nor hath fellowship with any therein, nor is violence offered to the will of the creature, nor yet is the liberty or contingency of second causes taken away, but rather established, in which appears his wisdom in disposing all things, and power and faithfulness in accomplishing his decree.

2. Although God knoweth whatsoever may or can come to pass upon all supposed conditions, yet hath he not decreed anything because he foresaw it as future, or as that which would come to pass upon such conditions.

3. By the decree of God, for the manifestation of his glory, some men and angels are predestinated or foreordained to eternal

life, through Jesus Christ, to the praise of his glorious grace; others being left to act in their sin to their just condemnation, to the praise of his glorious justice.

4. These angels and men thus predestinated and foreordained are particularly and unchangeably designed; and their number so certain and definite, that it cannot be either increased or diminished.

5. Those of mankind that are predestinated to life, God, before the foundation of the world was laid, according to his eternal and immutable purpose, and the secret counsel and good pleasure of his will, hath chosen in Christ unto everlasting glory, out of his mere free grace and love; without any other thing in the creature as a condition or cause moving him thereunto.

6. As God hath appointed the elect unto glory, so he hath by the eternal and most free purpose of his will foreordained all the means thereunto, wherefore they who are elected, being fallen in Adam, are redeemed by Christ, are effectually called unto faith in Christ, by his Spirit working in due season, are justified, adopted, sanctified, and kept by his power through faith unto salvation; neither are any other redeemed by Christ, or effectually called, justified, adopted, sanctified, and saved, but the elect only.

7. The doctrine of this high mystery of predestination is to be handled with special prudence and care; that men attending the will of God revealed in his Word, and yielding obedience thereunto, may, from the certainty of their effectual vocation, be assured of their eternal election; so shall this doctrine afford matter of praise, reverence, and admiration of God, and of humility, diligence, and abundant consolation to all that sincerely obey the gospel.

•   •   •   •   •

IX. Of Free Will.—1. God has indued the will of man with that natural liberty and power of acting upon choice, that it is neither forced nor, by any necessity of nature, determined to do good or evil.

2. Man, in his state of innocency, had freedom and power to

will and to do that which was good and well pleasing to God; but yet was mutable, so that he might fall from it.

3. Man, by his fall into a state of sin, hath wholly lost all ability of will to any spiritual good accompanying salvation; so as a natural man, being altogether averse from that good and dead in sin, is not able, by his own strength, to convert himself or to prepare himself thereunto.

4. When God converts a sinner, and translates him into the state of grace, he freeth him from his natural bondage under sin, and, by his grace alone, enables him freely to will and do that which is spiritually good; yet so as that, by reason of his remaining corruptions, he doth not perfectly nor only will that which is good, but doth also will that which is evil.

．　．　．　．　．

XXVII. Of The Church.—1. The catholic or universal church, which, with respect to the internal work of the Spirit and truth of grace, may be called invisible, consists of the whole number of the elect that have been, are, or shall be gathered into one under God, the head thereof, and is the spouse, the body, the fullness of him that filleth all in all.

2. All persons, throughout the world, professing the faith of the gospel and obedience unto God by Christ according unto it, not destroying their own profession by any errors, everting the foundation, or unholiness of conversation, are and may be called visible saints; and of such ought all particular congregations to be constituted.

3. The purest churches under heaven are subject to mixture and error, and some have so degenerated as to become no churches of Christ, but synagogues of Satan; nevertheless, Christ always hath had and ever shall have a kingdom in this world, to the end thereof, of such as believe in him and make profession of his name.

4. The Lord Jesus Christ is the head of the church, in whom, by the appointment of the Father, all power for the calling, institution, order, or government of the church is invested in a supreme and sovereign manner; neither can the pope of Rome in

any sense be head thereof, but is that Antichrist, that man of sin and son of perdition, that exalteth himself in the church against Christ and all that is called God, whom the Lord shall destroy with the brightness of his coming.

5. In the execution of this power wherewith he is so intrusted, the Lord Jesus calleth out of the world unto himself, through the ministry of his Word by his Spirit, those that are given unto him by his Father, that they walk before him in all the ways of obedience which he prescribeth to them in his Word. Those thus called he commandeth to walk together in particular societies or churches, for their mutual edification and the due performance of that public worship which he requireth of them in the world.

6. The members of these churches are saints by calling, visibly manifesting and evidencing in and by their profession and walking their obedience unto that call of Christ; and do willingly consent to walk together according to the appointment of Christ, giving up themselves to the Lord and to one another by the will of God, in professed subjection to the ordinances of the gospel.

7. To each of these churches thus gathered according to his mind, declared in his Word, he hath given all that power and authority which is any way needful for their carrying on that order in worship and discipline which he hath instituted for them to observe, with commands and rules for the due and right exerting and executing that power.

8. A particular church, gathered and completely organized according to the mind of Christ, consists of officers and members; and the officers, appointed by Christ to be chosen and set apart by the church so called and gathered, for the peculiar administration of ordinances and execution of power or duty which he intrusts them with, or calls them to, to be continued to the end of the world, are bishops, or elders, and deacons.

9. The way appointed by Christ for the calling of any person, fitted and gifted by the Holy Spirit, unto the office of bishop, or elder, in a church, is that he be chosen thereunto by the common suffrage of the church itself, and solemnly set apart by fasting and prayer, with imposition of hands of the eldership of the

church, if there be any before constituted therein; and of a deacon, that he be chosen by the like suffrage, and set apart by prayer and the like imposition of hands.

10. The work of pastors being constantly to attend the service of Christ in his churches, in the ministry of the Word, and prayer, with watching for their souls as they that must give an account to him, it is incumbent on the churches to whom they minister not only to give them all due respect but also to communicate to them of all their good things, according to their ability, so as they may have a comfortable supply, without being themselves entangled in secular affairs, and may also be capable of exercising hospitality towards others; and this is required by the law of nature and by the express order of our Lord Jesus, who hath ordained that they that preach the gospel should live of the gospel.

11. Although it be incumbent on the bishops or pastors of the churches to be instant in preaching the Word, by way of office, yet the work of preaching the Word is not so peculiarly confined to them but that others also gifted and fitted by the Holy Spirit for it, and approved and called by the church, may and ought to perform it.

12. As all believers are bound to join themselves to particular churches, when and where they have opportunity so to do, so all that are admitted unto the privileges of a church are also under the censures and government thereof, according to the rule of Christ.

13. No church members, upon any offense taken by them, having performed their duty required of them towards the person they are offended at, ought to disturb church order, or absent themselves from the assemblies of the church, or administration of any ordinance, upon the account of such offense at any of their fellow-members, but to wait upon Christ in further proceeding of the church.

14. As each church and all the members of it are bound to pray continually for the good and prosperity of all the churches of Christ in all places, and upon all occasions to further it, every one within the bounds of their places and callings, in the exercise of

their gifts and graces, so the churches, when planted by the providence of God, so as they may enjoy opportunity and advantage for it, ought to hold communion among themselves for their peace, increase of love, and mutual edification.

15. Cases of difficulty or differences, either in point of doctrine or administration, wherein either the churches in general are concerned, or any one church, in their peace, union, and edification; or any member or members of any church are injured in or by any proceedings in censures not agreeable to truth and order; it is according to the mind of Christ that many churches, holding communion together, do, by their messengers, meet to consider and give their advice in or about the matter in difference, to be reported to all the churches concerned; howbeit these messengers assembled are not intrusted with any church power, properly so called; or with any jurisdiction over the churches themselves, to exercise any censures either over any churches or persons; or to impose their determination on the churches or offices.

. . . . .

XXIX. OF BAPTISM AND THE LORD'S SUPPER.—1. Baptism and the Lord's Supper are the ordinances of positive and sovereign institution, appointed by the Lord Jesus, the only Lawgiver, to be continued in his church to the end of the world.

2. These holy appointments are to be administered by those only who are qualified and thereunto called, according to the commission of Christ.

. . . . .

XXX. OF BAPTISM.—1. Baptism is an ordinance of the New Testament ordained by Jesus Christ, to be unto the party baptized a sign of his fellowship with him in his death and resurrection; of his being engrafted into him; of remission of sins; and of his giving up unto God, through Jesus Christ, to live and walk in newness of life.

2. Those who do actually profess repentance towards God, faith in, and obedience to our Lord Jesus, are the only proper subjects of this ordinance.

3. The outward element to be used in this ordinance is water, wherein the party is to be baptized, in the name of the Father, and of the Son, and of the Holy Spirit.

4. Immersion, or dipping of the person in water, is necessary to the due administration of this ordinance.

. . . . .

XXXII. Of the Lord's Supper.—1. The Supper of the Lord Jesus was instituted by him the same night wherein he was betrayed, to be observed in his churches unto the end of the world, for the perpetual remembrance and showing forth the sacrifice of himself in his death, confirmation of the faith of believers in all the benefits thereof, their spiritual nourishment and growth in him, their further engagement in and to all duties which they owe unto him, and to be a bond and pledge of their communion with him and with each other.

. . . . .

7. Worthy receivers, outwardly partaking of the visible elements in this ordinance, do then also inwardly, by faith really and indeed, yet not carnally and corporeally, but spiritually, receive and feed upon Christ crucified and all the benefits of his death; the body and blood of Christ being then not corporeally or carnally, but spiritually present to the faith of believers in that ordinance, as the elements themselves are to their outward senses.

The New Hampshire Declaration of Faith

I. Of the Scriptures.—We believe that the holy Bible was written by men divinely inspired, and is a perfect treasure of heavenly instruction; that it has God for its author, salvation for its end, and truth without any mixture of error for its matter; that it reveals the principles by which God will judge us, and therefore is, and shall remain to the end of the world, the true center of Christian union, and the supreme standard by which all human conduct, creeds, and opinions should be tried.

II. OF THE TRUE GOD.—We believe that there is one, and only one, living and true God, an infinite, intelligent Spirit, whose name is Jehovah, the Maker and Supreme Ruler of heaven and earth, inexpressibly glorious in holiness, and worthy of all possible honor, confidence, and love; that in the unity of the Godhead there are three persons,—the Father, the Son, and the Holy Ghost,—equal in every divine perfection, and executing distinct but harmonious offices in the great work of redemption.

III. OF THE FALL OF MAN.—We believe that man was created in holiness, under the law of his Maker; but by voluntary transgression fell from that holy and happy state; in consequence of which all mankind are now sinners, not by constraint but choice; being by nature utterly void of that holiness required by the law of God; positively inclined to evil; and therefore under just condemnation to eternal ruin, without defense or excuse.

IV. OF THE WAY OF SALVATION.—We believe that the salvation of sinners is wholly of grace; through the mediatorial offices of the Son of God; who by the appointment of the Father, freely took upon him our nature, yet without sin; honored the divine law by his personal obedience, and by his death made a full atonement for our sins; that having risen from the dead, he is now enthroned in heaven; and uniting in his wonderful person the tenderest sympathies with divine perfections, he is every way qualified to be a suitable, a compassionate, and an all-sufficient Saviour.

V. OF JUSTIFICATION.—We believe that the great gospel blessing which Christ secures to such as believe in him, is justification; that justification includes the pardon of sin, and the promise of eternal life on principles of righteousness; that it is bestowed, not in consideration of any works of righteousness which we have done, but solely through faith in the Redeemer's blood; by virtue of which faith his perfect righteousness is freely imputed to us of God; that it brings us into a state of most blessed peace and favor with God, and secures every other blessing needful for time and eternity.

VI. OF THE FREENESS OF SALVATION.—We believe that the blessings of salvation are made free to all by the gospel; that it is the immediate duty of all to accept them by a cordial, penitent, and obedient faith; and that nothing prevents the salvation of the greatest sinner on earth but his own determined depravity and voluntary rejection of the gospel; which rejection involves him in an aggravated condemnation.

VII. OF GRACE IN REGENERATION.—We believe that in order to be saved sinners must be regenerated, or born again; that regeneration consists in giving a holy disposition to the mind; that it is effected in a manner above our comprehension by the power of the Holy Spirit, in connection with divine truth, so as to secure our voluntary obedience to the gospel; and that its proper evidence appears in the holy fruits of repentance, and faith, and newness of life.

VIII. OF REPENTANCE AND FAITH.—We believe that repentance and faith are sacred duties, and also inseparable graces, wrought in our souls by the regenerating Spirit of God; whereby, being deeply convinced of our guilt, danger, and helplessness, and of the way of salvation by Christ, we turn to God with unfeigned contrition, confession, and supplication for mercy; at the same time heartily receiving the Lord Jesus Christ as our Prophet, Priest, and King, and relying on him alone as the only and all-sufficient Saviour.

IX. OF GOD'S PURPOSE OF GRACE.—We believe that election is the eternal purpose of God, according to which he graciously regenerates, sanctifies, and saves sinners, that being perfectly consistent with the free agency of man, it comprehends all the means in connection with the end; that it is a most glorious display of God's sovereign goodness, being infinitely free, wise, holy, and unchangeable; that it utterly excludes boasting, and promotes humility, love, prayer, praise, trust in God, and active imitation of his free mercy; that it encourages the use of means in the highest degree; that it may be ascertained by its effects in all who truly believe the gospel; that it is the foundation of Christian assurance; and that to ascertain it with regard to ourselves demands and deserves the utmost diligence.

X. OF SANCTIFICATION.—We believe that sanctification is the process by which, according to the will of God, we are made

partakers of his holiness, that it is a progressive work; that it is
begun in regeneration; and that it is carried on in the hearts of believers by the presence and power of the Holy Spirit, the Sealer
and Comforter, in the continual use of the appointed means—
especially, the Word of God, self-examination, self-denial, watch-
fulness, and prayer.

XI. OF THE PERSEVERANCE OF SAINTS.—We believe that such
only are real believers as endure unto the end; that their persevering attachment to Christ is the grand mark which distinguishes
them from superficial professors; that a special providence
watches over their welfare; and they are kept by the power of
God through faith unto salvation.

XII. OF THE HARMONY OF THE LAW AND THE GOSPEL.—We believe that the law of God is the eternal and unchangeable rule of
his moral government; that it is holy, just, and good; and that
the inability which the Scriptures ascribe to fallen men to fulfill
its precepts, arises entirely from their love of sin; to deliver them
from which, and to restore them through a mediator to unfeigned
obedience to the holy law, is one great end of the gospel, and of
the means of grace connected with the establishment of the visible church.

XIII. OF A GOSPEL CHURCH.—We believe that a visible church
of Christ is a congregation of baptized believers, associated by
covenant in the faith and fellowship of the gospel; observing the
ordinances of Christ; governed by his laws; and exercising the
gifts, rights, and privileges invested in them by his Word; that
its only scriptural officers are bishops or pastors, and deacons
whose qualifications, claims, and duties are defined in the epistles
to Timothy and Titus.

XIV. OF BAPTISM AND THE LORD'S SUPPER.—We believe that
Christian baptism is the immersion in water of a believer, into
the name of the Father, the Son, and the Holy Ghost; to show
forth, in a solemn and beautiful emblem our faith in the crucified,
buried, and risen Saviour, with its effect, in our death to sin and
resurrection to a new life; that it is prerequisite to the privileges
of a church relation; and to the Lord's Supper, in which the
members of the church by the sacred use of bread and wine, are

to commemorate together the dying love of Christ; preceded always by solemn self-examination.

XV. Of the Christian Sabbath.—We believe that the first day of the week is the Lord's day, or Christian Sabbath; and is to be kept sacred to religious purposes, by abstaining from all secular labor and sinful recreations; by the devout observance of all the means of grace, both private and public; and by preparation for that rest that remaineth for the people of God.

XVI. Of Civil Government.—We believe that civil government is of divine appointment, for the interests and good order of human society; and that magistrates are to be prayed for, conscientiously honored, and obeyed; except only in things opposed to the will of our Lord Jesus Christ, who is the only Lord of the conscience, and the Prince of the kings of the earth.

XVII. Of the Righteous and the Wicked.—We believe that there is a radical and essential difference between the righteous and the wicked; that such only as through faith are justified in the name of the Lord Jesus, and sanctified by the Spirit of our God, are truly righteous in his esteem; while all such as continue in impenitence and unbelief are in his sight wicked, and under the curse; and this distinction holds among men both in and after death.

XVIII. Of the World to Come.—We believe that the end of this world is approaching; that at the last day, Christ will descend from heaven, and raise the dead from the grave to final retribution; that a solemn separation will then take place; that the wicked will be adjudged to endless punishment, and the righteous to endless joy; and that this judgment will fix forever the final state of men in heaven or hell, on principles of righteousness.

JOHN A. BROADUS, D.D., LL.D.

A Catechism of Bible Teaching
For a biographical sketch of Dr. Broadus see page 142.

LESSON I. GOD

1. Who is God? God is the only Being that has always existed, and He is the Creator and Preserver of all things.

2. How do we know that God exists? We know that God exists from the worlds He has made, and from our own sense of right and wrong; and the Bible above all tells us of God.

3. Have men any reason for denying God's existence? It is foolish and wicked to say there is no God. Ps. 14:1; Rom. 1:20.

4. How may we learn the character of God? We learn the character of God partly from His works, mainly from His Word.

5. What does God know? God knows all things, even the secrets of our hearts; God is omniscient. Heb. 4:13; Eccles. 12:14.

6. What power has God? God has all power; God is omnipotent.

7. Where is God? God is everywhere, and all things are present to Him; God is omnipresent. Gen. 16:13; Ps. 139:7.

8. What do we know as to the holiness of God? God is perfectly holy; the angels praise Him as holy. Isa. 6:3; Rev. 4:8.

9. Is God just? God is always perfectly righteous and just. Ps. 145:17.

10. Is God loving and good? God is love, and He is good to all. I John 4:8; Ps. 145:9.

11. Is God all love? God's justice is as truly a part of His nature as His love. Rev. 15:3.

12. How ought we to feel and act toward God? We ought to love God with all our heart and serve Him with all our powers. Deut. 6:5; I John 5:3.

13. Is it our duty to fear God? It is our duty to obey God in filial fear, and to fear His wrath if we sin. Eccles. 12:13; Heb. 10:31.

LESSON II. PROVIDENCE OF GOD

1. What is meant by the providence of God? God cares for all His creatures and provides for their welfare.

2. Does God's providence extend to the wicked? God gives to the wicked, sunshine and rain and all the common blessings of life, thereby calling them to repentance. Matt. 5:45; Ps. 145:9; Rom. 2:4.

3. Does God exercise any special providence over the righteous? God makes all things work together for good to them that love Him. Rom. 8:28; Ps. 23:1.

4. Is God's providence confined to great things? God notices and provides for even the least things. Luke 12:7.

5. Is there really any such thing as chance or luck? There is no such thing as chance or luck; everything is controlled by the providence of God.

6. Does God act according to purposes formed beforehand? God has always intended to do whatever He does. Eph. 1:11; I Pet. 1:20.

7. Do God's purposes destroy our freedom of action? We choose and act freely, and are accountable for all we do. Josh. 24:15; Rom. 14:12.

8. Does God cause evil? God permits evil, but does not cause it.

9. Does God ever check and overrule evil? God often prevents evil, and often brings good out of evil. Gen. 45:5; Ps. 76:10.

10. What is the greatest example of God's bringing good out of evil? The crucifixion of Christ is the greatest example of God's bringing good out of evil.

11. How ought we to think and feel about the providence of God? We ought always to remember our dependence on God, and to trust His providential guidance. James 4:15; Jer. 10:23.

12. When God in His providence sends upon us something painful, how ought we to feel? When God sends on us something painful we ought to be patient, obedient, and thankful. I Sam. 3:18; I Thess. 5:18.

LESSON III. THE WORD OF GOD

Part I. *The Books of the Bible*

1. How many separate books are there in the Bible? There are thirty-nine books in the Old Testament, and twenty-seven in the New Testament.

2. What are the five books of Moses? The five books of Moses are Genesis, Exodus, Leviticus, Numbers, Deuteronomy.

3. What are the other historical books in the Old Testament? The twelve other historical books in the Old Testament are Joshua, Judges, Ruth, I and II Samuel, I and II Kings, I and II Chronicles, Ezra, Nehemiah, Esther.

4. What are the five poetical books? The five poetical books are Job, Psalms, Proverbs, Ecclesiastes, Song of Solomon.

5. Which are the four greater prophets? The four greater prophets are Isaiah, Jeremiah (with Lamentations), Ezekiel, Daniel.

6. Which are the twelve lesser prophets? The twelve lesser prophets are Hosea, Joel, Amos; Obadiah, Jonah, Micah; Nahum, Habakkuk, Zephaniah; Haggai, Zechariah, Malachi.

7. What are the five historical books of the New Testament? The five historical books of the New Testament are Matthew, Mark, Luke, John, Acts.

8. What are the fourteen epistles of Paul? The fourteen epistles of Paul are Romans, I and II Corinthians, Galatians; Ephesians, Philippians, Colossians; I and II Thessalonians; I and II Timothy, Titus; Philemon; Hebrews.

9. What are the seven other epistles? The seven general epistles are James, I and II Peter, I, II, and III John, Jude.

10. What is the last book in the Bible? The last book in the Bible is Revelation.

Part II. *Inspiration and Authority of the Bible*

11. Were the books of the Bible written by men? The books of the Bible were written by men, but these men were moved and guided by the Holy Spirit. II Pet. 1:21; I Cor. 14:37.

12. What special proof have we that the entire Old Testament

is inspired? Christ and his apostles speak of "Scripture," or "the Scriptures," as inspired by God, and we know that they meant exactly what we call the Old Testament. John 10:35; II Tim. 3:16.

13. Does the Bible contain any errors? The Bible records some things said by uninspired men that were not true; but it is true and instructive that these men said them.

14. What authority has the Bible for us? The Bible is our only and all-sufficient rule of faith and practice.

15. What things does the Bible teach us? The Bible teaches all that we need to know about our relations to God, about sin and salvation.

16. How ought we to study the Bible history? We ought to study the Bible as a history of providence and a history of redemption.

17. Who is the central figure of the Bible history? The central figure of the Bible history is Jesus Christ, the Hope of Israel, the Saviour of mankind.

18. What does the Bible do for those who believe in Jesus Christ? The Bible makes those who believe in Jesus wise unto salvation. II Tim. 3:15.

19. What does the Bible contain besides history? The Bible contains doctrines, devotional portions, precepts, and promises; it teaches us how to live and how to die.

20. With what disposition ought we to study the Bible? We ought to study the Bible with a hearty willingness to believe what it says and to do what it requires. John 7:17.

21. What great help must we all seek in studying the Bible? We must pray that the Holy Spirit who inspired the Bible will help us to understand it. Ps. 119:18; Luke 24:45.

LESSON IV. MAN

1. How did men begin to exist? God created Adam and Eve, and from them are descended all human beings.

2. What sort of character had Adam and Eve when created? Adam and Eve were made in the image of God, and were sinless.

3. Who tempted Eve to sin against God by eating the forbidden fruit? Eve was tempted by the Devil, or Satan, who is the chief of the fallen angels, or demons.

4. What was the beginning of Eve's sin? The beginning of Eve's sin was that she believed Satan rather than God. Gen. 3:4, 5.

5. What was the first sign that Adam and Eve gave of having fallen into sin? Adam and Eve showed that they had become sinful by trying to hide from God. Gen. 3:8.

6. What was the next sign? Adam and Eve tried to throw the blame on others. Gen. 3:12, 13.

7. How did God punish their willful disobedience? God condemned Adam and Eve to death, physical, spiritual, and eternal. Gen. 2:17; Rom. 6:23; Eph. 2:1.

8. How does this affect Adam and Eve's descendants? All human beings are sinful and guilty in God's sight. Rom. 5:12.

9. How does this sinfulness show itself? All human beings actually sin as soon as they are old enough to know right from wrong. Rom. 3:23.

10. Will those who die without having known right from wrong be punished hereafter for the sin of Adam and Eve? Those who die without having known right from wrong are saved in the way God has provided.

11. Can any human beings be saved through their own merits from the guilt and punishment of sin? No; the second Adam, the Son of God, is the only Saviour of sinners. Acts 4:12; Gen. 3:15.

LESSON V. · THE SAVIOUR

1. Who is the Saviour of men? Jesus Christ, the Son of God, is the Saviour of men.

2. Was Jesus himself really a man? Yes, Jesus Christ was really a man; he was the son of Mary.

3. Was Jesus the son of Joseph? No, people called Jesus the son of Joseph, but he was really the Son of God. Luke 1:35.

4. Can you give any express statement that Jesus was God?

"The Word was God. . . . And the Word became flesh, and dwelt among us, full of grace and truth." John 1:1, 14.

5. What then is Jesus Christ? Jesus Christ is both God and man, the God-man.

6. How does this fit Jesus to be the Saviour of men? Jesus the God-man can stand between men and God as Mediator.

7. Can you tell the meaning of the two names, Jesus Christ? Jesus means Saviour, and Christ means Anointed, like the Hebrew word Messiah. Matt. 1:21; John 4:25.

8. What did Christ do on earth for us? Christ taught the highest truths, he lived as a perfect example, and he died and rose again to redeem us.

9. What is Christ doing now for us? Christ dwells in his people, intercedes for them, and controls all things for their good. John 14:23; Heb. 7:25; Matt. 28:18.

10. What will Christ do hereafter for us? Christ will come a second time and receive us unto himself, to be with him for ever. John 14:3; Heb. 9:28.

11. What must we do to be saved through Jesus Christ? We must believe in Christ, must turn from our sins to love and obey him, and must try to be like him.

LESSON VI. THE HOLY SPIRIT AND THE TRINITY

1. Who is the Holy Spirit? The Holy Spirit is the Spirit of God, and is called the third person in the Trinity.

2. What did the Holy Spirit do for the prophets and apostles? The Holy Spirit inspired the prophets and apostles to teach men their duty to God and to each other.

3. What did the Holy Spirit do for all the writers of the Bible? The Holy Spirit inspired them to write just what God wished to be written.

4. Did the Holy Spirit dwell also in Jesus Christ? Yes, the Holy Spirit was given to Jesus without measure. Luke 4:1; John 3:34.

5. When Jesus ascended to heaven, what did he send the Holy

Spirit to do? Jesus sent the Holy Spirit to take his place and carry on his work among men. John 14:16, 17.

6. What does the Holy Spirit do as to the world? The Holy Spirit convicts the world of its sin and its need of Christ's salvation. John 16:8.

7. What work does the Holy Spirit perform in making men Christians? The Holy Spirit gives men a new heart, to turn from sin and trust in Christ. John 3:5; Ezek. 36:26.

8. How does the Holy Spirit continue this work? The Holy Spirit helps those who trust in Christ to become holy in heart and life. Gal. 5:22; I Cor. 3:16.

9. Is the Holy Spirit himself divine? Yes, the Holy Spirit is God. Acts 5:3, 4.

10. If the Father is God, and the Saviour is God, and the Holy Spirit is God, are there three Gods? No, there are not three Gods; God is one. Deut. 6:4; Mark 12:29.

11. What then do we mean by the doctrine of the Trinity? The Bible teaches that the Father is God, and the Son is God, and the Holy Spirit is God, and yet God is one.

12. Are we able to explain the Trinity? We cannot explain the Trinity, and need not expect to understand fully the nature of God; we cannot fully understand even our own nature.

13. How is the Trinity recognized in connection with baptism? We are told to baptize "in the name of the Father and of the Son and of the Holy Spirit." Matt. 28:19.

14. How is the Trinity named in a benediction? "The grace of the Lord Jesus Christ, and the love of God, and the communion of the Holy Spirit, be with you all." II Cor. 13:14.

LESSON VII.   THE ATONEMENT OF CHRIST

1. What was Christ's chief work as Saviour? Christ died and rose again for his people. II Cor. 5:15; Rom. 4:25.

2. Did Christ voluntarily allow himself to be slain? Yes, Christ laid down his life of himself. John 10:17, 18.

3. Was this Christ's design in coming into the world? Our Lord says that he came "to give his life a ransom for many." Mark 10:45.

4. For what purpose did the loving God give His only Son? God gave His only Son "that whosoever believeth on him should not perish, but have eternal life." John 3:16.

5. How could Christ's dying give us life? Christ took our place and died like a sinner, that we might take his place and be righteous in him. II Cor. 5:21.

6. Was it right that the just should die for the unjust? The Saviour was not compelled, but *chose*, to die for the benefit of others.

7. Is it right for God to pardon men because the Saviour died? God declares it to be right for Him to pardon men if they seek salvation only through Christ. Rom. 3:26.

8. May a man go on in sin, and expect to be saved through Christ's atoning death? No, we must live for Him who died for us. II Cor. 5:15.

9. Is salvation offered to all men through the atonement of Christ? Yes, salvation is offered to all, and all are saved who really take Christ for their Saviour. Ezek. 18:23; 2 Pet. 3:9.

10. What is Christ now doing for men's salvation? Christ is interceding for all those who trust in his atonement. Heb. 7:25; Rom. 8:34.

LESSON VIII.   REGENERATION

1. What is meant by the word regeneration? Regeneration is God's causing a person to be born again.

2. Are such persons literally born a second time? No, the regenerated are inwardly changed as if they were born over again.

3. In what respect are men changed in the new birth? In the new birth men have a new heart, so as to hate sin and desire to be holy servants of God. Ezek. 11:19, 20.

4. Is this new birth necessary in order to salvation? Without the new birth no one can be saved. John 3:3.

5. Who produces this great change? The Holy Spirit regenerates. John 3:5, 6.

6. Are people regenerated through baptism? No, only those whose hearts are already changed ought to be baptized.

7. Are people regenerated through Bible teaching? Yes, peo-

ple are usually regenerated through the Word of God. I Pet. 1:23; James 1:18.

8. Can we understand *how* men are born again? No, we can only know regeneration by its effects. John 3:8.

9. Does faith come before the new birth? No, it is the new heart that truly repents and believes.

10. What is the proof of having a new heart? The proof of having a new heart is living a new life. I John 2:29; II Cor. 5:17.

LESSON IX. REPENTANCE AND FAITH

1. What is it to repent of sin? Repenting of sin means that one changes his thoughts and feelings about sin, resolving to forsake sin and live for God.

2. Does not repenting mean being sorry? Everyone who truly resolves to quit sinning will be sorry for his past sins, but people are often sorry without quitting.

3. What is the great reason for repenting of sin? The great reason for repenting of sin is because sin is wrong, and offensive to God. Ps. 51:4.

4. Is repentance necessary to a sinner's salvation? Those who will not turn from sin must perish. Luke 13:3; Ezek. 33:11.

5. What do the Scriptures mean by faith in Christ? By faith in Christ the Scriptures mean believing Christ to be the divine Saviour, and personally trusting in him for our salvation.

6. Is faith in Christ necessary to salvation? No person capable of faith in Christ can be saved without it. John 3:6; Heb. 11:6.

7. Can those who die in infancy be saved without faith? Yes, we feel sure that those who die in infancy are saved for Christ's sake.

8. Are they saved without regeneration? Infants are not saved without regeneration, for without holiness no one shall see God.

9. Can we see why persons capable of faith cannot be saved without it? Persons capable of faith must by faith accept God's offered mercy; and His truth cannot become the means of making them holy unless it is believed.

10. Is refusing to believe in Christ a sin? It is fearfully wicked

to reject the Saviour and insult God who gave His Son in love. John 3:18; I John 5:10.

11. Do faith in Christ and true repentance ever exist separately? No, either faith or repentance will always carry the other with it. Acts 20:21.

LESSON X. JUSTIFICATION AND SANCTIFICATION

1. What is meant in the Bible by justification? God justifies a sinner in treating him as just, for Christ's sake.

2. Can any person be justified by his own works? By works of the law shall no flesh be justified. Rom. 3:20.

3. How are we justified by faith? Believing in Christ our Saviour, we ask and receive justification for his sake alone. Rom. 3:24; 5:1.

4. Has this faith that justifies any connection with our works? The faith that justifies will be sure to produce good works. Gal. 5:6; James 2:17.

5. What is meant by sanctification? To sanctify is to make holy in heart and life.

6. What connection is there between sanctification and regeneration? The new birth is the beginning of a new and holy life.

7. Is justification complete at once? Yes, the moment a sinner really believes in Christ he is completely justified.

8. Is sanctification complete at once? No, sanctification is gradual, and ought to go on increasing to the end of the earthly life. Phil. 3:13, 14.

9. Is it certain that a true believer in Christ will be finally saved? Yes, God will preserve a true believer in Christ to the end. John 10:28; Phil. 1:6.

10. What is the sure proof of being a true believer? The only sure proof of being a true believer is growing in holiness and in usefulness, even to the end. II Pet. 1:10.

11. To what will justification and sanctification lead at last? Justification and sanctification will lead at last to glorification in heaven. Rom. 5:2; 8:30; Matt. 25:21.

LESSON XI. BAPTISM AND THE LORD'S SUPPER

1. Who ought to be baptized? Every believer in Christ ought to be baptized.

2. Why ought every believer in Christ to be baptized? Because Christ has commanded us to declare our faith in him by being baptized. Matt. 28:19; Acts 8:12; 10:48.

3. What is the action performed in Christian baptism? The action performed in Christian baptism is immersion in water. Mark 1:9, 10; Acts 8:39.

4. What does this signify? The water signifies purification from sin, and the immersion signifies that we are dead to sin, and like Christ have been buried and risen again. Acts 22:16; Rom. 6:4.

5. Does baptism procure forgiveness or the new birth? No, baptism only represents regeneration and forgiveness like a picture. John 3:5; Acts 2:38.

6. What is meant by our being baptized "in the name of the Father and of the Son and of the Holy Spirit"? It means that we take God the Father, the Son, and the Spirit as our Sovereign and Saviour. Matt. 28:19.

7. What is the solemn duty of all who have been baptized? It is the duty of all who have been baptized to live that new life of purity and obedience which their baptism signifies. Rom. 6:4.

8. What is the Lord's Supper? A church observes the Lord's Supper by eating bread and drinking wine to represent the body and blood of our Saviour. I Cor. 11:20, 26.

9. Why ought the bread and wine to be thus taken? Because Christ has commanded us to eat bread and drink wine in remembrance of him. Luke 22:19.

10. Who ought to partake of the Lord's Supper? Those ought to partake of the Lord's Supper who have believed in Christ, and have been baptized, and are trying to live in obedience to Christ's commands.

LESSON XII. THE LORD'S DAY

1. What does the word Sabbath mean? The word Sabbath means rest.

2. Why was the Sabbath at first appointed? The Sabbath was at first appointed to represent the rest of God after finishing the creation. Gen. 2:3.

3. What says the fourth commandment given through Moses at Mount Sinai? Remember the Sabbath day to keep it holy. Ex. 20:8, 11.

4. What does this show? The fourth commandment shows that the children of Israel knew about the Sabbath, but were apt to neglect it.

5. When the Saviour was charged with breaking the Sabbath, what did he teach about it? The Saviour taught that it was not breaking the Sabbath to heal the sick, to provide food for the hungry, or to do any work of necessity or mercy. Matt. 12:3; Mark 3:4; Luke 13:15, 16.

6. What change was gradually made under the direction of the apostles as to the day to be observed? The day to be observed was changed from the seventh day to the first day of the week, the day on which the Lord Jesus rose from the dead. John 20:1, 19, 26.

7. What is this day called? The first day of the week is called the Lord's day. Rev. 1:10.

8. What do we find the first Christians doing on the Lord's day? They met for public worship, heard preaching, took the Lord's Supper, and gave money for religious objects. I Cor. 16:2; Acts 20:7.

9. Ought we to keep the Lord's day as the Sabbath? Yes, we ought to keep the Lord's day as a day of rest and holy employments.

10. Ought we to keep the Lord's day as the first Christians did? Yes, we ought to keep the Lord's day as a day for public worship, with Bible study and preaching, for religious gifts and ordinances, and for doing good in every way.

LESSON XIII. SOME DUTIES OF THE
CHRISTIAN LIFE

1. What is our duty as to speaking the truth? We must always speak truth and never lie. Eph. 4:25; Ex. 20:16; Rev. 21:8.

2. Is it possible to act a lie without speaking it? Yes, to act a lie may be one of the worst forms of falsehood. Acts 5:3.

3. What is our duty as to speaking evil of others? We must never speak so as to wrong any person. James 4:11.

4. What is meant by profane speech? Profane speech is cursing or swearing, or speaking in an irreverent way of God, or of the Bible, or of anything sacred.

5. What does the Bible say about stealing? "Thou shalt not steal." Ex. 20:15; Eph. 4:28.

6. Can you tell some things which this forbids? The commandment forbids all unfair buying and selling, and any failure to pay promised wages or perform promised work.

7. Is it wrong even to wish to take away another person's property? Yes, the Bible says we must not covet what belongs to another. Ex. 20:17.

8. May we properly strive to do better than others? Yes, we may strive to excel others, but we must not envy others nor try to pull them back. I Pet. 2:1.

9. May we revenge ourselves on those who have wronged us? No, revenge is very wicked, and we must leave punishment of those who have wronged us with God. Rom. 12:19.

10. Ought we to love our enemies just as we love our friends? We ought to love our enemies as God loves His enemies, and so be ready always to do them a kindness. Matt. 5:44, 45.

11. What is our duty as to purity? We must avoid all impure actions and words, thoughts and feelings.

12. How may Christians hope to perform these and all duties of the Christian life? Christians may hope to perform their duties by watchful effort and constant prayer for the help of the Holy Spirit. Matt. 26:41; Luke 11:18.

LESSON XIV. IMITATION OF CHRIST

1. Did the Saviour live a real human life? Yes, the Saviour lived a real human life, but without sin of any kind.

2. Was he tempted to sin? He was tempted in all points just as we are, but he always overcame the temptation. Heb. 4:15.

3. Is it the duty of Christians to imitate Christ? Yes, Christ has left us a beautiful and perfect example, which we ought to imitate. I Pet. 2:21; I Cor. 11:1.

4. How may we hope to imitate Christ? We may hope to imitate Christ by the help of the Holy Spirit. Luke 4:1.

5. What example did the Saviour set as to obeying parents? The Saviour did as his parents directed, and "was subject unto them." Luke 2:51.

6. What example did he set as to the Scriptures? The Saviour attended a Bible class, and had great knowledge of the Scriptures even when a child. Luke 2:46, 47.

7. Did he use the Bible when tempted or suffering? Yes, the Saviour quoted the Bible three times against the tempter, and twice while on the cross.

8. What is his example as to public worship? Our Lord's *custom* was to go into the synagogue on the Sabbath day and worship. Luke 4:16.

9. What example did Christ set as to private praying? Christ prayed often and much, sometimes through a whole night.

10. What example in doing good to men? Jesus all the time "went about doing good." Acts 10:38.

11. What example as to the love of enemies? Jesus prayed for the men who were crucifying him, "Father, forgive them, for they know not what they do." Luke 23:34.

12. What example as to loving Christians? Christ laid down his life for us, and we ought to lay down our lives for the brethren. I John 3:16; John 13:34.

13. What is our highest hope for the future life? "We shall be like him." I John 3:2.

LESSON XV. THE FUTURE LIFE

1. Do men everywhere believe in a future life? In all nations and races men have generally believed in a future and endless life.

2. Does the Bible confirm this belief? The Bible leaves no room to doubt that every human being will always continue to exist.

3. What becomes of the soul at death? The soul is undying, and passes at once into blessedness or suffering. II Cor. 5:8; Luke 16:23, 28.

4. What becomes of the body after death? The body returns to dust, but it will rise again. Gen. 3:19; Eccles. 12:7; Acts 24:15.

5. Will the same body live again? Yes, the very same body will live again, but greatly changed as to its condition and mode of life. I Cor. 15:42-44.

6. What is meant by the day of judgment? The day of judgment means a great and awful day, on which the living and the dead will stand before Christ to be judged. Acts 17:31; Matt. 25:31; II Cor. 5:10.

7. To what will Christ condemn the wicked? Christ will send the wicked away to everlasting punishment in hell. Matt. 25:41, 46.

8. To what will Christ welcome the righteous? Christ will welcome the righteous to everlasting blessedness with him in heaven. Matt. 25:34, 46.

9. Will there be different degrees of punishment? The future punishment will be greater according to the degrees of sin, and the knowledge men had of God's will and of the way of salvation through Christ. Luke 12:47, 48; Mark 12:40.

10. How is hell described in the Bible? Hell is a place of darkness and torment, of endless sin and endless suffering.

11. How is heaven described? Heaven is a place of light and holiness, of freedom from all sorrow and temptation, of blessed society and thankful praise to God. Rev. 7:9, 10; 21:4.

PASSAGES FOR LEARNING BY HEART

It is an excellent thing for the young to commit to memory many portions of Scripture. The following passages are recommended as suitable, and it is hoped that many will learn some of them, and add other selections as thought best.

The Ten Commandments, Ex. 20:1-17.

Psalms 1, 16, 19, 23, 25, 27, 32, 34, 51, 84, 90, 92, 95, 100, 103, 115, 116, 130, 139, 145.

Proverbs 3:1-20; 6:6-11; chap. 10; chap. 11; chap. 20; Ecclesiastes, chap. 12.

Isaiah, chap. 40; chap. 53; chap. 55.

Matthew 5:3-16; chap. 6; chap. 7; chap. 25; 28:18-20.

Mark 14:22-25; 32-42.

Luke 15:11-32; 16:19-31; 18:1-14; 24:13-35.

John 1:1-18; 14:1-15; 20:1-23.

Acts 17:22-31; 20:17-38.

Romans 5:1-11; 8:28-39; chap. 12.

I Corinthians, chap. 13; chap. 15; II Corinthians, chap. 5.

Ephesians 3:14-21; 6:10-20; Colossians 3:1-4; 4:2-6.

I Thessalonians 4:13-18; Titus 2:11-14.

Hebrews 4:14-16; 11:1 to 12:3.

I John 1:5 to 2:6; 3:13-24; chap. 4.

Revelation 1:9-20; 7:9-17; 20:11-15; chap. 21; chap. 22.

TWO CHURCH COVENANTS

Covenant of the Second Baptist Church, Richmond, Virginia

We solemnly covenant together, God helping us, that as strangers and pilgrims we will abstain from fleshly lusts that war against the soul; that we will put away from us all bitterness, and wrath, and anger, and clamor, and evil speaking, and be kind to one another, tender-hearted, forgiving one another, even as God for Christ's sake hath forgiven us; that as we have opportunity we will do good unto all men, especially unto them that are of the household of faith; that we will have no fellowship with the unfruitful works of darkness, but will rather reprove them; that we will contend earnestly for the faith which was once delivered to the saints; will bring our children up in the nurture and admonition of the Lord; will not forsake the assembling of ourselves together as the manner of some is; will keep the ordinances as they were delivered unto us; will confess our faults one to another and pray one for another; that we will remember them which have the rule over us, who speak unto us the Word of God, whose faith we will follow, considering the end of their conversation, Jesus Christ; that we will give as God hath prospered us, not grudgingly or of necessity, for God loveth a cheerful giver, that we be not eased and others burdened; that whatsoever things are honest, whatsoever things are of good report, if there be any virtue, and if there be any praise, we will think on these things; and that whatsoever we do, we will do it heartily, as to the Lord, and not unto men; knowing that of the Lord we shall receive the reward of the inheritance: for we serve the Lord Christ.

Church Covenant [1]

First. We believe that the Holy Scriptures were given by inspiration of God, and that they are the only certain rule of faith and practice.

Second. Whereas various interpretations of the Sacred Word have been given by different denominations of professed Christians, we hereby declare that the foregoing Articles of Faith (the covenant follows the articles) express our views of the meaning of the Word of God, which Holy Word we promise to search diligently and to make the man of our counsel.

---

[1] Widely used. Source unknown.

Third. We agree to contribute towards the support of the worship of God in our own church, and to spread the knowledge of Jesus in our own country and throughout the world according to our ability.

Fourth. We hereby covenant and agree to walk in love and to live in peace, to sympathize with each other under all conditions and circumstances in life, to pray with and for one another, and to exhort and stir up each other unto every good word and work.

Fifth. We solemnly promise, by the assistance of the Holy Spirit, to watch over each other with all kindness and Christian affection; not suffering sin to rest upon a brother, but as far as God in his providence shall make it known to us, we will, in all cases of offense, take our Lord's direction in the 18th chapter of Matthew, which says, "Moreover, if thy brother shall trespass against thee, go and tell him his fault between thee and him alone; if he shall hear thee, thou hast gained thy brother. But if he will not hear thee, then take with thee one or two more, that in the mouth of two or three witnesses every word may be established. And if he shall neglect to hear them, tell it unto the church: but if he neglect to hear the church, let him be unto thee as an heathen man and a publican." And we will urge our utmost endeavors to maintain a scriptural discipline in the church.

Sixth. Moreover, we covenant to meet on the first day of the week for public worship, and to fill up our places at all the appointed meetings of the church, as God shall give us health and opportunity. All and each of these duties we freely and most solemnly promise (by the assistance of the great Head of the church) to observe, until we are planted in the glorious church above.—Amen.

III

SOME BAPTIST
CONTROVERSIES

————————•◦•————————

THE JOHN BUNYAN (1628-1688)—
WILLIAM KIFFEN (1616-1701)
DEBATE ON THE ORDINANCES

The editor of A Baptist Treasury *ventures to publish here a part
of his previously unpublished paper,* Controversies among Eng-
glish Baptists on the Ordinances, *rather than presenting many
short excerpts from the writings of the two famous early Particular Baptists. It seems best for Baptists to know that divergen-
cies of opinion which persist till now have long been present
among our people. The presentation of the early arguments may
give many readers better grounds for clarifying their own views.*

From the beginning there was no agreement among our Baptist
forefathers on the question of how definitely they should separate from Pedobaptists. Should Pedobaptists remain in, or be
received into, church membership? Should they be welcomed
to communion services even if not admitted to full membership?
Does the ordinance of the Lord's Supper depend upon that of
baptism, or are they quite independent ordinances? Is love a

sufficient basis for full fellowship? Was baptism before Pentecost Christian baptism? How should scripture passages like Romans 14:1-3 and I Corinthians 12:13 (for by one spirit are we all baptized into one body) be interpreted? Baptists disagreed vigorously on the answers.

Armitage tells us (without documentation) that Bunyan's publication of his confession of faith in 1672 started matters with Kiffen who attacked in 1673 in a work called *Serious Reflections*, in which he was aided by a colleague named Paul. Bunyan then published his famous *Differences in Judgment Concerning Water Baptism* and Kiffen's final argument was made in *A Sober Discourse of Right to Church Communion*, a copy of which, printed in 1681, we use as a source, along with the two Bunyan works mentioned.

Bunyan was baptized in the church in Bedford which earnestly heeded the dying words of a pastor named Gifford that the church should never separate on "baptism, laying on of hands, anointing with oil, psalms (singing)" or any externals. This advice Bunyan as pastor and denominational leader ever heeded. Such an open position evidently antagonized many Baptist brethren. Bunyan wrote in 1673 of "being assaulted for more than sixteen years, wherein the brethren of the baptized way, as they had their opportunity, have sought to break us in pieces" and says his opponents had called him "a machiavellian, a man devilish, proud, insolent, presumptuous, and the like." Evidently the tension was high before written shots were fired, for Bunyan's church refused letters to strict Baptist churches, while granting them to almost all others. His language during the controversy sometimes reveals more self-confidence and stridency than one might expect from the author of *Pilgrim's Progress*, but we remember the character of the times and make allowances. He was at his best when he wrote the paragraph which reveals the central ideas of his position:

"Touching shadowish, or figurative ordinances; I believe that Christ hath ordained but two in his church, viz., Water baptism and the supper of the Lord: both of which are of excellent use to the church in this world; they being to us

representations of the death and resurrection of Christ; and
are as God shall make them, helps to our faith therein. But
I count them not the fundamentals of our Christianity, nor
grounds or rule to communion with saints: servants they are,
and our mystical ministers, to teach and instruct us in the
most weighty matters of the kingdom of God: I therefore
here declare my reverent esteem of them; yet dare not remove them as some do from the place and end, where by
God they are set and appointed; nor ascribe unto them more
than they were ordered to have in their first and primitive
institution. It is possible to commit idolatry, even with
God's own appointments."

Throughout the controversy Bunyan tried to maintain this
essential position by exegesis of Scripture and logical reasoning.
He considered himself a good Baptist. He held firmly to salvation by faith and resented the charge that he had belittled water
baptism. "That I deny the ordinance of baptism, or that I have
placed one piece of an argument against it, though they feign it,
is quite without color of truth. All I say is, That the Church
of Christ hath not warrant to keep out of their communion the
Christian that is discovered to be a visible saint by the word, the
Christian that walketh according to his light with God."

Bunyan denied that baptism is the door to the church. "John
(the Baptist) gathered no particular church." And, "Philip baptized the eunuch, but made him by that no member of any particular church." In answer to the question, Why then are they
baptized? he replies, "That their own faith by that figure might
be strengthened in the death and resurrection of Christ. And
that themselves might see, that they have professed themselves
dead, and buried, and risen with him to newness of life." His
own requirement for church membership was that one be discovered to be a visible saint by confessing faith and by obedience
to the moral precepts of the gospel.

Bunyan granted "that water baptism hath formerly gone first;
but that it ought of necessity so to do, I never saw proof." (He
doubted that all earliest Christians were given Christian baptism

before being received into fellowship. Hall later attempted formal proof of this point.) He distinguished between the forms of baptism and was willing to grant room for error on the matter of form, provided one had the doctrine which the outward form signifies, namely, "MY DEATH WITH CHRIST. . . . The best of baptisms he hath; . . . he hath the heart of baptism, he wanteth only the outward shew, which if he had would not prove him a truly visible saint, it would not tell me he had grace in his heart."

Basic to this position on the ordinances is the fact that all Baptists acknowledged that Pedobaptists may be saved. "God hath received them," Bunyan says again and again. He includes under the term "weak" (see Rom. 14, 15; I Cor. 8) errors of judgment in such matters as baptism and would apply to Pedobaptists the injunction, "We then that are strong ought to bear the infirmities of the weak, and not to please ourselves." (Rom. 15:1) Differences over the interpretation of this term are about the hottest in the centuries of controversy.

Time prohibits discussion of many interpretations of Scripture used by Bunyan to sustain his cause, but one may consult his use of Colossians 3:12-14, I John 1:3; I Corinthians 3:1, 2 and John 16:12 in his *A Reason for My Practice in Worship* to determine the strength of his proposition for open communion, "because love, which above all things we are commanded to put on is of much more worth than to break about baptism."

A summary of further points must suffice. The Bedford tinker shrewdly uses Paul's words, "For whereas there is among you envying, and strife, and divisions, are ye not carnal?" (I Cor. 3:3) to declare that divisions about things more serious than outward baptism were severely rebuked by the apostle and to press home the point that division into parties is the sad result of the "strict" position.

He is very insistent that it is the duty of Christians to instruct and edify one another and that open communion provides opportunity for this, whereas close communion begets "janglings, contentions, murmurings, and evil surmising."

He points out, finally, that if Pedobaptists are condemned for lack of light on water baptism, then next it will be for lack of light in giving and next for the breaking of a commandment, and so on until there is no end of breaking of fellowship. The right way is rather to bear with brethren unless they can safely be judged to be disfellowshiped by God.

Naturally the question comes as to the fruits of the Bunyan way. As long as Bunyan lived, his church administered believers' baptism by immersion, but his successor, Ebenezer Chandler, introduced infant baptism. The church split on the issue several times and finally became a Congregationalist Church. But the strict Baptists that split off from the original church later practiced close membership with open communion. The Bunyan tradition affected many in all England and has become of late years more influential than ever, practically all English Baptist churches practicing now open communion and many of them open membership.

William Kiffen, Bunyan's great opponent, was the grand old man among early English Baptists. He was a pastor of a Particular Baptist church in London and a man of big business interests too, the wealthiest Baptist of his generation. He always stood squarely for believers' baptism as the only true baptism, and just as strongly for closed communion. His Calvinistic eyes saw these positions, and these alone, in the Scriptures; so for him, God had spoken words of commandment.

At the beginning of his *Sober Discourse* he lays down the invariable order of true worship as being first baptism and then communion, and then says, "I doubt it will be no sufficient plea to say, that if we have erred in any Punctilios of Divine Truth, it was for Peace and Unions sake, & c. For, *No motions of Peace are to be made or received with the loss* of Truth. Nor may the Laws, Orders, and Prescriptions of Christ be altered, or varyed, in any tittle, upon any pretence whatsoever, God never having given any such Prerogative to mankind, as to be arbiters how he may be best and most decently worshiped." Here we see the type of theologian which Dr. E. Y. Mullins used to describe as "Latin minded," one to make the most of the letter of Scripture. The contrast with Bunyan's "Greek" type of mind is immediately striking and the passages of Scripture cited and the interpretation given by each are in accord with this difference of general attitude. These two types Christianity has ever had in her midst, and never the twain seem to meet.

Kiffen deeply feared Bunyan's teachings. He felt that Bunyan minimized the importance of that view of baptism which Baptists alone were emphasizing. He was sure that if "the Sanctity of the Party" (which Bunyan had called "faith and obedience to the moral precepts of the gospel") that proposes himself for communion were the only requirement, then "This sort of thing moves toward Anarchy." To him there was a necessary connection between the two ordinances and baptism *must* precede the Lord's Supper, because of the New Testament precedent.

Bunyan had said that to excommunicate because of lack of baptism would lead to excommunication for countless causes for which no Scripture could be given. Kiffen reasons that to open communion to the unbaptized because Scripture does not expressly prohibit such action will open the door to "Popish Purgatory, and Monkery and ten thousand other things." Not only so, but to lay aside a positive order of the New Testament would, Kiffen thinks, be to lose one of the "Sacraments" (sic) which would make easy way for the loss of the other and "lastly Religion itself."

To break Scripture here is to make it possible to break it elsewhere, and soon Baptists will cease to base on "what we find written." To dispense with baptism is to lessen esteem also for Christ, because Christ commanded it. Still further, he argues that baptism represents to the eye and understanding by a visible sign or figure what has been preached to the ear and heart. It also is the chief witness to repentance and the evidence of regeneration, "which is called in allusion to it the washing of Regeneration," as well as a symbol of death, burial and resurrection. "It is therefore a symbol of very great significancy, and such as go about it to lay it aside (as this opinion in its tendency and Consequence must needs do) deserve no thanks from the Churches of Christ."

On Bunyan's point that Romans 14 and 15 teach that we should bear with the weak in this matter, Kiffen answers that the words

of Paul do not include things relating to the "*worship* of God."
In support of this he quotes Hebrews 8:5: "See that thou make
all things according to the pattern shewed to thee in the mount,"
and then comments, "And no less exact are Christians to be in the
Administration of Gospel Ordinances; since to deviate from the
express Rule is branded with the odious Title of Will-worship
and Human Tradition."

For a man of little formal education Kiffen shows a remarkable knowledge of Christian history. He strongly uses the historical abuses of infant baptism to warn against any compromises
of the Baptist position. He reminds that charity and brotherly
love were the arguments used to introduce both infant and clinic
baptism. The list of quotations he uses in Chapter IV is astonishing.

In his final chapter in which he considers objections to closed
communion, Kiffen faces several issues raised by Bunyan. For
example, Bunyan used I Corinthians 12:13 to argue that "spiritual
baptism" was sufficient grounds for communion. Kiffen bluntly
replies "None where Inchurched without water baptism." He
had no patience with Bunyan's contention that baptism is an individual matter only. Again, when Bunyan asserts that baptism
was practiced in the early church but is not necessarily binding
upon us now, Kiffen asks, "Where is another rule for us? This
is the pretence by which infant baptism & all traditions of men
are brought in." Still another objection is that strict communion
is a dividing principle. Kiffen answers: "God's word sets the
order. To do differently is real dividing from God."

The victory, as far as the number of churches following close
communion is concerned, undoubtedly goes to Kiffen. His influence in his generation seems to have been unmatched. Strict
communion held most of the churches until it was challenged
again by Robert Hall in 1815. Yet, in Kiffen's day, when the
first Assembly of the Particular Baptists met in London, it was
agreed to accept into membership churches which practiced open
communion, though not those which had open membership.
Kiffen seemingly agreed. Was his contention primarily to pre-

vent open membership only? Or was his debate with Bunyan possibly based upon mutual personal dislike?

In any case the main and permanent issues that have continued through the long controversy were made fairly clear in this first clash. They are:

1. Agreement that only believers' baptism is true New Testament baptism.
2. Agreement that Pedobaptists are accepted of God.
3. Agreement that the order practiced in the primitive church was first baptism and then the Lord's Supper (but Hall disagrees), but disagreement that such New Testament practice sets an absolute requirement.
4. Disagreement as to whether baptism is an individual or a church matter.
5. Disagreement on interpretation of significant passages of Scripture (e.g. Rom. 14, 15; Eph. 4:16).
6. Disagreement as to the tendencies and effects following upon either practice.
7. Disagreement as to which practice is best adapted for enlightening and winning Pedobaptists.
8. Disagreement as to whether or not open communion minimizes the significance and importance of baptism.
9. A lack of clarity as to whether or not the term open communion includes open membership.

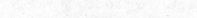

DR. JOHN GILL (1697-1771)

Baptists, both General (those who followed Smyth and Helwys in believing with the Arminians, in a general atonement) and Particular (Calvinistic followers of such leaders as Spillsbury, Kiffen and Bunyan, who believed that the atonement of Christ

*was for the elect only) prospered under hardships and persecu-
tions until toleration was won in 1689 and then rapidly showed
signs of weakness. The General Baptists tended toward Uni-
tarianism and the Particulars developed a killing hyper-Calvinism.
The early evangelistic zeal of the Particulars was lost almost
entirely. John Gill is the outstanding example of those who ex-
pounded doctrine but never invited men to accept Christ. He
was probably the most learned man of his age, by his own efforts
in the main, but his church in London dwindled sadly during the
more than fifty years of his ministry. His strong emphasis on
election and reprobation, summarized in our selections, tended toward Antinomianism and dry rot. This grip of hyper-Calvinism
was loosened by the Wesleyan revival, and the New Connexion
General Baptists, and was finally broken by the practical theology of Andrew Fuller and by Carey's missionary zeal.
(See selection from Fuller.)*

A Body of Doctrinal Divinity

ON ELECTION

The several properties of election may be gathered from what
has been said of it; as:

1. That it is eternal; it does not commence upon believing, and
much less at perseverance in faith and holiness; but it was an act
in God before the foundation of the world (Eph. 1:4).

2. It is free and sovereign; God was not obliged to choose any;
and as it is, he chooses whom he will, and for no other reason
excepting his own glory, but because he will; . . . and the difference in choosing one and not another is purely owing to his will
(Rom. 9:18, 22, 23).

3. It is absolute and unconditional; clear of all motives in man,
or conditions to be performed by him; for it *stands not of works,
but of him that calleth*, the will of him that calls (Rom. 9:11).

4. It is compleat and perfect; it is not begun in eternity and
completed in time, nor takes its rise from the will of God, and is
finished by the will of man; nor is made perfect by faith, holiness,

obedience, and persevering in well doing, but has its complete being in the will of God at once.

5. It is immutable and irrevocable; God never repents of, nor revokes the choice he has made; some choose their friends and favourites, and alter their minds and choose others; but God is in one mind, and never makes any alteration in the choice he has made; and hence their state is safe and secure.

6. It is special and particular; that is, those who are chosen are chosen to be a special people above all others, and are particular persons, whose names are written in the book of life; not in general, men of such and such characters, but persons well known to God, and distinctly fixed on by him.

7. Election may be known by the persons, the objects of it; partly by the blessings flowing from it, and connected with it, before observed, bestowed upon them; for to whomsoever such blessings of grace are applied, they must be the elect of God (Rom. 8:30). They may know it from the efficacy of the gospel upon them, in their vocation and conversion (I Thess. 1:4, 5) and by the Spirit of God testifying their adoption to them, to which they are predestinated (Rom. 8:15, 16) and they may be able to make it known to others by their holy lives and conversations; which is meant by making their calling and election sure, even by their good works, as some copies read (II Pet. 1:10) since both calling and election are to be made sure, and therefore by some third thing: indeed no man can know his election of God until he is called; it would be presumption in him to claim this character, until he is born again; nor should any man conclude himself a reprobate because a sinner, since all men are sinners; even God's elect, who are by nature, and in no wise better than others, but children of wrath, even as others.

There are many things objected to this doctrine of election; but since it is so clear and plain from scripture, and is written as with a sun-beam in it, all objections to it must be mere cavil. It is urged, that God is said to be *good to all, and his tender mercies over all his works* (Ps. 145:9), which seems inconsistent with his choosing some and leaving others; but this is to be understood not of his special grace, but of his providential goodness, which extends to the elect and non-elect, the evil and the good, the just and the unjust (Matt. 5:45), and in this sense he is the saviour, preserver and bountiful benefactor of all men, but especially of them that believe (I Tim. 4:10). It is observed that Christ says he was sent not to *condemn the world, but that the world through him may be saved,* and therefore not some only but all; but to understand this of all the individuals in the world is not true, because all are not saved; and so this end of Christ's mission, so understood, is not answered; but by the world is meant the world of God's elect, whom he was reconciling in Christ, and for whom Christ gave his life, and became the propitiation for their sins, even for all the chosen throughout the whole world, and particularly among the Gentiles.

Nor is I Tim. 2:4 any objection to this doctrine, *Who will have all men to be saved, and to come unto the knowledge of the truth;* for all men are not eventually saved, nor do all come to the knowledge of the truth of the gospel; nor indeed have all the means of that knowledge: but the sense is, either, that all that are saved, God wills to be saved; or that it is his will that men of all sorts and of all nations, Jews and Gentiles, should be saved; which agrees with the context 1, 2, 7.

And when it is said of God, that he is *not willing that any should perish, but that all should come to repentence* (II Pet. 3:9), this must be interpreted, not of all mankind, but of the elect, to whom this and the preceding epistle are inscribed, and who are in verse 8 stiled *beloved,* and in this verse, the *us* towards whom *God is long-suffering;* now it is the will and pleasure of God that none of those should perish, but all in due time be brought to faith in Christ, and to repentance towards God: but objections from hence, with others of the like kind, are not sufficient to overturn this truth, so abundantly established in the sacred scriptures.

ON REJECTION OR REPROBATION

The moving, or impulsive cause of God's making such a decree, by which he has rejected some of the race of Adam from his favour, is not sin, but the good pleasure of his will: sin is the meritorious cause of eternal death, wrath, and damnation; wrath is revealed from heaven against all unrighteousness and ungodliness of men, and comes upon the children of disobedience, whom God leaves in it; the wages, or demerit of sin, is death, even death eternal: but then it is not the impulsive cause of the decree itself; not of preterition, because that, as election, was before good or evil were done, and irrespective of either; nor of pre-damnation, God, indeed, damns no man but for sin; nor did he decree to damn any but for sin; but yet, though sin is the cause of damnation and death, the thing decreed, it is not the cause of the decree itself; it is the cause of the thing willed, but not the moving cause of God's will; for nothing out of God can move his will; if it could, the will of God would be dependent on the will and actions of men; whereas, his purpose, whether with respect to election or rejection, stands not on the works and will of men, but on his own will and pleasure: besides, if sin was the cause of the decree itself, or of God's will to reject men, then all would be rejected, since all fell in *Adam;* all are under sin, all have sinned, and come short of the glory of God; all are, by nature, children of wrath, and deserving of it: what then could move God to choose one and reject another, but his sovereign good will and pleasure? that then is the sole moving and impulsive cause of such a decree; when we have searched the scriptures most thoroughly, and employed our reasoning powers to the highest pitch, and racked our invention to the uttermost; no other cause of God's procedure in this affair can be assigned, but what Christ has expressed; *Even so, Father, for so it seemed good in thy sight;* as to hide the things of his grace and gospel from some, and reveal them to others; so to decree and determine within himself, to act in this manner (Matt. 11:25, 26).

The final cause, or end of this decree, is his own glory; this is the ultimate end of all his decrees and appointments, and so of this, appointing the wicked for the day of evil; it was for this purpose he raised up *Pharaoh,* and decreed all he did concerning him, that he might shew his power in him, his sovereignty and dominion over him, and that his name and glory might be declared throughout all the earth: and the same view he has with respect to all the vessels of wrath, namely, to shew his wrath, and to make his power known, in their destruction, which is of themselves; it is not the death and damnation of the sinner, in which he delights not, that is his ultimate end; it is his own glory, the glory of his perfections, and particularly the glory of his justice and holiness (Prov. 16:4; Rom. 9:17, 22).

The date of this decree is as ancient as eternity itself; wicked men are *before of old* said to be *ordained to condemnation* (Jude 4). . . . And, indeed, there can be no new decree, appointment or purpose, made by God in time; if the decree of election was from eternity, that of rejection must be so too; since there cannot be one without the other; if some were chosen before the foundation of the world, others must be left, or passed by, as early; and, indeed, those whose names are left out of the book of life, are expressly said to be not written in the book of life, from the foundation of the world (Rev. 17:8). . . .

The properties of this decree will appear to be much the same with those of the decree of election, and need be but just mentioned: as,—1. That it is an eternal decree of God. This did not arise in the mind of God in time, as no new act does, but was made before the foundation of the world. —2. That it is free and sovereign, owing to his own will and pleasure, not moved to it by any thing out of himself; *He hath mercy on whom he will have mercy, and whom he will he hardeneth* (Rom. 9:18), and so he determined to do. —3. It is immutable and irrevocable; is it expressed by a decree, a preordination? all the decrees of God are unalterable, there is an immutability in his counsel, let it be concerning what it may. Is it expressed by a writing or a fore-writing, as in Jude 4? It is such a writing as ever remains in full force. Did *Pilate* say, *what I have written, I have written*, signifying it should remain without any alteration (John 19:22)? Then it may be concluded, that what God has written shall remain, and never be revoked; for he is in one mind, and none can turn him. —4. It is of particular persons; it does not merely respect events, characters, and actions; but the persons of men; as they are persons who are chosen in Christ, and appointed, not to wrath, but to obtain salvation by him; so they are persons who are foreordained to condemnation, whose names are left out of the book of life, whilst others are written in it. —5. It is a most just and righteous decree; and no other but such can be made by God, who is righteous in all his ways, and holy in all his works.

ANDREW FULLER (1754-1815)

The "high and dry" hyper-Calvinism of pastors like Dr. John Gill, which almost completely dominated and stagnated the Particular Baptists up to 1785 was at last broken, chiefly by the influence of one man—Andrew Fuller. His modification of high Calvinistic doctrine to the extent that preachers began preaching the responsibility of every man for heeding the call of Christ and then of extending that call to the uttermost parts of the earth was set forth first in 1785 when he published his Gospel Worthy of All Acceptation, *which he had written several years before. Fuller's views spurred on the missionary zeal of Carey, and the two friends won others until they were able to organize, however feeble at first, the Missionary Society in Kettering in 1792. Fuller did the work of enlistment at home while Carey carried on his labors in India.*

Baptists owe Andrew Fuller a double debt: He led them forth in evangelism and in missions. Big in body, he was strong in mind, indefatigable in labors, and tender of heart. Truly one of our greatest men. Our brief excerpt from the concluding paragraphs of his great work should be read in contrast to the excerpts from Dr. Gill.

An excerpt from *The Gospel Worthy of All Acceptation* (concluding reflections)

The work of the Christian ministry, it has been said, is to "preach the gospel," or to hold up the free grace of God through Jesus Christ, as the only way of a sinner's salvation. This is, doubtless, true; and if this be not the leading theme of our ministrations, we had better be any thing than preachers. "Woe unto us, if we preach not the gospel!" The minister who, under a pretence of pressing the practice of religion, neglects its all-important principles, labours in the fire. He may enforce duty till duty freezes upon his lips; neither his auditors nor himself will greatly regard it. But, on the contrary, if by "preaching the gospel" he means the insisting solely upon the blessings and privileges of religion, to the neglect of exhortations, calls, and warnings, it is sufficient to say that such was not the practice of Christ and his apostles. It will not be denied that they preached the gospel; yet they warned, admonished, and entreated sinners to "repent and believe"; to "believe while they had the light"; to "labour not for the meat that perisheth, but for that which endureth unto everlasting life"; to "repent, and be converted, that their sins might be blotted out"; to "come to the marriage supper, for that all things were ready"; in fine, to "be reconciled unto God."

If the inability of sinners to perform things spiritually good were natural, or such as existed independently of their present choice, it would be absurd and cruel to address them in such language. No one in his senses would think of calling the blind to look, the deaf to hear, or the dead to rise up and walk; and of threatening them with punishment in case of their refusal. But if the blindness arise from the love of darkness rather than light; if the deafness resemble that of the adder, which stoppeth her ear, and will not hear the voice of the charmer, charm he never so wisely; and if the death consist in alienation of heart from God, and the absence of all desire after him, there is no absurdity or cruelty in such addresses.

But enforcing the duties of religion, either on sinners or saints, is by some called "preaching the law." If it were so, it is enough for us that such was the preaching of Christ and his apostles. It is folly and presumption to affect to be more evangelical than they were. All practical preaching, however, is not preaching the law. That only, I apprehend, ought to be censured as preaching the law, in which our acceptance with God is, in some way or other, placed to the account of our obedience to its precepts. When eternal life is represented as the reward of repentance, faith, and sincere obedience (as it too frequently is, and that under the complaisant form of being "through the merits of Christ"), this is preaching the law, and not the gospel.

But the precepts of the law may be illustrated and enforced for evangelical purposes; as tending to vindicate the Divine character and government; to convince of sin; to show the necessity of a Saviour, with the freeness of salvation; to ascertain the nature of true religion; and to point out the rule of Christian conduct. Such a way of introducing the Divine law, in subservience to the gospel, is, properly speaking, preaching the gospel; for the end dominates the action.

If the foregoing principles be just, it is the duty of ministers not only to exhort their carnal auditors to believe in Jesus Christ for the salvation of their soul; but IT IS AT OUR PERIL TO EXHORT THEM TO ANYTHING SHORT OF IT, OR WHICH DOES NOT INVOLVE OR IMPLY IT. I am aware that such an idea may startle many of my readers, and some who are engaged in the Christian ministry. We have sunk into such a compromising way of dealing with the unconverted as to have well nigh lost the spirit of the primitive preachers; and hence it is that sinners of every description can sit so quietly as they do, year after year, in our places of worship. It was not so with the hearers of Peter and Paul. They were either "pricked in the heart" in one way, or "cut to the heart" in another. Their preaching commended itself to "every man's conscience in the sight of God."

How shall we account for this difference? Is there not some important error or defect in our ministrations? I have no reference to the preaching of those who disown the Divinity or atonement of Christ, on the one hand, whose sermons are little more than harangues on morality, nor to that of gross Antinomians on the other, whose chief business it is to feed the vanity and malignity of one part of their audience, and the sin-extenuating principles of the other. These are errors the folly of which is "manifest to all men" who pay any serious regard to the religion of the New Testament. I refer to those who are commonly reputed "evangelical," and who approve of addresses to the unconverted.

I hope no apology is necessary for an attempt to exhibit the Scriptural manner of preaching. If it affects the labours of some of my brethren, I cannot deny but that it may also affect my own. I conceive there is scarcely a minister amongst us whose preaching has not been more or less influenced by the lethargic systems of the age.

Christ and his apostles, without any hesitation, called on sinners to "repent, and believe the gospel"; but we, considering them as poor, impotent, and depraved creatures, have been disposed to drop this part of the Christian ministry. Some may have felt afraid of being accounted legal; others have really thought it inconsistent. Considering such things as beyond the "power" of their hearers, they seem to have contented themselves with pressing on them things which they "could" perform, still continuing the enemies of Christ; such as behaving decently in society, reading the Scriptures, and attending the means of grace.

Thus it is that hearers of this description sit at ease in our congregations. Having done their duty, the minister has nothing more to say to them; unless, indeed, it be to tell them occasionally that something more is "necessary" to salvation. But as this implies no guilt on their part, they sit unconcerned, conceiving that all that is required of them is "to lie in the way, and to wait the Lord's time." But is this the religion of the Scriptures? Where does it appear that the prophets or apostles ever treated that kind of inability which is merely the effect of reigning aversion as affording any excuse? And where have they descended, in their exhortations, to things which might be done, and the parties still continue the enemies of God?

Instead of leaving out every thing of a spiritual nature, because their hearers "could" not find in their hearts to comply with it, it may safely be affirmed they exhorted to "nothing else"; treating such inability not only as of "no account," with regard to the lessening of obligation, but as rendering the subjects of it worthy of the severest rebuke. "To whom shall I speak, and give warning, that they may hear? Behold, their ear is uncircumcised, and they 'cannot' hearken: behold, the word of the Lord is unto them a reproach, and they have no delight in it." What then? Did the prophet desist from his work, and exhort them to something to which, in their present state of mind, they "could" hearken? Far from it. He delivers his message, whether they would hear, or whether they would forbear.

"Thus saith the Lord, Stand ye in the ways, and see, and ask for the old paths, where is the good way, and walk therein, and ye shall find rest for your souls. But they said, We will not walk therein." And did this induce him to desist? No: he proceeds to read their doom, and calls the world to witness its justice: "Hear, O earth! behold, I will bring evil upon this people, even the fruit of their thoughts, because they have not hearkened unto my words, nor to my law, but rejected it" (Jer. 6:10-19). Many of those who attended the ministry of Christ were of the same spirit. Their "eyes were blinded," and their "hearts hardened," so that they COULD NOT BELIEVE; yet, paying no manner of regard to this kind of inability, he exhorted them "to believe in the light while they had the light." And when they had "heard and believed not," he proceeded, without hesitation, to declare, "He that rejecteth me, and receiveth not my words, hath one that judgeth him: the word that I have spoken, the same shall judge him in the last day."

. . . . .

When did Jesus or his apostles go about merely to form the "manners" of men? Where do they exhort to duties which a man may comply with and yet miss of the kingdom of heaven? If a man "kept their sayings," he was assured that he "should never see death." In addressing the unconverted, they began by admonishing them to "repent and believe the gospel"; and in the course of their labours exhorted to all manner of duties; but all were to be done "spiritually," or they would not have acknowledged them to have been done at all. Carnal duties, or duties to be performed otherwise than "to the glory of God," had no place in their system.

The answer of our Lord to those carnal Jews who inquired of him what they "must do to work the works of God" is worthy of special notice. Did Jesus give them to understand that as to believing in him, however willing they might be, it was a matter entirely beyond their power? that all the directions he had to give were that they could attend the means and wait for the moving of the waters? No: Jesus answered, "This is the work of God, that ye believe on him whom he hath sent." This was the "gate at the head of the way," as the author of *The Pilgrim's Progress* has admirably represented it, to which sinners must be directed. A "worldly-wise" instructor may inculcate other duties, but the true "evangelist," after the example of his Lord, will point to this as the first concern, and as that upon which every thing else depends.

JOHN CLIFFORD (1836-1923)

Dr. John Clifford *is one of the mightiest giants of Baptist history, even though not well known in America. For fifty-seven (1858-1915) years he was pastor of Westbourne Park Baptist Church in London. From that pulpit he influenced all England and all the Baptist world by his evangelical fervor and his unremitting and uncompromising fights for religious liberty, human freedom, rights of conscience, social justice, and Christian understanding. He was a personal soul-winner all his life. He studied hard for a formal education and then continued hard study in spite of stupendous pastoral and public services. He was very*

active in the Baptist World Alliance from the time of its forma-
tion (1905) until his death. He knew well many national and
world leaders of every sort. Lloyd George was a familiar friend.
He led the New Connexion Baptists into the Baptist Union in
1891.

When in 1888 Clifford delivered the address which appears
below at his inauguration as president of the Union, Baptists in
England were experiencing a period of theological unrest. Some
believed that a portion of the leadership of the Union had been
too much affected by the new studies in criticism, and it was
feared that they were forsaking the old fundamentals. Clifford's
statesmanlike utterance defended progress and research, reaf-
firmed fundamental gospel, and thus prevented a disastrous split
within the denomination.

From "The Great Forty Years; or, the Primitive Christian Faith: its Real Substance and Best Defence"

We meet this morning, fathers and brethren, at the impulse, and
with many of the anxieties, of internal controversy. The experience is mainly if not wholly new within the bounds of this Christian organization; but, as you know, it is extremely common in
the longer story of our aggressive religion. Therefore, though
our strife is sad and forbidding in many of its aspects, yet we
need not enter upon our proceedings with weakening dread or
corrupting timidity, as if "some strange thing had happened to
us."

Study of the ages of controversy ought to quiet our alarm,
enlarge patience, extirpate self-seeking, exclude personal recrimi-
nations, exalt brotherly love, quicken joyful trust in, and large
expectancy from, the Gracious Ruler of His Church. But, above
all, since the sinuous subtlety with which sin assails even the purest theological combatants is so palpable, we can scarcely do
amiss if we cry out, as beneath the fierce blaze of the Eternal
Holiness, "Search me, O God, and lead me the way everlasting."

Robert Hall says, "The evils of controversy are all temporary, and its benefits are all permanent." It is a consolatory message. We accept it with thankfulness; but it remains "a hard saying," and amid the din of actual and on-pressing conflict we can scarcely receive it. Nor is it rendered more welcome when we add the mysterious word of Paul: "There must be heresies among you, that they which are approved may be made manifest among you." We are, therefore, on our trial *now*.

Today we stand before the judgment seat of Christ. The great white throne is here. I see it; and seated on it one like to the Son of Man, from whose mouth goes the sharp two-edged sword, and whose eyes are as a flame of fire. The books are opened. Every man's word, yours and mine, is going down; "for by thy words thou shalt be justified, and by thy words thou shalt be condemned."

The existence of church parties is the severest test of our loyalty to the Lord Jesus. Nothing puts a heavier strain on our self-suppression, holy discipline, and sweet charity; or so acutely tests our powers of discrimination between the vanishing forms and the actual substance of truth, or checks our swift-rushing eagerness to anticipate one another in kindly word and deed, or accurately fixes the measure in which we are filled and swayed by the Spirit of Christ. Fortunate indeed, is he who whatever else he may lose in this warfare, carries in his heart, unbeguiled by the devices of Satan, the sure approbation of the Holy Judge Himself.

O Christ Jesus! our Redeemer! more actually here than we ourselves are, fill us so with the fear and love of Thee that we may seek first Thy kingdom and Thy righteousness, and care for nothing else in heaven, or earth, or hell than Thy "Well done!"

God has not given the spirit of fear. More mischief comes of it than of boldness. Cowardice corrupts; courage saves. Timorous is the brother of Ready-to-halt, and cousin to Facing-both-ways. Frank, manly, and grace-filled speech is the salt of life. Controversy is far better than stagnation. Even strife is a sign of vitality—uncomfortable, irritating vitality, perhaps; exceed-

ingly disagreeable to fossil theologians and actual tyrants; but still
it is vitality, and one of the various forms of that law of the
struggle for existence which runs into the realm of ideas and of
spirit as surely as into that of gigantic icthyosaurs and pterodac-
tyls.

He is not the typical Christian who is forever hugging the
shores in search of the quietest harbors, but he who braves the
storm and tempest with his lifeboat that he may save; not John
Mark running from his work to his mother, but the apostle who
charms the music of the evangel out of the clanking chains on
his wrist for the soldier of Caesar's guard, and converts the
Roman prison into a study, from underneath whose dark shadows goes forth a literature which for evermore illumines the
path of all heroic and death-daring men. True saints of God, like

> Castilian gentlemen,
> Chose not their work; they choose to do it well——

sowing seeds, or fighting a foe; healing the sick, or contending
for the faith; solacing the weary, or driving to death and a deserved grave the smug respectabilities and hollow orthodoxies of
the Jewish and modern worlds. The sharpest challenges of Christianity have elicited its irresistible energy and secured its most
masterly advances. It was in a day of stress and storm John
wrote, "This is the victory that *overcometh* the world, even our
faith."

The history of Christianity is the history of controversy. Our
Master said, "I came to cast *fire* on the earth;" and here, as everywhere, He has kept His word. The fire has gone burning and
cleansing on, consuming the falsehoods and partialisms of ages,
and making more luminous the revelation of God in Christ, the
Divine Fire-bringer. Disputes with the Temple party at Jerusalem are the setting of the sublimest speech of the Son of the
Highest concerning Himself and His relations to the souls of
Men.

Philosophic debates at Colossae give rise to the awe-inspiring
portraiture of the ineffable glory of "the fullness of the Godhead bodily." Peter and Jude make palpable the central position

of the Cross in our religion when they denounce with scorching energy those who privily bring in destructive heresies, denying even the Master that bought them, and who is therefore their rightful Lord. John exposes the capital heresy of this and every age when he signalizes as deceivers all those who refuse to acknowledge "that Jesus Christ is come in the Flesh," an actual man amongst common men; and so detaches us from that teaching, abiding in which "we have *both* the Father and Son."

Nor is this all. Internal controversy has often expanded the sway of truth, freed souls, quickened missionary zeal, and purified the Church. Even the first friends of Christianity were never perfectly agreed as to its whole contents. *Living* men differ. It is the dead who agree. Poor shattered fragments that we are! Why! truth would have no chance at all on the earth if each man were nothing but the sibilant echo of his fellow. God sets men at different angles to the truth, so that one may see what others cannot, and, thereby, more of her virginal beauty and perennial loveliness be revealed to men.

The four Gospels are four mirrors placed over against the Christ at different positions, and revealing different aspects of the One Unique Figure. They are not echoes, but voices, each living and distinct in tone and timbre, quality and message; but all speaking in perfect harmony, and contributing to the sweetness and fullness of the majestic music. Peter is not a plaster cast of the Apostle John. Paul does not always endorse Peter; he does us good, and the world too, by withstanding him to the *face* when he is to be blamed. Practical James does not copy the *Romans;* he writes his own letter in his own way, and differs with and completes Paul. . . .

Pluck the fruits of controversy from the New Testament tree, and you have not only stripped it of its most precious growths, but left the branches so bare that they cease to be a sheltering home for the wearied nations of the earth.

The first century is a sample. The Jews are not out of the arena before other combatants appear eager for the fray. Lucian of Samosata, with his caustic satire, lofty scorn, and profane parody of Christian martyrdom; Celsus, as bitter and disdainful as he is able; Fronto, sardonic and satirical; Apollonius, with his formal philosophy and speculative genius; Porphyry, critical, penetrating, and damaging; these and their compeers used all the weapons of the armory of attack on the religion of the Cross— fierce rancor, pessimistic cynicism, coarse rationalism, and super- cilious hauteur. It was a painful struggle. Men who loved truth and adored the Christ were forced to fight for the citadel of Christianity; and they fought long and courageously, leaving their mistakes for our warning, their zeal for our imitation, and their victories for our solace and inspiration.

And whilst the battle raged without there was anything but peace at home. Theological debate was as rife in Antioch and Rome as political is in Liverpool and Bradford. Men talked as freely about the relations of the Father and of the Son as we do about the union of hydrogen and oxygen in water. Romanists and Evangelicals have both tried to make out that the Christians of the early centuries were perfectly agreed as to the significance of the Christian revelation, and moved on the same lines of theo- logical doctrine.

It is a vain attempt. Historical study has shown the utter false- ness of the position, and historical theology is becoming one of the most healing of the forces of Christian literature. Dr. New- man, in his remarkable book on *The Development of Christian Doctrine*, "has attempted to lead contemporary Catholicism into this more liberal and scientific track by admitting without hesi- tation the variations of primitive theology."

Indeed, nothing is more certain than that our Christianity was born in stillness and cradled in obscurity, developed its great strength by sustained combat with the Goliaths of Paganism and Philosophy, and incessant efforts to clear itself from the crudities and exaggerations of its own expositors and defenders. The "Kingdom" came without observation; but it had not been here long when the clash of arms was heard; and the sword of con- troversy has not been sheathed from that day to this.

God educates His Church, if I may say it, by the Socratic method. He forces us to face the questions that test us, and at- tack the problems which try our strength; and thereby brings

the sleeping energies of His living words into wakeful and beneficent activity. The Sphinx is one of our best teachers. "Easy
come, easy go," is true of knowledge as well as of money; and
true of even more precious things—of faith and hope, self-
mastery and inward calm, resolute will and character. Even He,
the pattern for us all, learned obedience by the things He suffered, and we must go through much tribulation to the kingdoms
of truth and service. God will not suffer us to get our best beliefs as we do our coats. He forces our unrealized creeds through
the furnaces of criticism, and they come forth in us as soul-
propelling convictions. Give men a ready-made faith, paid for by
pen subscription, or lip affirmation, and it is *on* them, not in
them; on them like a garment, not in them as a life.

Give us a Bible about which two opinions are not possible, and
we treat it as we do the multiplication table, use it for our grosser
needs; but never think of it for the splendid hours of spiritual
aspiration and redeeming service. Give us a Book full of truths
we can never master, and depths we can never fathom, and it is
exactly like our human life, and part of it; and as we use it so we
are built up in strong convictions and inspiring faiths. The effort
educates. The pain cleanses. The overpowering sense of weakness flings us in glad and unhesitating trust on the omnipotent
forces of the Spirit, and so we become stronger and stronger.

For myself I will say that, whilst I feel it impossible to exaggerate the gravity of this occasion, yet I do not look on with
pessimistic fears. I believe in the living Christ, the Redeemer and
Ruler of men. According to His promise, the Spirit is leading
us along rugged paths to the fuller enjoyment and use of the
truth. His Kingdom rules over all; over all men and all churches,
and He will be exalted over all. Sustained by that faith, let us be
true in speech, resolutely honest in exposition, and loving and
forgiving in spirit, and these things shall fall out rather to the
progress of the Gospel, and share in making more manifest the
*Primitive Christian Faith in its real substance and best defense,
just as it was in the Great Forty Years of Original Christianity.*

II

But whatever the issues may be for ourselves as individuals, and as a Union of Churches, it ought to encourage us, in the present distress, that *the controversies of Christendom are gravitating with accelerated energy around the Lord Jesus, the Divine Redeemer and Ruler of men.* This is as undeniable as it is prophetic of final victory. The battles of religion and of man are really battles about Christ and for Christ; for Christ's ideas and Christ's methods; for the sway of Christ's spirit in the whole of life, home and Church, nation and world; for the perpetual and universal incarnation of the passion and power of the Cross on the floor of this broad earth; and in actual touch of sinning and suffering men.

God is compelling us to answer all our questions in the terms of Jesus Christ. Our controversies on ethics and politics, ritual and theology, ecclesiastics and eschatology, are rooted in spiritual facts and ideas; and spiritual facts and ideas have their sublime ideal and infallible revelation in the Son of Man, the supreme creative personality of the religious life. We can settle no difficulties of that life without His help; we cannot even understand them. Without Him, the "service of man" is a code of rules hung on a factory wall, to be evaded as soon as the foreman is out of sight. Without Him, our "culture" is a cheap veneer with a fine polish; and our "ethical idealism" only an intellectual luxury. Without Him, business is a fight for pelf, politics a scramble for place, ritual a pleasant performance, a creed a coffin for a faith, and theology a death's head. . . .

And we know, from ever accumulating evidence, that the perfectest conceptions of duty, and the highest inspirations to obedience to the Best, are in Him who is Godhood and manhood revealed to, and dwelling with, the sons of men. Hegel says: "The heritage a great man leaves the world is to *force* it to explain him." On that scale Christ is unmatched, and His legacy unparalleled, and this the splendid hour in which beyond all preceding times, He is *forcing* all men, in churches and out of them, to take part in explaining His simple and unique relations to the whole life of mankind.

Viewed in patches, and in our sadder moments, it may seem as if all men were rebelling against Christ, and would not have Him to reign over them. Looked at along narrow lines, it may appear as though skepticism and unbelief were conquering men of education; mammon, men of business, and vacuity the remainder; ay, and examining the churches, one might imagine they had forgotten they are not their own, but are bought with a price and under unescapable obligations to save other people, whether they themselves are saved or not; but when the age is beheld in its depth and inwardness, in its yearnings and hopes, in its substantial faith and quiet service, it is clear that Jesus Christ is going everywhere, that His teachings are being sown in all soils. His power is present to heal in the synagogues of debate, His pavilion is at the very center of the world's life, and His disciplined hosts are marching, as of old, from strength to strength and from victory to victory. The contest is between Christ and the age, and "He must reign till He has put all His enemies under His feet."

III

That fact is light as well as solace, and defines and demonstrates our immediate work. We must go where Christ is, get at the very heart of His religion, and fight for it with all our wisdom and might. We must have "the old Gospel"—the Gospel of the Great Forty Years—the years from thirty to seventy in the first century, the sublime creative era in the history of mankind and in the annals of Christianity.

If the Spirit of Christ is bearing us on through all controversies, ourselves often not knowing it, towards Christ, we surely, who are His men, must reach Him, sit at His feet, and learn of Him who is meek and lowly in spirit. Then we must represent Him, interpret His heart, make His idea of God regnant in the life of man, His thoughts of sin a fire in the conscience, His message of forgiveness a medicine, His ideal of duty a law, and His salvation in its length and breadth a living world-wide experience. The Gospel was given for that.

God uses us to help each other so
Leading our minds out.

Somebody has said ninety per cent of modern wars originated
in mistakes. Should I go far astray if I said ninety per cent of
the controversies of Christians started with misconceptions,
thrived on confusion and bitterness, and became perpetual
through the power of "vested interests"? The *first* requisite, then,
is not to fight, but to be *perfectly sure that we have, and therefore can fight for, "the faith which was once for all delivered to
the saints,"* and not for that which somebody, who may not
know any better than ourselves, has labeled and handed to the
world as "the faith."

We must fight for "the thing itself," not something like it,
not something that may perhaps be it and is not, but for that
which Jesus Christ put into the custody of His disciples, and
charged them to carry to all peoples on earth. Christ is God,
and gives the thought of God. The thought of God makes or
mars the man; corrupts and destroys him if it be false and bad;
if it be true and good, builds him up in love and trust and hope
and service for evermore.

This is the "one thing needful." Before all things we must
possess ourselves of the imperishable substance of the primitive
Christian faith.

It is this momentous task I feel myself compelled to attempt:
but not as claiming any authority. My work has too wide a
sweep, is beset with too many difficulties, to allow me to feel
like one having authority. I do not even ask anyone to agree
with me; I seek to discharge what I feel to be a duty, remembering that the sources of evidence are open to you as they are
to me, but fervently praying that my words may contribute to
that real Christian unity, strong love of God and souls and society, we all have at heart.

IV

But how can we be sure of the original Christianity of the Great Forty Years?

Fortunately inquiry is neither new nor unfamiliar. When Martin Luther arose from his knees, on the holy staircase at St. John's Lateran, in Rome, he was a new man. New men put new questions; and his new question broke the spell of the ages, and forced Europe to ask, with quickened interest and alluring hope, "What is Christianity?" "What is the faith that saves?"

The question has not slept for long since, and is today more wakeful than ever. Accustomed to take their answer from the lips of the Pope and his accomplices, men had sunk into a weakening content, and Europe into a deepening decay. The monk reformed their *method* of studying religion, lifted their horizon, quickened penitence, and changed their life. They looked to Rome; he turned their eyes to Jerusalem. They listened to "councils" and "fathers"; he bade them hear the living oracles of God. They lost conscience, character, and Christ through the priests; he urged them back to the Saviour, and they became new men in Him, "created in righteousness and holiness of truth."

That impact is still upon us, and we move forward by its unspent energy. "The greatest gift a hero leaves his age is to have been a hero"; but surely the next greatest is to have invented a new and fruitful method of work. Lord Bacon served the generations of men in many ways; but the inductive method of scientific study is his everlasting memorial. So modern Christianity has been enriched by the massive sense and contagious enthusiasm of Martin Luther in manifold forms; but most of all in his use and vindication of the best method of finding an answer to the question "What is the substance of the Christianity of Jesus Christ?"

By a new experiment, a scientist obtains the confirmation of his first result, and thus vindicates his way of working; so a fresh application of the Lutheran method was given of God in the last century, which made its value indisputable. That century was one of spiritual darkness, decay, and death. It was the era of revolution; the incarnation of the spirit of denial. Everything was in debate; the foundations of life and thought were shaken out of course. Hume attacked knowledge; Voltaire assailed the Church; Rousseau carried fire and sword into the very citadel of society. The philosophers examined man and found no mind, as they had investigated the universe and found no God. Theology was reduced to criticism, and Christianity to acrid syllogisms.

. Now, it is not given to one man to tell everything. Mill has shown that Bacon's method is insufficient to detect the most obscure and difficult laws of nature. But our God is not poor; His resources are infinite and His Spirit is never dumb. So in the fullness of time He raised up that greatest of modern apostles, John Wesley, and that prince of Baptist theologians, Andrew Fuller.

Wesley made Methodism by his thoroughgoing application of Luther's method; and Fuller introduced a change scarcely less fruitful by his treatment of theology. That theology began the renewal of our churches; roused the collective life of the Baptists of several Midland counties through their Associations; increased prayer, inflamed zeal, and inspired the modern missionary enthusiasm for humanity. Conscience, the stronghold of missions to the heathen, was rediscovered and rebuilt. Christians felt with Paul that they were "debtors" of men, and owed to the millions of Hindostan and China the "Gospel worthy of all acceptation."

Faithful Samuel Pearce set it aflame in the fires of his seraphic devotion; Robert Hall made it luminous with his brilliant genius; John Foster set it foursquare to the whole of man's ethical life; Sutcliffe, Ryland, and the immortal Carey put it to work for the salvation of India.

Men have doubted for a long time whether the red flames seen in total eclipses of the sun belong to the sun or the moon. An eclipse is an experiment in Nature's vast laboratory. In a recent one a trained eye noticed that the flames *moved with the sun*, and were gradually covered by the moon at successive instants of the eclipse. Nothing could be more conclusive. Doubt fled. The fact was established. So in the more interesting lab-

oratory of human life, a religious experiment with changed conditions has been conducted through the last half century. A
new and beneficent impulse came into play fifty years ago, and
is mightily operative still. Partly from physical science and its
eternal insistence on the *fact*—first the *fact*, and always and everywhere the fact—and partly from the reaction against the unreal-
ities and hollownesses and insincerities of the preceding age, there
was born that intense and domineering love of fact which is the
characteristic of our day. . . .

The conclusion is established with all the severity of scientific
processes. To get a living and real Christianity today, one that
will work out the salvation of the individual and the race, we
must find out what Christianity is; to know what it is we must see
it in its original integrity. Christ Himself is its Expositor as well
as its Creator—Christ in the New Testament, Christ in the Church
of the first days. Luther made Europe anew by going back to
Paul and Christ. The fact is typical. Every approximation to
Christ leads to the simplicity that is in Christ. Stop short of Him,
and in the degree of your distance you are exposed to the corruptions of a Romanistic conception of the Gospel and of the
Church.

The sole invariable antecedent of a Christianity serviceable in
the highest degree to man and men is the actual Christianity of
Jesus Christ in the New Testament; and the method that compels us to study those writings is the one that supplies the best
answer to the questions, "What is the Christianity for today?"
"What was the Christianity of Jesus Christ, the Christianity of
the Great Forty Years?"

Get that method to work. Use it with exactness and thorough-
ness. Do not forget that, though the facts of original Christianity face us today as they have not faced any century except the
first, yet they are often hard to interpret; though they look simple, they are complex; though few, yet they have far-reaching
ramifications. But fling *theories* to the winds with the energy of
science; eliminate all known chances of error; move with un-
sleeping alertness; omit nothing; add nothing; learn all; and we

ought to establish a conclusion on which we can rest as on
granite.

Take three cases.

1. Begin at the beginning, with the first utterance by man of
the Christian faith, "the primordial germ" of the Christian creeds;
and of which we have the guarantee that Christ Himself approved it, hailed its expression with rapturous joy, and directly
and distinctly attributed it to the inspiration of the Father.

a. Listen to the First Christian Confessor! He starts on the
solid base of fact. "*Thou* art the Christ, the Son of the living
God." "*Thou*"! the Man, loved and glad of love, the Friend of
young men, the Reformer of the Jewish religion, the working-
man Jesus.

b. "Thou art the Christ!" The outburst is alive with soul. It
is a hymn of adoration even more than a statement of belief;
throbs with the whole heart of Peter, and the impulsive energies
of the Holy Ghost. "Flesh and blood hath not revealed it unto
thee!" Peter has not been to the Rabbis. He is not fresh from
a theological debate. This Creed is not of human origin elab-
orated by reasoning, a scholastic proposition, the starved child
of a pinched logic: it is the actual gift and the veritable inspiration of the Father.

c. Fathom its meanings. Thou art the Christ; the anointed of
Jehovah; the key to all human struggle; the ideal of all aspiration;
the authentic interpretation of the past; the supreme satisfaction
for the coming ages. Peter is the typical—the most typical man
of a typically religious people. He has been brought by Christ's
training to the summit of the Hebrew race, and is the qualified
representative of the Hebrew prophets. The highest man has
the largest constituency, the widest representation; hence Peter
gives utterance to the joy of humanity in the fulfillment of the
hope of the world. Humanity has its Christ, and therefore history is not a chaos, but an order; not a chapter of accidents but
a veritable progress; not a confusion, but a sure, if slow, evolution in His Divine Person and Work of the Divine idea of Redemption.

d. Not only so, this primary creed is one of those luminous

soul-sentences that flash light on a universe of thought. In compactest form it packs the fullness of evangelic ideas. *"Thou art the Christ, the Son of the living God!"* Mind of His mind, thought of His thought, heart of His heart, will of His will; One with Him who lives in every movement, is in contact with every soul; the living Lord and Ruler of the eternities; the beloved *Son* of the *Father;* the perfectest manifestation of Deity; God coming out of His Eternal Invisibility to get hold of us and save us; uttering His highest speech to our heart; responding to the pathetic hunger of souls for His "bread of life"; demonstrating that Deity is not cold, dead law, but warm, glowing life; not an impassive majesty, a distant spectator, but an ineffable Father-Heart, suffering to redeem, and redeeming to reign in love and righteousness for evermore.

There you have it—*Facts, Forces, Ideas;* not less, not more; not facts only, and so nothing but a retrospect, a page of history; not ideas only, and so nothing but an effort of intellect; but ideas, facts, and forces—the forces which are above, and come to us men bringing an everlasting salvation. Ah, brothers! get that creed as Peter got it; let it be in you by the power of the Father, and come forth in adoring trust and worshiping love; and whoever may condemn you, one voice will be heard in the silence of your spirit, saying, "Blessed art thou; flesh and blood hath not revealed it unto thee, but My Father who is in Heaven."

2. At the *close* of our Lord's ministry another original and irresistible expression of the primitive Christian faith meets us. It follows the Crucifixion, and has been cleansed and energized in the fires of agonizing doubt. More concise than Peter's, it is not more comprehensive. Like Peter's, it is not an echo, but a voice; not a recitation, but a conviction; not an act of memory, but the articulate breath of a living soul; and, therefore, it is immediately appreciated and expressly approved by Jesus Christ—endorsed as to its tremendous contents, but guarded and protected against possible misuse by cautionary and enlarging words. There is, however, this difference; Peter's confession places us at the birth of a creed; the exclamation of Thomas puts us at the rebirth of faith after the paralyzing shock of the death on the Cross.

Here, again, the same contents confront us. First, we stand on the solid rock of historic *fact*. Thomas is secure. The risen Christ is before him, responsive to his finger touch, as well as to his skeptical anxiety. But *how* a man says his creed is often more than what he says. Devils have creeds and say them tremblingly. A creed may be held by the sense and not by the soul. The whole being of Thomas is alive with conviction and feeling, and clothes itself with warm and quickening speech, as the life-sap of the trees bursts into bud and leaf, blossom and fruit. He believes and adores. The man Christ is King and God: Ruler because Revealer, and complete Ruler because Revealer in the completest and intensest degree of the Eternal—"My Lord and my God."

Sixty years have elapsed since this confession when John cites it. Nearly two generations have come and gone. Changes of the most decided and revolutionary character have occurred. Christianity is the most regal fact of the century; it has been preached and denied, betrayed and opposed, misunderstood and accepted. Three memoirs of Christ are in circulation, and various brief sayings—"faithful and worthy of all acceptation"—are current concerning the cardinal facts and ideas of Christianity. Christ Himself is more fully known than ever, and now comes the edifice of New Testament literature. The Gospel of John brings on the top stone with a device, not new, but the very words used by the first Christian: "For these things are written"—concerning the doubt and faith of Thomas—in part—"that ye may believe that Jesus is the Christ, the Son of God, and that believing ye may have life through His name."

John stands at the end of the century where Peter stood sixty years before. Ephesus and Caesarea Philippi join hands. The Christian faith of the aged pastor, with all his ripe experience, saintly devotion, and unsurpassable inspiration, is, in its core and substance, the same as that of the young, eager, large-souled, and God-taught pupil of Jesus, when he exclaimed: "Thou art the Christ, the Son of the living God."

3. And now, what about Paul? His is no case of "primordial germs." There you have Christianity developed, stated in its

broad inclusiveness. He is the theologian of Christianity. Yes, in a sense; but it is characteristic of minds of the highest order to combine wide knowledge and breadth of view with unchanging centers of thought. They do not shift their center, though they may travel along different radii to the far-off points on the edge of the far-spreading circle of their teaching.

It is Paul who sums up Christianity in the brief and compact teaching of Romans 10:8-13—"The word is nigh thee, even in thy mouth, and in thy heart, that is the word of faith which we preach: That if thou shalt confess with thy mouth the Lord Jesus, and shalt believe in thine heart that God hath raised Him from the dead, thou shalt be saved. For with the heart man believeth unto righteousness, and with the mouth confession is made unto salvation. For the scripture saith, Whosoever believeth on Him shall not be ashamed. For there is no difference between the Jew and the Greek; for the same Lord over all is rich unto all that call upon Him. For whosoever shall call upon the name of the Lord shall be saved." Here, again, are the *facts* exemplified in and crowned by the resurrection of Christ from the dead; the *forces* bringing righteousness to the heart; and the all-comprehensive *ideas* of the saving sovereignty of Christ over all souls.

But hear him again. To Paul we owe the completest creed of the Scriptures. I may call it the model creed; as to the facts it embraces, the form it takes, the beauty of its setting, the sweetness of its notes, the superlative wealth of its contents, and the gracious and devout uses to which it is put.

Oh! how blessed are we if we know by experience the meaning of the benediction, "the grace of the Lord Jesus Christ, and the love of God, and the communion of the Holy Ghost be with you all!" Standing again, then, at the beginning of the Great Forty Years he sees in the tenderness and pitiful compassion of the Saviour's ministry and death the revealing of the heart of God and the advent of souls to partnership in the powers of the Holy Spirit. The historical Christ is for him the object lesson given by the Eternal to men, so that they may apprehend and enjoy His love, and share the gifts of His Spirit. God is in Jesus,

Teacher, Redeemer, Pattern, Son of Man, Son of God. God is
known by Jesus as the Father, essentially love—love, not as a
passive and luxurious emotion, but active, healing, and redeeming. Jesus opens the heart of man by the love of God to the
inflow of God, the Inspirer and Energizer, to renew, transfigure,
and perfect. "So through Jesus we have our access in one Spirit
unto the Father."

In the mouth of three witnesses, Peter, John, and Paul, it is in-
disputably established that the primitive Christian faith, the religion given once for all in those pre-eminently creative years,
consisted, first, of a body of sensible, verifiable facts, centering
in a life of captivating beauty and grace, matchless purity and
love; secondly, of a mass of spiritual forces, inherent in and inseparable from that Personality; and, thirdly, a set of formative
ideas, contained in His life, and words, and work. On Herder's
tombstone, at Weimar, are the words, "Life, Love, Light." In
the Christianity of the Forty Years, and constituting its real substance, are the facts of the Eternal Life, the forces of the Eternal
Love, and the ideas of Eternal Light.

VI

Of the *facts* themselves we are more sure today than men have
been since the death of the Apostle John. The critic, thinking
to discredit their supernatural reality, has only lifted them into
clearer radiance, and enabled us to see the Son of Man "in His
habit as He lived," with unsurpassable fullness of detail and defi-
niteness of outline. Strauss and his co-workers cleared the ground
for the reconstruction of the story of that Life, which is the
wonder and the redemption of the world; so that it throbs again
with impressive humanness, and stirs our hearts with thrilling
proofs of its perfect and pathetic divinity.

We are not more certain of the enthroned Augustus than of
the crucified Redeemer. The "facts" of the "faith" have been
committed to the custody of the mightiest and most characteristic literary creation of the centuries—the Gospels and Epistles
of the New Testament. "That which was from the beginning,

that which men heard, what they saw with their eyes and handled with their hands, concerning the Word of Life; for the life was manifested, and seen, and attested, even the eternal life which was with the Father," is now so sure and steadfast, that our nineteenth century has nothing, in all its wide sweep, more indestructible or more indubitable than the history of Jesus—the fourfold witness to the exalted character and marvelous work of the Son of God.

God's best gifts are men. His supremest gift is the Man Christ Jesus. "The Word was made flesh." Christ "came to His own." He was seen and heard, trusted and hated, adored and crucified. Obscure and humble as were His surroundings, He drew men to Him in affectionate discipleship, and cast over them the spell of His sweet authority. He lived a workman's life, spoke but rarely; and yet His words were so wise that we have not yet fathomed their significance, and His ideals so high that we are still panting to realize them.

"Good society" despised Him and cast Him out; and yet He constructed a social organism so just and brotherly in its laws, so free and noble in its spirit and beneficent in its work, that it has become the social ideal of the best men of every age and of every land. Respectability sneered at Him; orthodoxy boycotted Him; astute church leaders tried to ensnare Him, and were themselves caught; flung baseless charges at Him, and were themselves condemned; and, when they could do no more, they plotted for and secured His death. He was despised and rejected of men; and crushed with defeat, He passed away. And yet, marvel of marvels! His very death had such merit in it that it eclipsed His living, and the sacrifice of His life accomplished more than His use of it.

Living, He wrought many wonderful works on the bodies of men and more astonishing changes in their thought and life; living, He made His disciples feel He was pervaded with an undimmed sense of His own sinlessness, and marked by perfect obedience to the will of His Father. But dying, He puts away the world's sin, and makes an end of it, and so fills and sways the

minds of His followers that the record of His last days is the
most touching picture and the highest glory of the Gospels.

There is but a glimpse of the facts of His boyhood, a bright
ray out of its sweet purity. A paragraph describes His baptism;
a few sentences portray His warfare with the devil; and even His
speeches only appear in fragments; but wide spaces of revelation
are replete with His pity toward the lost, compassion for the out-
cast, and help for the needy; and more than half of the Gospel
of John is absorbed with the loving talk, tender sympathy, and
perfect sacrifice of His last days; so that we almost expect Him
to appear again, as He does, triumphant over death, and dedicat-
ing His few followers to the gigantic task of preaching His Gospel to "all the nations" of the earth.

It fits with the nature of His life that His deepest humiliation
should be transfigured into His chief victory, and the cross on
which He dies become the throne from which He reigns to save
and renew the world. Brothers! *we* have not followed cunningly
devised fables. They are the fabulists who deny Jesus. Our
"faith" is in its pith and reality, *fact*—historical, verifiable, undeniable fact. Men doubt and deny, resist and repudiate, but our
faith does not stand in the wisdom of men or the reasonings of
the learned, but on the irremovable basis of the facts of the Great
Forty Years. Not more surely does geology rest on the solid
strata of this globe, and astronomy on suns and stars and satel-
lites, than the new religion of Christ on the unique and creative
facts centering in Jesus, the Christ, the Son of the living God!

VII

. . . . .

His is a beggarly account of the faith that has not so much as
heard whether there be a Holy Ghost. Oxygen and lime, iron
and hydrogen, though primal parts of earth and sun, do not make
a world without the energies of light and heat—*i.e.*, without the
Eternal One—active in all forces, operative through all laws, and
using all materials. Thirty years ago the Christian watchword
was, "Fight for the facts of original Christianity." The battle is
ended, and we have won in every part of the field. Our trophies

abound, our conquests are secure; our well-arranged museums are of immense value; but

"We who are men as men are now,
Must feel with men in the agonizing present,"

and value the facts for the sake of the forces; verify the tragedy of Calvary, because it is not only a death but a cleansing sacrifice; preach the Christ of the Testament for the sake of the energies of the Spirit, and study the typical men of Christianity, so that we may share their supernatural life, and be clad in the strength and graced with the beauty of their God.

Primitive Christianity was charged in every fiber of it with living force. It had not a dead particle in it, but throbbed and bounded with the fullness of life.

"It is not for you," said the newly risen King, "to know the times and the seasons, but ye shall receive *power* after that the Holy Ghost is come upon you." Paul described the revolution as "the Kingdom of God, not in word but in *power.*"

A new Epoch has dawned. A new society starts into conquering life; a new and quickening speech, creative of a new literature, is heard in Jerusalem and Rome, in Corinth and Philippi. A new type of manhood appears. A new spirit is abroad softening the hearts of men, cleansing the imagination, inspiring reverence and trust and self-sacrifice; singing to the sorrowful and heavy laden the sweet song of Divine love in tones of tenderness; laying its hands of companionship on the head of the lonely, bidding the weary to hope, and the despairing to be of good cheer, in sight of the day of deliverance and glory now at hand.

Approach the Forty Years from the opposite side. Take stock of the moral condition of "all the nations" when Christ Jesus sends His few disciples to evangelize them. Register your facts carefully. Give a high place to all that is noble and pure, exalted and inspiring; for it, too, is of God.

Generously estimate the splendid heritage and unspent energies of Greece in such lofty singers as Homer and Aeschylus, Sophocles, and Euripides; such unequaled philosophers as Plato and Aristotle and Zeno, and the unforgettable chief of ethical apostles, Socrates. Reckon up every power for good in old Rome—disciplined soldiery, perfected municipal privilege, fine roads, irresistible might, political supremacy, and the stimulating memory of the masterly and mighty Caesar, eloquent and thoughtful Cicero, stern and unbending Cato, and the accomplished Scipio. Without prejudice, because of the obscurity of the people, add to your stock every ounce of serviceable strength in the possession of the Jews—a race with the highest ideals of character in Moses the Lawgiver, David the royal poet, Solomon the wise, and Isaiah the prophet; a race that has come, by the painful but gracious discipline of Divine revelation, to yearn for a Deliverer from sin, and a King who shall reign in righteousness. Face these forces for culture and conduct, for beauty and strength honestly, and set down their exact value and probable issues; and what have you? Let one unbiased in favor of Christianity answer. Dr. Draper says:

"In the reign of Augustus violence paused only because it had finished its work. Faith was dead, morality had disappeared. Around the shores of the Mediterranean the conquered nations looked at one another, partakers of a common misfortune associated in a common lot; not one of them had found a God to help her in her day of need. Europe, Asia, Africa, were tranquil; but it was *the silence of despair*."

May the historian Lecky be cited concerning the much-praised worth of human thought in its higher forms? If so, he says: "Philosophy was admirably fitted to dignify and ennoble, but it was altogether impotent to regenerate mankind."

But, instead of accumulating evidence to show that you might as well attempt to bind a lion with a cobweb as trust to man the work of his own redemption, go to the other end of the Forty Years and ask what has happened in the brief but tremendously impressive and reproductive interval. What has happened? Why, there is not a space like it in the annals of men. Not Attica in the century of its glory, when it produced one great genius for every five thousand of the population, and amongst them Demosthenes in eloquence, Phidias in sculpture, Plato in thought, Pericles in statesmanship—not Attica in all its glory can equal it.

First comes the *new society*, leaping into life full-armed, inspired and victorious on the day of Pentecost. A new institute is itself a new force, as well as a new product. It lifts the individual to the maximum of power, goes far to make twice one not into two, but two hundred, or two thousand. In Jerusalem, Rome, Corinth, Colossae, Galatia, Philadelphia, Asiatic Ephesus, and European Philippi are these societies, with representatives in Caesar's bodyguard and in Lydia's purple trade, at the gate of Europe and in the center of the empire.

But wide geographical distribution is their least important feature. A new type of manhood reigns. "My greatest discovery," said Faraday, "was a man." Christ's greatest discovery was Paul— the cultured, massive, eagle-eyed, enthusiastic, heroic, indescribable Paul. But Paul is only the full flowering of the Christian tree, the ripest fruit in the Garden of God.

Next *a new literature* is born. The Hebrew Scriptures are rediscovered, their fettered energies unloosed; the long frozen river melts, and again its streams make glad the city of God. The Old Testament is revised by the pupils of Christ, and renews the vigor of its ancient days. Nearly the whole of the New Testament is produced. James has written for direct, practical, out-and-out Christianity; Peter has comforted and warned the Christians of the Dispersion; Theophilus is reading Luke's memorabilia of Jesus and Peter and Paul; Christians at Corinth and Rome and Galatia are listening to the incisive sentences of the pupil of Gamaliel. . . .

But, best of all, in this new literature and in these new men of the new society reigned, supreme and irresistible, the *new spirit* of self-sacrificing love to God and men. Culture and civilization were cold as death in the presence of the evils of the world, and, like Greek philosophy and Roman religion, did not care. That was their character and condemnation. They did not burn with passion to save men and women disinherited by avarice, plunged into the abyss of cruelty by polytheism, and robbed of all the joys of the heart by despair.

Whatever may be said of the churches of our own day—and God knows they have sins enough!—the Church of those Forty Years—O Divine Renewer!—did not permit the poor to rot, meet tyrannous strength with truculence, bend on supple-knee to wealth and state, or luxuriate in its own glad emotions. No, it made

"All men's good
Each man's rule, and universal love
Lie like a shaft of light across the land,
And, like a line of beams athwart the sea,
Through all the circle of the golden years."

Mohammedanism consecrated slavery, polygamy, and despotism. Christianity *began* the abolition of the first by the death of Christ for each lost man, and the proclamation of the infinite sacredness of the human unit; undermined the second by its emancipation and coronation of woman; and made the government of states, the welfare of the world, by its promulgation of the brotherhood of all men with the Christ. That new spirit expelled cruelty by gentleness, passion by self-control, hardness by pity, pride by humility, impurity by chivalrous fight against the flesh, and hatred by love. As when by some vast secular change the life-destroying glacial epoch gives place to an era of tropical warmth and splendor, and a new flora and fauna appear, so in these four decades humanity had received a new and a glorious start towards its predestined goal. The religion of Jesus proved itself in power, even the fourfold power of a new spirit, a new literature, a new manhood, a new society, and so gave birth to a new world.

Hear a parable. From the clouds leaps a force on to the cross fixed at the summit of yonder spire; that force is seen as a flash of light; away it runs down the metal as a current of electricity; but in its journey it melts the metal as heat; as it moves forward it changes the positions of the atoms of the metal towards one another as magnetism, and at last it bursts through the stone-work as motion. It is one fontal energy from first to last, but varies its modes of action and manifestation; it is light, electricity, heat, magnetism, and motion; it is all and it is one. So, the one Christ in these Forty Years poured out of His fullness, and men received peace and joy, patience and zeal, truth and grace. He teaches truth as no ordinary Rabbi. He only has the words of *eternal* life, and is the *light* of the world. He dies the death of the cross, but His offering is the sacrifice for the sins of the world, and draws and magnetizes all men. He loves, and His glowing affection softens hard hearts, melts to penitence, *constrains* to self-repression, and impels to the service of man. He rises from the dead, and the Resurrection is the beginning of the Ascension to the Kingly rule of the Spirit which convinces the world of sin, of righteousness, and judgment.

This, then, is at the core of our "faith." We cling to the facts with unrelaxed tenacity, and proclaim the ideas with growing clearness; but for importance to sinful men we place in the first rank the redeeming forces of the Sacrifice of Christ and the regenerating energy of the Holy Spirit. We believe in the Holy Ghost. He is the breathing formative Soul of the body of the primitive faith.

VIII

But now, we must ask for the Ideas, given once for all—*i.e.*, with irreversible finality—to the "saints" of the first Forty Years of our Christian story.

Ah! says the critic, now you are on the shifting sand. Here the rock base forsakes you. Your history I cannot deny; it is an impregnable fortress. The play of unsubduable energies I admit; the evidence is irrefutable; but when you talk of Truths and Ideas, I see you have fallen on the loose and jarring shingle of contradictory human opinion.

Wait! Not so fast! Are you not mistaken? Do not imagine that modern scientists have the monopoly of certitude, and toil in totally different ways from their fellow workers in art and religion; as though, because they experiment with metals and gases and not brushes and Bibles, they do not work with ideas. It is a glaring absurdity. Science is as supersensible as the paintings of Turner, or the discussions of Mill and Hamilton, and is as surely built up with ideas as aesthetics or ethics. Laws of matter are not matter. A trilobite is not science. Botany does not grow in the garden, but in the man. The light of optics is of the soul, although the light of this building is of the sun. To say earth is full of laws and every common bush aflame with science is an utterance of mental conception, although not so beautiful or opulent with deep meanings as the lines of Mrs. Browning:

> "Earth's crammed with heaven,
> And every common bush afire with God."

The fair and beautiful temple of science, of which our generation is so proud, has been built up, every stone of it, by the invisible fingers of thinkers like Bacon and Newton, Herschel and Joule, Brewster and Faraday. Remove from that edifice the ideas expressed in laws of motion, chemical equivalents, correlative forces, and the like; and the building returns to its primeval chaos. The solid structure made up of observed facts and indestructible forces is, as a structure, as thoroughly the product of *mind* as the ethics of Aristotle, the philosophy of Hegel, or the Christianity of Jesus Christ.

Therefore let no man take offense at our quest for the Ideas of the primitive faith, as though we were about to wander in the wild wastes of Will-o'-the-Wisp, or the scarcely less innutritious fields of angry debaters. We are still on sure ground. The rock is beneath our feet. Our data are the positive, spontaneous, and massive results of that MIND OF CHRIST which fills and informs the Christian facts, inspires and directs the Christian forces of the first years of original Christianity.

. . . . . .

A religion is as its conception of God. With that it rises or falls, lives or dies, saves or destroys. The core of the faith delivered to the Palestine saints is the *Idea of God*.

What then is it?

Is it that God is Almighty, First Cause and End of Things, Irresistible and Eternal? Nature uttered that message with irresistible cogency. The Greek heard and fashioned the inexorable will of Zeus.

Does Christianity merely proclaim the moral God, "a power making for righteousness?" That was the gospel of the Old Testament, of the history of Moses, the song of the Psalmists, the vision of the prophets, and the philosophy of Job.

What, then, does Christ add to the teaching of nature? How does He fulfill, *i.e.*, fill out the sketch of the Old Testament?

In a brief, poor sentence that only hints the essential fact, it seems to me, He shows the moral God victoriously dealing with immoral, sinful men. Jesus, the Son of God, on *the cross* gives the Christian conception of God in its most luminous, universal, human, and satisfying form.

"We preach," said the most speculative, myriad-thoughted and fine-spirited of the saints, who received "the faith," "*we preach Christ crucified, the wisdom of God, and the power of God*"— *i.e., the philosophy of God*, the revelation of His nature, the key to His administration of man's life, and the rule of souls.

We preach Christ crucified; the Messiah, but crucified; the Son of Man, but crucified; the Son of God, but crucified; the Holiest of the Holy, but crucified; God in Christ, but in Christ crucified, humiliated, marred, broken, slain in His war against sin, giving Himself to an escapable doom, choosing it in His love for men, giving Himself for our sins, not for His own, that He might deliver us by His sacrifice from this present evil age, with all its awful tyrannies of sin and the devil. God in His Son, His beloved Son; in Christ, His Essential Self making atonement, reconciling the world unto Himself; restoring its ideal harmony, getting rid both of the love of sin and the guilt of it; identifying Himself with man in his saddest plight and sorest need; sorrowing and suffering for his wrong, and so cleansing and making him anew; revealing his possibilities of righteousness and service. That is the beating heart of the "faith" of the great Forty Years.

Now the core of the Pagan idea of God is pitilessness, destiny sweeping on with resistless might against wrong, without heart, and without aim other than that of the destruction of men. There is no atoning God, no Cross in the Pagan conception. Islam has gone back to Paganism, for it denies the Crucifixion. The God of Mohammed is "solitary, severe, stern"; a fighter not a redeemer. There is no cross in Mohammedanism. But in the Gospels the mind is fixed on the *crisis* of Christ's suffering, sacrificial life; suffering freely chosen; sacrifice eagerly coveted for the sake of the loved prize, a world's redemption. That is God, says Paul; that is how He feels towards you, that's what He will do for you, that's the measure of His hatred of sin, of His love for your soul, of His desire and will to redeem and renew you. "God hath sent His only begotten Son into the world that we might live through Him. Herein is love, not that we loved God, but that He loved us, and sent His Son to be a propitiation for our sins, and not for ours only but for the sins of the whole world." Character is read by the heart, by the feelings that lie at the back of the intellect. The Cross appeals to the heart; it does not affront the reason; indeed, it satisfies man when he is keenest and most alert rationally; but its direct appeal is to the universal heart, by which character is swiftly understood and moral change effected; therefore we preach Christ crucified, the wisdom of God and power of God.

. . . . . .

Surely, then, all appearances in our perplexed and troubled life to the contrary, *love* is the source and root of all things, stronger than hate and mightier than sin; and the end of all our pain and discipline is *righteousness*. Even Christ learned obedience by the things which He suffered, and so became the Pattern and Comforter of suffering souls in all ages. "Grief is joy misunderstood." Tribulation is a gate to the Kingdom. Defeat is not failure. The Crucified rises again and lives for evermore; and He who sacrifices Himself for the welfare of the world can never really die or His work come to nought. It will live in the Kingdom for evermore.

. . . . . .

Ah! friends, *it is true;* the sore malady of our time is that we have failed at the Cross. But how? Thus: We glory in opinion, idolize intellect, canonize genius, worship brute force and fleeting fashion, and practically deny the Cross. The word is on our lips, the meaning is not in our hearts, and the reality not on our wills. We do not see God as He is there; and, therefore, we do not judge sin as God does, nor treat it as He does *there*. We do not even behave to our friends as Christ did to His *foes*. The suffering Jesus is too far away from the actual life of the Church, and so Christ is kept out of the hearts of men. Oh! that with the intense passion and full truth of Paul every man of us could say: "God forbid that I should glory, save in the cross of our Lord Jesus Christ, by whom the *world* is crucified unto me, and *I* unto the world."

Such, then, is, in outline, the veritable substance of the Primitive Christian faith, delivered by its Author and Finisher to saints like Peter and Thomas, James and John, Matthew and Jude, Dorcas and Lydia, Mary and Phoebe, Euodias and Syntyche, Timothy and Titus, Luke and Paul. They knew whom they believed. Christ Himself, in His glorious fullness, was their Christianity. He was their Redeemer and Leader, and they were all brothers and friends and followers. Alike they held Him Sovereign; wanted no other, and refused any other, even though one of themselves.

In His love they trusted, by His word they were cleansed, in His Cross they gloried—a shame and a folly to men; but an atonement, wisdom, and victory for all who believed. By His risen life they lived one strong, compacted life, distributed but not divided, multitudinous yet single, enthusiastic but yet controlled, sublimely heroic and yet tender as a mother's love, and gracious as the heart of God. "*I live*," said each one, conscious of the new onward pulsing force in him; and yet scarcely is the sentence off his lips than it is fetched back by the dominant sense of the present Redeemer, to whom he owes all. "I live, yet not I, but *Christ liveth in me*." Filled with the powers of the Holy Ghost, illumined and guided by the Ideas received through His anointing, they hazarded their lives to save men everywhere, and to fill up that which was behind of the sufferings of Christ.

．　．　．　．　．

And what is it we hear in the latter ages but the glad and exultant cry of faith in the same Sacrifice! That is the everlasting experience, and, therefore, the everlasting faith. Summon ecclesiastics like Andrews and Usher, Jeremy Taylor and Hooker, and the last, speaking for them all, says, "We care for no knowledge in the world but this, that man hath sinned and God hath suffered; that God hath made Himself the Son of Man, and that men are made the righteousness of God."

Register the witness of stalwart souls such as Wycliffe and Latimer, Luther and Cromwell, expressed in the dying words, thrice repeated, of the pure-hearted Protector, "It is a fearful thing to fall into the hands of the living God." But, "all the promises of God are in Him. Yes, in HIM; Amen. To the glory of God by us—by us in Jesus Christ." Let Bunsen gather up the judgment of the wide and well-drilled scholarship of Origen and Athanasius, Augustine and Anselm, Melanchthon, and hundreds more, as, standing on the very brink of the river of death, he tells us there is no way across except by the "Bridge of the Saviour."

. . . . . .

And are *we* changed? Have we lost our center? Are Carey, and Fuller, and Foster no longer represented? Have we given up the Cross? Have we moved from the substance of the faith of our fathers? Do we not stand on the Facts and Forces and Ideas of the Great Forty Years? Then God forgive us. We are lost, and our labor is a folly, an irritation, and a menace. Given up? A thousand times, No! Given up? Come, dear Charles Stovel, from your place in the glory, and tell men "what was your business upon earth." "I have spent," he says, a little before his departure, "a large portion of my life in bringing the words of Christ to the test of experience. I bear my witness that the claims of Christ are justified by the declarations of experience. I have also been constantly observing the words of Christ passing into successful experiment in the lives of believers. If you ask me what is my business here upon earth, I answer: I am working out the grand experiment of the Redeemer's love. If that fail me—

> "The pillared firmament is rottenness,
> And earth's base built on stubble."

. . . . .

IX

And now may we go to the same prolific field for guidance as to the best methods for securing the acceptance of Christ by all men, and the enthronement of His religion as the religion of mankind? Different as our circumstances are from theirs, does their way of working afford infallible proofs of Divine inspiration, and so come to us with all the authority of a Divine mandate?

I unhesitatingly answer, Yes. . . .

First, then, joyously and with splendid abandon live your Christianity in your own life, in the whole of it, in the free subjection of your thought to the discipline of Christ, in the surrender of will to His unquestioned sovereignty, in conforming behavior to His example, in utter detachment from self and the world, and the exquisite play of your new life in His service, and you take the surest course to establish His religion at the springs and sources of the world's life. A bright, joyous religion, filled with the radiance of the love of God, kills despair, kindles hope, slays self, begets obedience to law, and creates a boundless love. "We love because He first loved us." "The love of Christ constrains us not to live to ourselves." The soldier who bids us "contend earnestly for the faith" has in one sentence, brief as a telegram, compact as a general's order, summed up his directions for warfare in the words, "Keep yourselves in the love of God."

That is the way to take care of the faith. Get out of that love, and shout as you may, fight as you will, you are lost, and the "Faith," so far as you are concerned, is lost too. Sunshine is life, nourishment, medicine. Love is the sunshine of God. Catch the sun. Never wander out of it. Move your positions till you get in it and so that you may keep in it. Do your man-building in its brightness. For your faith is to be used as the soldier uses bread and water, as the invalid the breezes of the sea and of the mountainside, as the sick man the healing medicine.

Build yourselves on your faith, but in the love of God. That is the builder's living and working "environment." Out of it he and his work perish, in it he builds for time and eternity; and the gates of hell cannot prevail against it. Here is the first great commandment: "By this shall all men know that ye are My disciples, if ye have love one to another."

Better lose all than lose love. He wins who keeps that supreme. He loses who says one bitter word, writes one selfish line, or moves one inch out of the love of God and of his brother. "If any man have not the *Spirit* of Christ he is none of His." He may be the Church's, and belong to all the unions of Christendom, and have the applause of all men, but he is not Christ's in so far as he lacks His spirit. We hurt the faith more by hardness and self-will and unbrotherly behavior than by confused opinions or false definitions.

Ruskin says, "We have been taught a religion of pure mercy, and we must either now betray it or learn to defend it by fulfilling it." So did the first Christians defend the faith, filling out its sublime program with the golden splendors of their devotion, the burning fires of their love to God and to souls, the passionate aggressive effort to bring all men to the knowledge of Him who, by the grace of God, tasted death for everyone.

O Lord Jesus, shed abroad that love in our hearts by the Holy Ghost, and fuse our souls in the blessed unity of an unbroken devotion to Thee in the salvation and service of men!

Set Christianity to work in and on others, is the *second* great commandment in the New Testament law. It is palpable beyond all dispute that the saints of the original Forty Years held that they had received a religion not for show, but for work—not as a creed for debate, but as the power of God unto salvation; a working force intended to renew and conquer. . . .

Again I say, if any one ask me to describe the chief vice of present-day Christendom, I should affirm it to be *that men do not believe in Christ Jesus enough to use Him and His Gospel always, everywhere, and out and out.* They dare not do as He would if He were visibly here, or say what He would say of wealth, and orthodoxy, and ecclesiasticism, and trade, and poverty, and of our inmost selves. We distrust Him, not as the Saviour from guilt, but as the Saviour from sinning—from all kinds, and sorts, and degrees of sinning. We keep Him out of our politics, and go on in wrong; out of our trade, and make bad paper, bad clothes, bad buildings; out of our social life, and grind the poor, and stop our ears with cotton wool, so that the cries of agony and misery may not disturb us, and we let drink and harlotry flourish; out of our pleasures, and allow them to debase and sensualize our fellows; out of our churches, and so perish of our conventionalisms and respectabilities.

He cannot do the mighty works wanted because of our unbelief. His religion fails to become the personal and social force it is meant to be because we do not use it. If a "declaration" about it would do it, we could make dozens; if creed passing would do it we could get patent machines by the score. But it has to be *worked* day and night, amongst the thriftless and the cultured, in the slums and in the universities, at home and on the exchange; and for this simple and homely task we are poor, alas! unspeakably poor.

We discuss where we should live, persecute where we should sympathize, put a system where we want a heart, appeal to men as critics where we ought to speak to their higher faculties, regal conscience, moral intuitions, craving for God, for the sight of His love, for His free pardon, and the assured sense of His sweet aid. We give a sermon, and the world asks for soul; a tract, and it wants quickening life; a talk, and it sighs for work; a machine, and it still calls for a MAN. *The incarnation of the Christ of the Cross is the one thing needful;* the Gospel of the Atonement translated into the vernacular of the world; the Christ of Galilee and Gethsemane, the street preacher, the comrade of the working man, the friend of the fallen woman, brought into actual touch of the real life of the dwellers in the cities and villages of the world. "Keep yourselves in the love of God, and on some have mercy that are in doubt; and some save, snatching them out of the fire; and on some have mercy with fear, hating even the garment spotted by the flesh." O zeal of Christ, seize us, absorb us, consume us! Give us no rest night or day, except as we are saving our fellows and glorifying Thee!

But we must not forget that only less urgent was the task of the first teachers of adjusting the new ideas received from Christ with all preceding teaching, and *clearing the revelation of God* of the confusions and mists with which it was overcast by men. Though Peter had lived in the bracing air of the north, was so open-minded as not to be offended at the astounding claims of Christ, and, moreover, was illumined by the Holy Ghost, yet it was necessary he should be freed from his misconceptions of the mission of Christ, due to his misreading of the older revelation, before he could preach the Gospel to Cornelius. Did not Saul go to Arabia for three years that he might fit the vaster meanings of the Son of God revealed in him with all he had learned from his most revered teachers of the Judaism in which he was cradled?

Say what we will about "progressive theologies," no one need look far to discover *retrogressive* ones. So corrupt is man that he cannot hold the revelation of God in his mind without staining it through and through. The purest Divine ray is soon laden with the dust of man's depravity. The history of religion is the history of frequent falls. Get a few paces from the original fount, and the stream has lost its pellucid clearness. A current of cold air turns the floating moisture into crystals and flings them at us, sometimes, with the deadly force of a blizzard; so the frosts of our human life crystallize the thoughts of God, and the winds of passion drive them along the lanes of life to the grave hurt of souls. Clearing the revelation of God in Christ from the confusions of men has ever been one of the necessary ways of defending the faith.

The leaders of Christianity *did* it by two processes. First, *they gave clear exposition of the older speech of God in the light of the newer; and, secondly, two of their number—Paul and John— set the Gospel in its true relations as the center of all available and usable truth, and began building a coherent and ordered system of Christian thought.*

To this day our Scriptures require "opening," so that men may see their profound meanings, and enjoy their exhaustless fruitfulness. Bad systems of interpretation confuse and bewilder many minds. Exaggeration distorts, prejudice blinds, materialism degrades, tradition clouds, and laziness confounds—and so the Word of the Lord is bound. Delitzsh, the patriarch of expositors, says: "By a continually deepened exegesis can we prepare the way for the Church of the Future." That is the Divine plan; obeyed, with infinitely blessed results, in apostolic times, and sure to lead to light and progress in our own.

Let the Bible be studied with every appliance of modern criticism, and every result of modern research. Encourage your best young men to give their nights and days to the study of the complex facts of Scripture and Christian history. Sustain strenuous and disciplined preachers in their search for the veritable Word of the Lord. Let every pastor be made to feel that you rejoice when he is more afraid of misrepresenting a single line or a single word of the Bible than of all the anathemas of Christendom. "Glasgow prospers by the preaching of the Word." The churches and the kingdom prosper by the clear, full, and luminous exposition of the revelation of God in Christ.

Not so readily does this generation accept the second method. It is disposed to repudiate the foremost saint of the Forty Years, the beloved John, when he discusses Jesus, as the Logos, the Eternal Word; and to turn from the foremost philosopher Paul, when he builds his philosophy of God on the broad basis of the sacrifice of the Son, and crowns the edifice with the consummation of all things in Him. Forsooth, we have become so scientific that we despise the science of theology! It is the most flagrant anachronism of our day! and yet it is not altogether surprising. The Church has had so many bad theologies, and loved them so tenderly, that we can hardly wonder that some of her sons should look on a theologian as a disguised enemy. . . .

.   .   .   .   .

In our day the perils of the young thicken on all sides, and the responsibilities of the churches increase proportionately. It is a time of religious crisis; and in times of crisis the young are the first to suffer, and their attitude determines the final issue of the campaign. Just from the schools, in which they have handled the new methods of science, studied the past in the dry light of reasoned accuracy, heard of the religions of mankind, spoken the new language and thought the new thought of this day of God, they pass into an atmosphere electric with doubt. Idolatry of intellect tempts them. The heart is in danger of being starved to make the head. Skepticism floats into their nature with the air they breathe, flattens life, narrows their horizon, paralyzes the conscience, fetters the will, and saps the character.

We need take the utmost care. We cannot save or help them by the clashing of our creeds; the noise bewilders. We shall not win their confidence by pounding scientists in the mortar of our criticism once a week; it only excites their ridicule. We shall not inspire reverence by talking of "evolution," as though Christianity were suspended on a South Kensington hypothesis; and setting up our interpretation of the Scripture as though it were a declaration straight from the lip of God; that way lies incredible mischief.

Worse than useless will it be for us to ban thinking and denounce inquiry; they will simply leave us to utter our priestly intolerance to the aged and apathetic. Why should we needlessly affront their reason? Better for us and for them to say, with Ambrose, "It hath not pleased the Lord to give His people salvation in dialectic." Better to bring them, by warm sympathy and direct heart-speech, to Jesus Himself, constraining them to touch Him, or, at least, to touch the hem of His garment, to trust in His work for their pardon, and obey the light which comes from His face as promptly as it reaches their eyes, believing that as they will to do His will, they shall know of the doctrine whether it be of God or men.

God sends us into the world, not to condemn it, but that the world may be saved through His Son, whom we preach; and He judges us by our faithfulness to that purpose of salvation. But, to be faithful to men, we must really love them, think with them, feel with them, enter into all their life, and so persuade them to count all things but loss for the excellency of the knowledge of Christ Jesus our Lord. The battle of Christianity will be fought and won amongst the young; and victory is assured in the measure in which we can bring souls to trust His work for them and in them, and so partake of the life of His everlasting love!

Called to be workers together with God in Christ, may all our churches, pastors, teachers, and officers rise to the height of this Divine vocation, steadfastly resting on the Facts, joyously experiencing the Forces, clearly teaching and powerfully embodying the Ideas of the Great Forty Years of the Christianity of Jesus Christ.

RESOLUTIONS ON CAMPBELLISM

The Dover Association in Virginia was outstanding in its opposition to the "Reform" movement under Alexander Campbell. In 1830, under the leadership of Andrew Broadus and Robert B. Semple, delegates accepted the following statement.

The Baptists as a denomination (making reasonable allowance for difference of opinion in minor matters) have professed and practiced certain leading principles which have been characteristic of them. . . . The system of religion known by the name of Campbellism has spread among our churches to a distressing extent. . . . The errors of this system are various, some of them comparatively unimportant while others appear to be of the most serious and dangerous tendency.

The Conference then resolved:

1. That we consider the gracious operations of the Holy Spirit, in the regeneration and salvation of a soul, as a funda-

mental doctrine of the Scriptures, and universally maintained by Baptists (such as we hold in fellowship) in all countries.

2. That to maintain baptism to be conversion—regeneration—the new birth, and that in baptism sins are actually (not figuratively) washed away, is a radical error, founded in popery, and ought not to be countenanced.

3. That we consider the doctrine of repentance (or penitence for sin) as held among us, and as set forth in the Scriptures, to be of vital importance; and that, in its room to substitute reformation (as is generally understood) tends to subvert one of the main pillars of the Christian religion.

4. That to maintain the sufficiency of human nature to purposes of salvation, with the mere written word, and without the gracious influence and aid of the Holy Spirit, is, in our view, a plain contradiction of the word of God, a denial of a fundamental doctrine held among Baptists, and a vain attempt to introduce the Pelagian scheme, long since exploded.

5. That we recommend to our churches, that when any of their membership shall maintain all or any of these radical errors, that, in love and tenderness, they endeavor to convince them of their errors; but in the event of failing in the object, that in the fear of God and in the spirit of faithfulness, and after reasonable forbearance, they declare non-fellowship with such, and separate them from their communion as offenders against God and truth.

6. That in regard to practice, we advise that our churches take a decided stand against the disorderly and disorganizing measures pursued by some of the preachers of this party, in going among the churches and administering baptism upon their new plan—flying in the face of all church order, trampling down all former usage among Baptist churches and disregarding the peace of the churches, and especially of the pastors. Such a course being subversive of all order and regular church government, ought to receive the most prompt and decided reprehension from the churches.

7. That persons thus baptized ought not to be received into any Baptist church of regular standing, but upon strict examina-

tion as to experience, moral standing and the motives which induced them to such a step. Conscious, however, that many pious and well meaning persons may be misled by these preachers, we would advise that every degree of gentleness and affection be exercised towards them.

IV

DISTINCTIVE BAPTIST PRINCIPLES

———◦◦◦———

FRANCIS WAYLAND (1796-1865)

Usually called President Francis Wayland; educated at Union College and Andover Theological Seminary; pastor of Boston First Church; President of Brown University (1826-1855), which he advanced greatly; pastor of Providence First Church (1856-7); strong missions advocate; conscientious defender of distinctive Baptist principles. His great sermon, "The Moral Dignity of the Missionary Enterprise," (see page 224), illustrates his logical thinking and deep convictions.

Selections from *Notes on the Principles and Practices of Baptist Churches.* (*1857*)

NOTE XXI

The points in which we differ from other sects important.— The manner in which we have escaped the errors into which others have fallen.

. . . . The nature of the difference which distinguishes us from others, is on this wise: it is evident that all disciples of Christ must hold essentially the same belief respecting the character of God, the obligations and character of man, and the way of salvation through the merits and atonement of the Redeemer. But it is also evident that, holding these truths, men may adopt sentiments at practical variance with them. These sentiments, in process of time, may encroach upon and undermine the truth, so that it becomes more and more inoperative, until, at last, a church once spiritual and heavenly-minded becomes formal, ritual, and worldly.

Of course we are to judge of any denomination not merely by what it believes, but also by the contradictory elements which it has associated with its belief, and which, in the long run, may cause it to swerve from the simplicity of the truth as it is in Jesus. This, we think, has been the misfortune of many of our Christian brethren, whose belief, according to their formularies, agrees quite closely with our own.

We, on the other hand, think that, by the grace of God, we have been enabled to exclude from our belief many of those principles which have exerted a deleterious influence on some of our brethren. In a word, we hope that we have followed more closely in the steps of the Master, excluding the errors derived from the traditions of the fathers, the decisions of councils, and the enactments of state, and cleaving more firmly to the simple teachings of Christ and his apostles. We utter this in no spirit of arrogance or self-esteem, but in devout thankfulness to the Great Teacher, who, we believe, has condescended to make known to us the truth more perfectly.

But it will be said, How can you ascribe this more perfect knowledge of the word of God to yourselves? You have not numbered among you profound philosophers, learned philologists, acute logicians, or any of those gigantic intellects to whom we look up as the lights of the advancing ages. I answer, we have arrived at a clearer knowledge of divine truth, for the very reason that we have had no such guides to follow.

Our fathers were, for the most part, plain, unlearned men. Having nowhere else to look, they looked up in humility to the Holy Spirit to teach them the meaning of the word of God.

They had no learned authorities to lead them astray. They mingled in no aristocratic circles, whose overwhelming public sentiment might crush the first buddings of earnest and honest inquiry. As little children they took up the Bible, supposing it to mean just what it said, and willing to practice whatever it taught. Thus they arrived at truth which escaped the notice of the learned and the intellectually mighty.

This is just what we might have expected. The New Testament was given as a revelation, not to the learned or the philosophically wise, but to every one born of woman. In it, God speaks to every individual of our race, as much as though that individual was the only being whom it addressed. Such a communication must evidently be made as plain and simple as language could make it. In the New Testament, Infinite Wisdom has put forth its power to render the truth by which we must be saved easy to be understood. Such being the nature of the revelation, it is manifest that the best of all interpreters must be a humble and childlike disposition. The mind which is most thoroughly purified from every desire to conform the word of God to its preconceived opinions or biases, will be, of all others, the most likely to discover the truth which the Spirit intended to convey. Such is clearly the teaching of our Saviour on this subject.

"I thank thee, O Father, Lord of heaven and earth, because thou hast hidden these things from the wise and prudent, and has revealed them unto babes. Even so, Father, for so it seemed good in thy sight."

I hope I have all due respect for learning, and especially for philological learning. I trust I am not wanting in reverence for the wise and good of our own and of preceding ages. But I would ask, in that age of robust scholars, which of them had so deep and thorough an understanding of the mind of the Spirit in the New Testament as John Bunyan? Shut up for twelve years in Bedford jail for the testimony of Jesus, his soul wrung with anguish by the tears of his starving wife and helpless babes, with no book but the Bible, a ray of light from the throne of God shone down on the sacred oracles, as he looked upon them, and revealed to him mysteries which the learned could not see, and which he has unfolded to the admiring gaze of all the coming ages.

Take another case of a different character. Neander was learned in philosophy, and in the history of the church, beyond any man of this age, perhaps of any age. Take up now his Commentary on John's First Epistle, the best of his works, of this character, with which I am acquainted. The excellency of this exposition is not at all owing to his marvelous learning, but to the childlike and loving temper which places him in so delightful harmony of spirit with the beloved apostle. If such be the law of the divine dispensation, it is not remarkable that the truth which was hidden from the wise and prudent has been revealed unto babes. And that this has been so, would seem to be evident, from the fact that the sentiments which we have maintained for generations, amid obloquy and contempt, are now admitted to be truths by the profoundest thinkers and the most learned Christian philosophers of the present age; by men of the logical acumen of a Whately, and the philological and historical learning of a Bunsen and a Neander.

NOTE XXII

Hereditary membership at variance with the idea of the spirituality of the church.—Tendency of infant baptism to establish hereditary membership.

In my last paper I stated, in general, the reasons why a Baptist should be thankful to God for the past history of his denomination. It may be expected that I should present the case more in detail. I trust I am prepared to do so, and will illustrate my meaning by examples.

In common with other evangelical denominations, we hold the doctrines of the depravity of man, the necessity of piety to church membership, and the necessity of regeneration, in order to render a man fit for the kingdom of God in heaven, or the church of Christ on earth. That is, we believe that the heart of man is estranged entirely from God, and is, therefore, in its natural state, incapable of holy affections, or of any act which fulfills the requirements of the law; that the church of Christ is made up, not of those who are members by profession, but only of those who are changed in their affections, who love God with a filial temper, and submit themselves in all things to the precepts and example of Christ, relying wholly on his merits for salvation. This change of heart is called, in the Scriptures, regeneration, and hence our belief is, that the church of Christ is made up wholly of regenerated persons.

To the truth of these doctrines we have always borne testimony, and we have always intended to reject every practice and ordinance at variance with them. On these doctrines rests the superstructure of a spiritual church, of that church whose members are "a royal priesthood, a holy nation, a peculiar people." Suffer them, for any cause, to be obscured or undermined, and the dividing line between the church and the world is removed, and what was once a church of Christ in reality, becomes such only in name. I do not say that such will be the result within a single generation, but such is the tendency, and as surely as things follow their tendencies, they must sooner or later arrive at this termination.

For instance, suppose a church of Christ, holding the doctrines I have referred to above, also admits the practice of infant baptism. It is granted that there is no precept commanding, or example sanctioning this rite in the New Testament. It must, therefore, if a duty, be such in consequence of some other truth which necessitates the obligation to perform it. What, then, are the doctrines on which this obligation rests?

Is it the covenant with Abraham? But all the children of Abraham, and the servants born in his house, were members of the patriarchal church. Why, then, should they not be members also of the Christian church, if it be formed on the same model?

Or, is the ground of infant baptism the rite of circumcision, under the Mosaic law? Every male, by this rite, and every female without it, became a member of the Hebrew church, entitled to eat the Passover, and enjoy all the immunities belonging to the theocratic commonwealth. If this be our model, why should not corresponding privileges be accorded to the children baptized under the New Testament dispensation?

Here the door is at once opened to hereditary membership. The practice and the principles of Christians holding these beliefs are at variance, and, in such cases, it commonly happens that the practice encroaches on the principle. This occurred in the time of President Edwards. In the first place, the children of those who were not church members were admitted to baptism. Then persons who had been baptized, and were of moral life, who professed a desire to be converted, were admitted to the church. And thus it came to pass that, at one period, every respectable householder of the town was expected to be a member of the church. Thus, at the same time, in the Reformed Dutch churches in this country, Mrs. Grant tells us that every young man, at the age of twenty-one, was married and joined the church, as a matter of course.

In the Established Church of England, confirmation, by which a person is admitted to communion, is expected of every one on arriving at a suitable age. In the Lutheran churches the custom is universal. Thus the doctrine of the spirituality of the church is, in the end, subverted by the doctrine of hereditary membership, introduced by the principle on which infant baptism is supported.

A striking illustration of the result of the admission of the doctrine of hereditary membership is seen in the history of the Friends, or Quakers. They had arrived at remarkably clear ideas of the religion of the New Testament, and of the obligations which it imposed. They, however, rejected ordinances altogether, observing that they had become merely a matter of form. Yet they adopted the principle of hereditary membership. In a few generations, the societies of these disciples, who, at the first, proclaimed the truth of the spirituality of the church, were filled with hereditary members destitute of the grace of God. Then ensued a division, by which the formal and the spiritual were separated from each other. But the spiritual, adhering to the doctrine of hereditary membership, were soon again overwhelmed by merely worldly professors. Other divisions ensued.

Thus, in spite of the purity and beauty of their original principles, they have been continually diminishing; and, it is to be feared, will before long cease to be a distinct denomination of Christians.

We can not but believe that a high honor has been conferred on us by the Master, in that we have been taught to bear testimony at all times, against what we believe to be an error so subversive of the doctrine of the spirituality of the church of Christ.

But take the other grounds on which the baptism of infants is enforced. It is said by some that baptism purifies the child from original sin. If it be thus purified, and its nature made holy, why should it not at once be admitted to a holy church? Or, is the doctrine of baptismal regeneration entertained, and is it said before baptism that "none can enter into the kingdom of God, except he be regenerated and born anew," and after baptism, "thanks are rendered to God that he has been pleased to regenerate this infant with his Holy Spirit, to receive him for his own child by adoption, and incorporate him into his holy church," why should he not be admitted to all the privileges of the church of Christ? But it is practically found that no moral change follows this ordinance, and hence the church is filled with worldly men, and the doctrine of the spirituality of the kingdom of Christ is virtually ignored.

Or, is it said, that setting aside all these views, we found the obligation of infant baptism on the traditions of the church, and its practice in the latter part of the second, and the beginning of the third centuries? We then concede the principle, that the acts of men of that period had power to bind the conscience, and we are obliged to receive as truth whatever they taught, and to follow their example in whatever they put in practice. Here, then, we abandon Protestantism, and adopt almost all the errors of the church of Rome.

Against these errors, as we conceive them, and the principles on which they are founded, we have had the honor of ever bearing our earnest and decided testimony.

JOHN A. BROADUS (1827-1895)

DR. BROADUS *was distinguished as a preacher, teacher, scholar, and denominational statesman. Educated at the University of Virginia and by study throughout life. One of the famous "Four Founding Fathers" of the Southern Baptist Theological Seminary in Louisville, Kentucky, where he taught from 1858 until his death.* His books include The Preparation and Delivery of Sermons; Commentary on the Gospel of Matthew; *and* Harmony of the Gospels. *Delivered Yale Lectures on Preaching in 1889. Our selection, first published in pamphlet form by the American Baptist Publication Society, is a masterly statement of Baptist distinctives and of how they should be propagated.*

The Duty of Baptists to Teach Their Distinctive Views

"Teaching them to observe all things whatsoever I have
commanded you."—Matthew 28:20.

The things he had commanded include the internal and the external elements of Christian piety. Of the latter, they include ethical instruction and directions as to the conduct of Christian societies. These directions were afterward supplemented by the inspired apostles giving instructions as to the constitution and government of the Christian societies, or churches, and the characteristic ceremonies they were to observe. These matters pertaining to the Christian societies are certainly not so important as the internal and spiritual elements of piety or as ethical principles and precepts, but still they are important. We may be sure they are, from the fact that Christ and his apostles gave direction concerning them; and we can see why they must be important.

It is impossible to maintain mental health if the body be abused or neglected, for bodily conditions react upon those of the mind.

And the externals of piety are the natural expression of its spiritual essence, which cannot be healthy if they are disregarded, exaggerated, or perverted. The tendency of human nature is usually not to neglect religious externals, but to exaggerate or pervert them. The New Testament gives us a very simple pattern in these respects—simple organization, simple government, simple ceremonies. But men early began to magnify their importance and to change their character and application.

EARLY JUDAIZERS AND THEIR SUCCESSORS

Did you ever consider what became of the Judaizers who gave Paul so much trouble? When we last observe them in the history, in connection with Paul's latest recorded visit to Jerusalem, they are really beaten, but still numerous and active. When, in the second century, we again get a clear view of the early Christians, the Judaizers seem reduced to a mere handful. But has the tendency really disappeared? Nay; it is beginning to strike through and through the Christianity of the day, and from that time onward a painfully large portion of Christendom has had only a Judaized Christianity.

When men began to exaggerate the importance of externals, they would soon begin to change their character. Coming to believe that baptism brings regeneration and is indispensable to salvation, they would of course wish to baptize as early in life as possible, and to make baptism practicable for the sick and the dying. Beginning to fancy that the bread and wine really became the glorified body and blood of the ascended Saviour, they not unnaturally took to withholding the cup from the laity, lest their awkward handling should spill some drops of the sacred fluid, which would have been profanation. And, in addition to these tendencies, the institutions of imperial Rome and the Roman genius for centralized government led the Christians to think it necessary that their societies should have a stronger government.

THE BAPTISTS OPPOSED TO JUDAIZING INFLUENCES

In opposition to all this, Baptists insist on holding to the primitive constitution, government, and ceremonies of the Christian societies, or churches; and this on the principle of recognizing no religious authority but the Scriptures themselves, and of strictly observing all that the Saviour has commanded. Now, the Saviour says in our text that we must *teach* them to observe all things whatsoever he commanded. These commandments include the matters just mentioned, concerning which the people who allow themselves to be called Baptists differ widely from large portions of the Christian world, and are persuaded that their own views are more scriptural, more in accordance with the Saviour's commands. They must therefore feel themselves required to *teach* these things as well as others. Hence, the text lays upon us the duty of which I have been requested to speak—*the duty of Baptists to teach their distinctive views.*

DISTINCTIVE VIEWS OF BAPTIST CHURCHES

It may be well to state briefly what I understand to be the leading distinctive views of the Baptist churches. The fact that certain of these are more or less shared by others will be remarked upon afterward.

1. We hold that the Bible alone is a religious authority; and in regard to Christian institutions the direct authority is of course the New Testament.

2. We hold that a Christian Church ought to consist only of persons making a credible profession of conversion, of faith in Christ. These may include children, even comparatively young children, for God be thanked that these do often give credible evidence of faith in Christ! But in the very nature of the case they cannot include infants.

The notion that infants may be church members because their parents are seems to us utterly alien to the genius of Christianity, not only unsupported by the New Testament, but in conflict with its essential principles; and we are not surprised to observe that our Christian brethren among whom that theory obtains are unable to carry it out consistently—unable to decide in what sense the so-called "children of the church" are really members of the church and subject to its discipline.

The other notion, that infants may be church members because so-called "sponsors" make professions and promises for them, seems to us a mere legal fiction, devised to give some basis for a practice which rose on quite other grounds. Maintaining that none should be received as church members unless they give credible evidence of conversion, we also hold in theory that none should be retained in membership who do not lead a godly life; that if a man fails to show his faith by works, he should cease to make profession of faith. Some of our own people appear at times to forget that strict church discipline is a necessary part of the Baptist view as to church membership.

3. We hold that the officers, government, and ceremonies of a Christian society, or church, ought to be such, and such only, as the New Testament directs. As to ceremonies, it enjoins the very minimum of ceremony; for there are but two, and both are very simple in nature and in meaning. We insist that baptism ought to be simply what Christ practiced and commanded. We care nothing for the mode of baptism, the manner of baptizing, if only there is a real baptism according to the plain indications of Scripture.

As to the significance of the ceremony, we understand it to involve three things: The element employed represents purification; the action performed represents burial and resurrection, picturing the burial and resurrection of Christ, and symbolizing the believer's death to sin through faith in Christ and his resurrection to walk in newness of life; and performing the ceremony in the name of the Lord Jesus—in the name of the Father and of the Son and of the Holy Ghost—makes it like an oath of allegiance, a vow of devotion, to Jesus Christ, to the Triune God.

The early Roman Christians had a good word for this idea if only the word could have remained unchanged in use: they called it a *sacramentum*, a military oath. As the Roman soldier in his oath bound himself to obey his general absolutely, so in baptism we solemnly vow devotion and obedience. But, alas! the word "sacrament," like many another word in Christian history has come to be employed in senses quite foreign to its original use.

As to the second Christian ceremony, we hold that not only the bread, but the cup also should be given, urging, as all Protestants do—and Baptists are Protestants in one sense, though in another sense distinct from Protestants—that our Lord commanded us to do both, and no one has a right to modify his commands. And the significance of the bread and wine is understood by us to be, not transubstantiation, nor consubstantiation, nor real presence in any sense, nor even according to the Calvinian view that a special spiritual blessing is by divine appointment attached to the believing reception of these elements, but simply according to the Zwinglian view that these are mementoes, remembrancers of Christ, and that, taking them in remembrance of him, we may hope to have the natural effects of such remembrance blessed to our spiritual good.

As to the order of the two ceremonies, we believe the New Testament to indicate that the second should be observed only by those who have previously observed the first and are walking orderly. This is in itself not a distinctive view of the Baptists, for they share it with almost the entire Christian world in all ages. The combination of this general Christian opinion, that the New Testament requires baptism to precede the Lord's Supper, with our Baptist opinion as to what constitutes baptism, leads to a practical restriction which many regard as the most marked of all our distinctive views; while for us it is only an incidental, though logically inevitable, result of that principle which we share with nearly all of those from whom it ceremonially separates us.

4. We hold that these societies called churches were designed, as shown in the New Testament, to be independent. They have no right to control one another. Ample warrant there is for cooperation in benevolence and for consultations as to questions of truth and duty, but without assuming to legislate or in any sense

to rule one another. And they must be independent of what we call the State as to their organization, faith, worship, and discipline, while, of course, amenable to the State if they violate those moralities which are essential to public welfare; nor must they suffer themselves to be dependent on the State in the sense of receiving from it pecuniary support.

Now, I repeat that we do not consider these externals to be intrinsically so important as the spiritual, or even the ethical, elements of Christianity. But they are important, because they express the spiritual and react upon it healthily or hurtfully, and because the Author of Christianity, in person or through his inspired apostles, appointed and commanded them. And we think it a matter of great importance that they should be practiced in accordance with, and not contrary to, his appointment —that, in the language of his text, his disciples should observe and conserve (for the word includes both ideas) all things whatsoever he commanded them.

We are glad that as to one or another of these distinctive views some of our fellow Christians of other persuasions agree with us more or less. We welcome all such concurrence, and it is not now necessary to inquire whether they hold those opinions with logical consistency. For ourselves, we do not claim to be fully *acting* upon these views, but we aim to do so, acknowledge ourselves blameworthy in so far as we fail; and we desire, notwithstanding our shortcoming in practice, to hold them up in due prominence before ourselves and others.

I wish now, first, to present reasons why Baptists ought to teach their distinctive views, and then to remark upon means and methods of performing this duty.

I. REASONS WHY BAPTISTS OUGHT TO TEACH THEIR DISTINCTIVE VIEWS

1. *It is a duty we owe to ourselves.* We must teach these views in order to be consistent in holding them. Because of these we stand apart from other Christians, in separate organizations— from Christians whom we warmly love and delight to work

with. We have no right thus to stand apart unless the matters of difference have real importance; and if they are really important, we certainly ought to teach them.

We sometimes venture to say to our brethren of some other persuasions that if points of denominational difference among evangelical Christians were so utterly trifling as they continually tell us, then they have no excuse for standing apart *from each other*, and no right to require us to stand apart from them unless we will abjure, or practically disregard, our distinctive views. But all this will apply to us likewise unless we regard the points of difference as having a substantial value and practical importance as a part of what Christ commanded, and in this case they are a part of what he requires us to teach.

And this teaching is the only way of correcting excesses among ourselves. Do some of our Baptist brethren seem to you ultra in their denominationalism, violent, bitter? And do you expect to correct such a tendency by going to the opposite extreme? You are so pained, shocked, disgusted at what you consider an unlovely treatment of controverted matters that you shrink from treating them at all. Well, the persons you have in view, if there be such persons, would defend and fortify themselves by pointing at you.

They would say, "I am complained of as extreme and bigoted. Look at those people yonder, who scarcely ever make the slightest allusion to characteristic Baptist principles, who are weak-kneed, afraid of offending the Paedobaptists, or dreadfully anxious to court their favor by smooth silence: do you want me to be such a Baptist as that?" Thus one extreme fosters another.

The greatest complaint I have against what are called "sensational" preachers is not for the harm they directly do, but because they drive such a multitude of other preachers to the other extreme—make them so afraid of appearing sensational in their own eyes, or in those of some fastidious hearers, that they shrink from saying the bold and striking things they might say, and ought to say, and become commonplace and tame. And so it is a great evil if a few ultraists in controversy drive many good men to avoid sensitively those controverted topics which we are all under obligation to discuss. The only cure, my brethren, for denominational ultraism is a healthy denominationalism.

2. *To teach our distinctive views is a duty we owe to our fellow Christians.* Take the Roman Catholics. We are often told very earnestly that Baptists must make common cause with other Protestants against the aggressions of Romanism. It is urged, especially in some localities, that we ought to push all our denominational differences into the background and stand shoulder to shoulder against Popery.

Very well; but all the time it seems to us that the best way to meet and withstand Romanism is to take Baptist ground; and if, in making common cause against it, we abandon or slight our Baptist principles, have a care lest we do harm in both directions. Besides, ours is the best position, we think, for winning Romanists to evangelical truth. Our brethren of the great Protestant persuasions are all holding some "developed" form of Christianity—not so far developed as Popery, and some of them much less developed than others, but all having added something, in faith or government or ordinances, to the primitive simplicity.

The Roman Catholics know this, and habitually taunt them with accepting changes which the church has made while denying the church's authority, and sometime tell them that the Baptists alone are consistent in opposing the Church. We may say that there are but two sorts of Christianity—church Christianity and Bible Christianity. If well-meaning Roman Catholics become dissatisfied with resting everything on the authority of the church and begin to look toward the Bible as authority, they are not likely, if thoughtful and earnest, to stop at any halfway house, but to go forward to the position of those who really build on the Bible alone.

Or take the Protestants themselves. Our esteemed brethren are often wonderfully ignorant of our views. A distinguished minister, author of elaborate works on church history and the creeds of Christendom, and of commentaries, etc., and brought in many ways into association with men of all denominations, is reported to have recently asked whether the Baptists practice trine immersion. A senator of the United States from one of the southern states, and alumnus of a celebrated university, was visiting, about twenty years ago, a friend in another state, who casually remarked that he was a Baptist.

"By the way," said the senator, "what kind of Baptists are the Paedobaptists?"

Not many years ago a New York gentleman who had been United States minister to a foreign country published in the New York *Tribune* a review of a work, in which he said (substantially), "The author states that he is a Baptist pastor. We do not know whether he is a Paedobaptist or belongs to the straiter sect of Baptists." Now, of course these are exceptional cases; but they exemplify what is really a widespread and very great ignorance as to Baptists. And our friends of other denominations often do us great injustice because they do not understand our tenets and judge us by their own.

As to "restricted communion," for example, Protestants usually hold the Calvinian view of the Lord's Supper, and so think that we are selfishly denying them a share in the spiritual blessing attached to its observance; while, with our Zwinglian view, we have no such thought or feeling. These things certainly show it to be very desirable that we should bring our Christian brethren around us to know our distinctive opinions, in order that we may at least restrain them from wronging us through ignorance.

If there were any who did not care to know, who were unwilling to be deprived of a peculiar accusation against us, with them our efforts would be vain. But most of those we encounter are truly good people, however prejudiced, and do not wish to be unjust; and if they will not take the trouble to seek information about our real views, they will not be unwilling to receive it when fitly presented. Christian charity may thus be promoted by correcting ignorance. And besides, we may hope that some at least will be led to investigate the matters about which we differ. Oh, that our honored brethren would investigate!

A highly educated Episcopal lady some years ago in one of our great cities, by a long and patient examination of her Bible, with no help but an Episcopal work in favor of infant baptism, at length reached the firm conviction that it is without warrant in the Scripture, and became a Baptist. She afterward said, "I am satisfied that thousands would inevitably do likewise if they would only examine."

But why should we wish to make Baptists of our Protestant brethren? Are not many of them noble Christians—not a few of them among the excellent of the earth? If with their opinions they are so devout and useful, why wish them to adopt other opinions? Yes, there are among them many who command our high admiration for their beautiful Christian character and life; but have a care about your inferences from this fact. The same is true even of many Roman Catholics, in the past and in the present; yet who doubts that the Romanist system as a whole is unfavorable to the production of the best types of piety?

And it is not necessarily an arrogant and presumptuous thing in us if we strive to bring honored fellow Christians to views which we honestly believe to be more scriptural, and therefore more wholesome. Apollos was an eloquent man and mighty in the Scriptures, and Aquila and Priscilla were lowly people who doubtless admired him; yet they taught him the way of the Lord more perfectly, and no doubt greatly rejoiced that he was willing to learn. He who tries to win people from other denominations to his own distinctive views *may* be a sectarian bigot; but he may also be a humble and loving Christian.

3. *To teach our distinctive views is a duty we owe to the unbelieving world.* We want unbelievers to accept Christianity; and it seems to us they are more likely to accept it when presented in its primitive simplicity, as the apostles themselves offered it to the men of their time. For meeting the assaults of infidels, we think our position is best.

Those who insist that Christianity is unfriendly to scientific investigations almost always point to the Romanists; they could not with the least plausibility say this of Baptists. And when an honest and earnest-minded skeptic is asked to examine with us this which claims to be a revelation from God, we do not have to lay beside it another book as determining beforehand what we must find in the Bible. Confessions of faith we have, some older and some more recent, which we respect and find useful;

but save through some exceptional and voluntary agreement we are not bound by them.

We can say to the skeptical inquirer, "Come and bring all the really ascertained light that has been derived from studying the material world, the history of man, or the highest philosophy, and we will gladly use it in helping to interpret this which we believe to be God's word"; and we can change our views of its meaning if real light from any other sources requires us to do so.

There is, surely, in this freedom no small advantage for attracting the truly rational inquirer. But, while thus free to search the Scriptures, Baptists are eminently conservative in their whole tone and spirit; and for a reason. Their recognition of the Scriptures alone as religious authority, and the stress they lay on exact conformity to the requirements of Scripture, foster an instinctive feeling that they must stand or fall with the real truth and the real authority of the Bible. The union of freedom and conservatism is something most healthy and hopeful.

4. There is yet another reason—one full of solemn sweetness: *To teach our distinctive views is not only a duty to ourselves, to our fellow Christians, and to the unbelieving world, but it is a duty we owe to Christ; it is a matter of simple loyalty to him.*

Under the most solemn circumstances he uttered the express injunction. He met the eleven disciples by appointment on a mountain in Galilee; probably the more than five hundred of whom Paul speaks were present also: "And Jesus came and spake unto them, saying, All authority is given unto me in heaven and in earth. Go ye, therefore, and disciple all the nations, baptizing them in the name of the Father, and of the Son, and of the Holy Ghost; teaching them to observe all things whatsoever I have commanded you."

The things of which we have been speaking are not, we freely grant, the most important of religious truths and duties, but they are a part of all the things which Jesus commanded; what shall hinder us, what could excuse us, from observing them ourselves and teaching them to others? The Roman soldier who had taken the *sacramentum* did not then go to picking and choosing among the orders of his general: shall the baptized believer pick and choose which commands of Christ he will obey and which neglect and which alter? And, observe, I did not quote it all:

Go, disciple, baptizing them, "teaching them to observe all things whatsoever I have commanded you: and lo, I am with you always, even unto the end of the world." Shall we neglect to teach as he required, and then claim the promise.of his presence and help and blessing?

II. MEANS AND METHODS OF PERFORMING
THIS DUTY

1. *One of the best means of teaching our distinctive views to others is the thorough instruction of our own people.* Brethren of other persuasions need not be repelled or offended if they find us taking suitable occasion in pulpit discourses to teach our young members what Baptists believe, and why. If they perceive we are not striking at them through our members, but in simplicity and sincerity feeding our flock, they may even listen with interest. And then, if they choose to take these things to themselves of their own accord and on their own responsibility, why, all the better, of course. But our young members greatly need such instruction for their own sakes, and it is often grievously neglected.

On a recent occasion a cultivated young lady stated that she had never in her life heard a word from the pulpit as to the relation between baptism and the Lord's Supper, and yet she was the daughter of a well-known Baptist minister, and her pastors had been men of marked ability and earnest Baptists. Do you think it a rare case? You can find such by thousands. And we ought to teach these things, in their measure, not only to our young members, but at home to the youth of our families.

Suffer another fact for illustration: I once knew a lad of sixteen, well educated for his years, whose father was a zealous and quite influential Baptist layman and his pastor an able and eloquent minister. The boy had been baptized, and with great joy and trembling had sat by his father's side and taken bread and wine in remembrance of Jesus. Some weeks later a Methodist preacher came through the country—a rare thing in that neighborhood—and after preaching he very tenderly invited all Christians to come to the Table of the Lord. The boy wanted to go, and knew of no reason why he should not, but thought he would wait till his older brother and sisters went forward; and, as they did not, he inquired on the way home why it was, and on reaching home asked his father about it. The argument was made plain enough, but it was all new to him. Pastors, parents, and all had never thought it necessary to explain that matter to anybody.

I mention these homely incidents with the hope of arousing such Baptists as my voice can reach to consider how it may be in their homes and their churches. Nor should this instruction be neglected in our Sunday schools. The current lesson system can, of course, make no immediate provision for such instruction, but it leaves ample room for it by giving lessons that embrace controverted matters, and it calculates that every denomination in its lesson-helps will explain these matters according to its views.

It is clear, then, that Sunday schools connected with Baptist churches ought to use Baptist helps for the study of the lesson. If some undenominational publications are so valuable for teachers as to be desired also, they ought to be used only in addition to those which explain according to Baptist beliefs. We do not withhold instruction in our Lord's other teachings till the pupil has become a believer, and why should we withhold it as to his commands regarding church membership and ordinances?

Three benefits ought to follow from thus teaching our youth:

First, it will restrain them from hereafter going to other denominations through ignorance. Some reasons for such change cannot be touched by instruction. But not a few take such a step because they were never taught the scriptural grounds for Baptist usage, and so they readily fall in with the plausible idea that "one church is good as another if the heart is right." There can be no doubt that well-meaning persons have in this way been lost to us whom early instruction might have retained.

Secondly, we may thus render them better Christians. I fully agree with an eminent Presbyterian minister who recently said, "We make people better Christians by making them better Presbyterians, better Methodists, Baptists, Episcopalians." There are some very excellent people in our time who think it a merit to be entirely undenominational, and who proclaim that they "love one church as well as another." But, where not deluded, such persons are few and quite exceptional; in general, the truest, most devoted, and most useful Christians are strong in their denominational convictions and attachments. I repeat, then, that by proper instruction in our distinctive views we shall really make our young people better Christians.

And, *thirdly*, we thus prepare them to explain and advocate these views in conversation—a thing which is often called for, and when properly managed may be very useful.

2. *If actions speak louder than words, we may practically teach our distinctive views by everything that builds up our churches in Christian character and promotes their legitimate influence.* Baptists are in some respects placed at serious disadvantage in consequence of trying to do their duty. They have not restricted their ministry to men who had a certain fixed grade of education, but have encouraged all to preach who felt moved to do so, and whom the churches were willing to hear. In this way they have greatly helped to meet the vast demand in our country, and have gained a powerful hold upon the masses.

What would have become of the scattered millions in this new country had it not been for the Methodists, the Baptists, and some others who have pursued a like course? But the result is, that we have a great mass of comparatively uneducated ministers and members. Moreover, our Episcopal and Presbyterian brethren brought over the sea the social influence derived from an established church; and this social superiority they have easily maintained in many of our cities, particularly as their ministry was at the same time restricted to men having considerable education. The result is that, while Baptists have many families of excellent social position and influence, and many ministers of high cultivation, yet, in virtue of having a great number who are in these respects comparatively wanting, they have to bear, as a denomination, the odium of social and educational inferiority. I do not regret this as regards our past. I think our principle as to the ministry is right, and I rejoice that we have been able to take hold of the multitude. But we must strive earnestly to better this situation in the future by steadily lifting up this great body of people as fast as we can. Whatever elevates the educational condition of our denomination or gives more of social influence, provided this be not gained by worldly conformity, will help in securing respect and attention for our distinctive tenets. And a like effect will be produced by the increasing development of benevolence among our churches, and by a completer report of what is actually done.

3. *If we wish to teach our distinctive views to others, it is necessary to understand those whom we propose to reach.* I remember a teacher of modern languages who would often elaborately explain some French or German or other idiom with which we had no difficulty at all, and then pass over as not needing explanation many a phrase we could not understand. He knew the language he was teaching, but was not well acquainted with the language of his pupils.

If we would in any way teach effectively, we must know how things look to the persons addressed; we must get their point of view. Now, Baptists are not, on the whole, so ignorant of the denominational opinions of other Christians as they are of ours, because our circumstances have compelled us to give some attention to that matter. Yet we need a much better acquaintance with them if we would speak to any purpose in public or private. I respectfully urge upon all ministers and upon intelligent private members of both sexes that they shall study, by reading and personal inquiry, each of the leading religious bodies with which they have to do—shall study them in three respects:

(a) Inquire what are the characteristic peculiarities of this body of Christians differencing them from others, and if possible get at the fundamental opinions which account for these peculiarities. (b) Consider in what respects they particularly deserve our admiration and, with the necessary changes, our imitation. Each denomination emphasizes certain aspects of truth or departments of duty, and will in regard to these present a very instructive and inspiring model. (c) Strive to ascertain how they regard our tenets, practices, and spirit—what things in us they especially dis-like, and with what they might easily feel sympathy.

Such inquiries will help us in several ways. They may re-strain the tendency to react from what we regard as the errors of others into an opposite extreme, as Protestants have done with reference to some errors of Popery, and many Baptists with reference to prelatical or pastoral domination, to clerical support, etc. They may check the unconscious adoption or imitation of opinions, sentiments, or phrases which are inconsistent, or at least incongruous, in us.

We rejoice in that "progress of Baptist principles" among Paedobaptists which Dr. Curtis's book so well describes, and per-haps fail to inquire whether there be not a counter-influence which deserves attention, and which may not be wholly bene-ficial. And then this study of other denominations will enable us better to adapt ourselves to those whom we would influence. When you address to Methodists an article suited to High Churchmen, or vice versa, what in the world are you thinking about?

4. *We should study the wise treatment of controverted topics.* Upon this point I venture to offer several practical suggestions for what they are worth.

(a) Years ago I asked the now lamented Dr. Jeter how he managed about matters in dispute between us and other denom-inations. His reply was, in substance, "I never go out of my way to avoid such topics, and never go out of my way to find them. When naturally suggested by my subject or the circumstances, I speak of them, and I try to speak without timid fear of giving offense, and without fierce vehemence, as if taking hostility for granted, but just treating these matters, so far as I can, in the same tone with which I speak of other things."

This seemed to me then, and still seems, an admirable state-ment of the course it is generally best to pursue. Some are con-stantly going out of their way to find such topics through a bred-and-born love of controversy or a mistaken judgment as to its necessity and benefits. Others go out of their way to avoid all disputed questions, and want nothing to do with controversy of any kind. This latter class might be advised to study the history and recorded writings of a man named Paul. He did not shrink from controversy. Yea, and his Master and ours is polemical on every page of his recorded discourses, always striking at some error or evil practice of the people around him.

(b) Dr. Jeter's plan may further suggest—what I think is true—that it is commonly better to treat these topics as they occur in our ordinary discourses. Set sermons have certain advantages; even public debates may still be useful in some few quarters, though most of us think their day of usefulness in this country is passed. But set sermons forewarn our hearers holding different opinions to come with armor buckled and visor closed, watching that no shaft shall reach them; while some excellent people take them as an invitation to stay away. They are no doubt sometimes appropriate and helpful, but in general the other course can scarcely fail to prove best.

(c) I think it very undesirable to connect sharp polemics with the actual administration of ordinances. Do not go into a defense of our restriction of the Lord's Supper when about to take the bread and wine. Whatever you can say will repel some hearers and deeply pain some others, while such a discussion can scarcely prove the best preparation for partaking. Try to bring out the sweet and blessed meaning of the ordinance and to observe it with unpretending reverence and solemnity, and it will itself teach all concerned.

I think Baptists often mar the wholesome solemnity of this ordinance through the persuasion that they ought then and there to defend their restricted invitation. And when about to baptize, it is usually best simply to read the New Testament passages which give the history and significance of the ordinance, and then with solemn prayer and a carefully prepared and reverent administration of the rite to leave it and the Scripture to make their own impression. If an address or sermon be given to present the practical lessons of baptism, especially that we should walk in newness of life, that will be more seemly, and often more convincing, than to argue the proper subjects and proper action of baptism. Of course, any such suggestion as this must be subject to exception, but I am persuaded it will generally hold good.

(d) We should use mainly arguments drawn from the English Scriptures and from common experience or reflection; only occasionally those which depend on learning. Scholarship is greatly to be desired in ministers—and may we have much more of it!— but the highest function of scholarship in preaching is to take assured results and make them plain to the general understanding, and certain thorough evidence which the unlearned can appreciate. If you pour a flood of learning about your hearer, and he remembers that two Sundays ago there was a torrent of learning from Dr. Somebody on the other side, then, as he does not understand and cannot judge, he is apt to conclude that he will not believe either of you. And do let us beware of using doubtful arguments as if they were conclusive.

(e) We may treat these subjects by other means as well as by preaching. Many opportunities will occur in conversation, for one who has a cultivated social tact and conversational skill, to relieve some prejudice, parry some thrust, or suggest some point for research or reflection, far more effectively than it can be done in the pulpit, and this without unpleasantly obtruding such subjects or in any wise violating the delicate proprieties of life. And carefully chosen tracts, books, or periodicals will often reinforce the sermon or conversation, or even reach some who would not listen to any public or private spoken words. We have already a great wealth of good literature of this kind, with which preachers and intelligent private members should make themselves as thoroughly acquainted as possible, so that they may know how to select precisely the most suitable for every case— a matter of the very highest importance.

(f) We must always speak of controverted subjects in a loving spirit. Baptists occupy, of necessity, a polemical position; let us earnestly strive to show that it is possible to maintain a polemical position in the spirit of true Christian love. This is really good policy; and, what is ten thousand times more, it is right.

5. *Let us gladly cooperate with our fellow Christians of other persuasions in general Christian work as far as we can without*

sacrificing our convictions. Men who think ill of us are sometimes sorely perplexed. They say, "Look at these narrow-minded, bigoted 'close-communion' Baptists! How zealously they work in our union enterprise! how loving they seem to be! I don't understand it."

It is well to increase this perplexity. At the same time, we must not allow our conscientious differences to be belittled. Sometimes in a union service you will hear a well-meaning and warm-hearted man begin to gush, till at length he speaks quite scornfully of the trifles that divide us. In such a case one must find some means of diverting the dear brother's mind to another topic, and either publicly or privately inform him that such talk will not quite do.

Indeed, this is coming to be better understood than was the case a few years ago. In Young Men's Christian Associations, for example, one seldom encounters now the unwise speeches in this respect that were once somewhat common. We must learn how to distinguish between abandonment of principles and mere practical concessions in order to conciliate—a distinction well illustrated for us in Acts 15 and in Paul's action as to Titus and Timothy. In the case of Titus the apostle would not yield an inch, would not give place for an hour, because a distinct issue of principle was made; and shortly after he voluntarily did, in the case of Timothy, what he had before refused, there being now no issue of principle.

It may sometimes be difficult to make the distinction, but that is a difficulty we may not shirk. One of the great practical problems of the Christian life, especially in our times, is to stand squarely for truth and squarely against error, and yet to maintain hearty charity toward Christians who differ with us. This assuredly can be done. The very truest and sweetest Christian charity is actually shown by some of those who stand most firmly by their distinctive opinions.

6. *Finally, let us cultivate unity among ourselves.* The Baptists of this vast country are, in fact, united. Dr. Barnas Sears, who had exceptional opportunities of observing, spoke to me not long before his death of the fact that our theological seminaries

are all teaching the same doctrines without any central authority to keep them united. And the fact is more general. Apart from mere excrescences, American Baptists are wonderfully agreed—wonderfully, if you remember it as an agreement reached and maintained in perfect freedom.

This unity becomes more manifest to any one in proportion as he gains a wider acquaintance. For example—pardon my taking local names to illustrate—there is many a brother in Mississippi with no knowledge of New England who, if he should spend a few weeks in Boston, would be astonished to find himself surrounded by real, right-down Baptists. And if some brethren in New England should go among those dreadful Landmarkers, whom they have seen so severely censured by newspapers that do not seem to know even the meaning of the term, they would conclude that most of the said Landmarkers are really very much like themselves, and not dreadful at all.

Dr. Fuller was fond of giving a story told by William Jay. Mr. Jay walked out one day in a dense English fog. Presently he saw approaching him a huge and monstrous object that made him start. As they drew nearer together it assumed the shape of a gigantic man; and when they met, it was his own brother John.

And American Baptists are becoming more united just now. A few years ago there was in some quarters a movement toward the propagation of "open communion" which at a distance awakened concern. But the estimable brethren engaged in that movement have gone in peace or have peacefully subsided into quiet. And in some other quarters ultraists are losing influence, and brethren who once followed them seem now disposed not at all to abandon any principle, but to avoid pushing differences among ourselves into an occasion of denominational disruption. So the general outlook is now very encouraging.

Let us cultivate, I say, this unity among ourselves. In order to do so, our watchwords must be freedom, forbearance, patience. There can be no constrained unity among us. The genius of our ideas and institutions quite forbids it. That newspaper, seminary, or society which undertakes to coerce American Baptists into unity will soon weary of the task.

We must be forbearing and patient, and not discouraged by many things which under the circumstances are to be looked for. Competing journals and other institutions may get up an occasional breeze; each great city may show a too exclusive interest in societies there located: that is natural, if not wise; personal rivalries may sometimes curiously complicate themselves with questions of principle and of general expediency: it may cause regret, but need not cause wonder; East and West may pull apart in some respects, and North and South; even the "celestial minds" of our noble women may not always perfectly agree about organizations; we cooperate fully in some matters, partially in some, perhaps work separately in others, yet with hearty fraternal kindness—but let us cultivate freedom, forbearance, patience, and we shall be substantially united more and more.

This growing unity among ourselves gives us increasing power to impress our denominational opinions upon others; and the more zealously we strive to teach our distinctive views to others, the more we shall become united among ourselves.

WALTER RAUSCHENBUSCH (1861-1918)

This son of German immigrants was well educated both in Germany and in America. He graduated from the Rochester Theological Seminary in 1886 and was then ordained to the Baptist ministry, the seventh in a direct line of ministers. He took a humble church among German immigrants in New York and studied how to help these and other common people. The depression of 1893 caused suffering among them that almost broke his heart. He became a leading protagonist of the "Social Gospel" and wrote many books that awakened American minds to needs for social change. Christianity and the Social Crisis, Prayers of the Social Awakening, *and* The Social Principles of Jesus *are among his great works. He taught New Testament and Church History in the Rochester Theological Seminary from 1897 until his death in 1918. We select his "Why I Am a Baptist" in order to acquaint Baptists better with the thorough denominational position of a great leader whose Baptist ties are often overlooked, and because it is one of the best statements ever written on our distinctive principles.*

"Why I Am a Baptist"

PRELUDE

Why am I a Baptist? Well, at the outset, because my father was one. He was a Lutheran minister in Germany; he came to America, got into contact with the Baptists, found in their teachings the truths that he had been groping for and, under great loss of position and trouble of soul, became a Baptist. If he had remained a Lutheran minister in Germany I should probably not be a Baptist minister in America. There is no use in denying that our family relations and the training of our childhood exert a very strong influence on all of us and determine our religious affiliations for us.

In countries that have an "Established Church" it is considered a horrible and impious thing for anyone to leave the religion of his fathers, and even in our country, which is the paradise of religious liberty and individualism, only a minority of persons are so strongly swayed by individual convictions that they can break the soft and twining bonds of family love and family tradition. Most men are Catholics or Protestants or Jews because their parents were Catholics or Protestants or Jews, and that's all there is of it.

. . . But that expresses only half of the truth. We are Americans because we were born so. But it is our duty and our right clearly and increasingly to understand what our country stands for and to adopt as our personal principles those ideals of democracy and equality on which our national life is founded. We are Americans by birth; but we must become Americans by personal conviction. In the same way we may be Baptists by birth, but we must become Baptists by conviction. And no man is a true Baptist until his inherited tendency has been transformed into conscious purpose. In a big freight yard you can watch a locomotive distributing a freight train over the various sidings. It will bunt a car along and let it roll along by itself. The car moves, but it moves by the power of inertia. It has no living energy in it. By and by it will slow up and stop. No Baptist boy or girl ought to grow up to resemble that car. They must develop their own Baptist convictions and run under their own steam. They have inherited a great legacy of truth; let them learn what is already theirs; let them hold by the surer title of personal acquisition what is theirs by hereditary right.

I began by being a Baptist because my father was, but today I am a Baptist, because, with my convictions, I could not well be anything else. I now stand on my own feet and am ready to give an account of the faith I hold.

It is a good thing to raise the question: "Why are you a Baptist?" I wish all our church members had to answer it clearly and fully. It is possible to be a Baptist on small grounds or on large grounds. Some man will say: "I am a Baptist because the Greek word *baptizo* means immerse." That is quite true, but that is a pretty small peg to hang your religious convictions on. A near-sighted child was taken to the zoo and stood in front of the lion's cage. The lion's tail was hanging down through the bars. "But I thought the lion was different," said the child, "it looks like a yellow rope." So there are Baptists who have hitherto discovered only the tail end of our Baptist ideals and convictions, and it is no wonder that they turn out as narrow as the tail they devoutly believe in. . . .

The minds of men are widening today. There are large thoughts pouring and flooding all about us. And men who have grasped great ideas in one part of their life feel impatient of petty ideas in any other part of their life, especially in their religion. Only a large faith, built on generous, gigantic lines will win the thoughtful men and women of the future. I do believe that we Baptists have a magnificent body of truth—free, vital, honest, spiritual, and wholly in line with the noblest tendencies of our age. But we must realize its largeness and present it in all its out-of-door greatness and freshness, and not show people a few dried plants and stuffed animals as exponents of the Promised Land to which God has led us and to which we invite them. . . .

MY FIRST REASON

Religion has taken a great variety of forms in the various Christian bodies. Take a solemn mass in a Roman Catholic cathedral, with the dim religious light, the swelling music, the candles, the trooping of the priests and acolytes, the wafting of the incense, the tinkle of the bell, the prostration of the people as the wafer is miraculously transformed into the very body of the Lord. Take on the other hand a little experience meeting in a country church where one simple soul after the other arises to tell in rude words of its dealings with God. How far apart they are! And yet it is only fair to believe that all Christian bodies aim at the same thing: to bring the human soul into saving contact with God through Christ and to secure for it the knowledge and power of a holy life. Let us rejoice that we are all one in that fundamental aim.

But on the other hand it is only true to assert that some religious bodies seek to attain that aim by means that hinder the soul from finding God more than they help it. Judaism, too, sought God with its elaborate temple worship, its bloody sacrifices, its detailed forms. But Christ taught us to approach God by a simpler and more spiritual way.

The all-important question of just where to worship and how to worship was relegated to the background as obsolete and outgrown for those who had learned to worship God in spirit and in truth. All religious bodies carry with them a good many clinging remnants of their childhood stage, beliefs and customs that were superstitious in their origin and never belonged to genuine Christianity. And some religious bodies have squarely refused ever to strip these things off; they cherish remnants of heathenism as their most precious and fundamental possessions. Thus it becomes a matter of importance for an intelligent Christian to inquire where he can find Christianity in its least adulterated form.

Where is the fundamental aim of bringing the human soul into saving fellowship with God attained most clearly? Where is worship most spiritual? Where is attention least diverted from what is essential in the religious and ethical life?

The Christian faith as Baptists hold it sets spiritual experience boldly to the front as the one great thing in religion. It aims at experimental religion. We are an evangelistic body. We summon all men to conscious repentance from sin, to conscious prayer for forgiveness. We ask a man: "Have you put your faith in Christ? Have you submitted your will to His will? Have you received the inward assurance that your sins are forgiven and that you are at peace with God? Have you had experience of God?"

If anyone desires to enter our churches we ask for evidence of such experience and we ask for nothing else. We do not ask him to recite a creed or catechism. The more simple and heartfelt the testimony is, the better we like it. If it is glib and wordy, we distrust it. Experience is our sole requisite for receiving baptism; it is fundamental in our church life.

We apply the same test to our ministry. The first thing we ask a candidate is about his conversion and Christian experience. The next thing we ask him is if he is conscious of being personally called to the work of the ministry; that also probes for experience with God. Finally we ask him for his views of doctrine, but there, too, we discourage any mere recitation of what is orthodox, and are best pleased if all his intellectual beliefs are plainly born of inward conviction and experience.

Thus our church membership and our ministry are both based on religious experience. So is the ordinary course of our church life. Take our churches right through and nothing so draws and wins them in preaching as the note of, personal experience of God; nothing so touches and melts them in the social meetings as the heart-note of experience. When we insist so strongly on true baptism, it is not an insistence on external forms, but a protest against any external form that has no experience back of it. Baptism of believers is an outward act plus an inward experience. Infant baptism, we believe, is an outward act minus any inward experience, and we will have none of it.

In this direct insistence on conscious personal experience a true Baptist Church is about as clear-cut and untrammeled as any religious body can well be. The Roman Catholic Church, for instance, also seeks to put a man in contact with the grace of God, but the grace of God is received through the sacraments. In the regenerating water of baptism, in the mysterious wafer of the communion, in the absolution pronounced by the priest in the sacrament of penance, they say a man meets God. But does he? Or does he only meet the Church? Has the Church not interposed a lot of man-made ceremonies between the soul and God, so that thousands who punctiliously go through all this ritual never experience God in fact, and are kept from doing so by the very things in which they are taught that they meet him?

I have repeatedly attended confirmation services in the Lutheran Church and was deeply interested in them. The children there are examined as to their knowledge of the catechism and of passages of Scripture. They recite them from memory. I wish Baptist children knew as much of the Bible and the hymns of the church by heart. I regard the systematic instruction given for months previous to confirmation as one of the finest features of the Lutheran Church and wish we could copy it. It offers an unrivaled opportunity for a devout pastor. But when the mental exercise of *memoriter* recitation is made the test for admission to the Church and its sacrament, personal experience is supplanted by something totally different and inferior. I know from personal contact with the people how many get the impression that such instruction makes a person a Christian.

Some churches make much of ritual and sacrament, in the belief that this furnishes access to God. Others make much of a formulated creed, in the belief that correct intellectual comprehension is the fundamental thing in the Christian life. Baptists have simplified ritual until we have only two obligatory ritual actions left, baptism and the Lord's Supper, and we insist on experience as the essential ingredient in these too. We believe in clear convictions of truth, but we have no formulated creed to which anybody, minister or layman, is required to assent. Intellectual statements of belief are useful if they are the outgrowth of personal experience; if not, they are likely to be a harmful substitute for experience.

Now consider how great a thing it is for a church body to assert that a man may and must come into direct personal relations with God, and to adapt all its church life to create such direct and spiritual experiences in men. I have met people in other churches who not only have no such experience themselves, but they doubt if anybody can have it. It seems presumption to them for a man to assert that he knows he has received pardon from God and is living in conscious fellowship with him. Yet what is all the apparatus of church life good for, if it does not help men to that experience?

. . . Experimental religion is necessarily free and voluntary. Men can compel attendance at the mass. They can compel subscription to a creed. They cannot compel an inner experience. It has to be free and spontaneous. And nothing has any value in the sight of God that is not the free outflow of the man's life. What would we care for the compulsory love of a wife or a child? What does God care for compulsory faith and adoration? When we insist on experience, and not on ritual or creed, we place religion where it is necessarily free, and then, if it is freely given, it has value in God's sight.

. . . I like to think also that a church body which demands religious experience and that alone is deeply democratic. It takes a trained mind to understand the fine distinctions of the creeds. It takes a good deal of historical information merely to understand the ritual and symbols of some of the old churches. If anybody knows just what each garment means which a Catholic priest wears before the altar, and how this garb originated and what changes it has passed through, he knows enough history to write a book. On the other hand, experience of God is open to the simplest mind, just as love is. A little child can love before it can think. A poor German or Italian mother cannot follow the new

learning which her children get in this country, but she can out-
class anybody in loving them. The intellect is aristocratic; human love and religious faith are both democratic.

When we Baptists insist on personal experience as the only
essential thing in religion, we are hewing our way back to original Christianity. The gorgeous ritual that drapes the limbs of
the ancient churches was wrought out piece by piece in later
generations, and modern historical scholarship is constantly making it clearer that the shimmering silk of which those garments
are made and the golden threads with which they are embroid-
ered, were taken from the heathenism of the ancient world. The
insistence on correct thinking, on exact orthodoxy of definition,
was likewise a product of Greek intellectualism after Christianity
had amalgamated with the Greek civilization of the heathen
world. These things were not a part of Christianity as the apostles knew it. Much less were they part of the Christianity of
Jesus himself.

Original Christianity was exceedingly simple; it was just a new
life with God and a new life with men. Faith in Christ was a
spiritual experience. Those who believed in him, felt a new spirit,
the Holy Spirit, living in their hearts, inspiring their prayers and
testimonies, melting away their selfishness, emboldening them to
heroism. Paul called that new life "faith." That word with him
does not merely mean an intellectual belief. It is a kind of al-
gebraic symbol, expressing the inner religious experience and
life in Christ.

I am a Baptist, then, because in our church life we have a
minimum of emphasis on ritual and creed, and a maximum of
emphasis on spiritual experience, and the more I study the history
of religion, the more I see how great and fruitful such a position
is.

When I claim such a purely spiritual religion for Baptists, I
am well aware that not all Baptists possess it. Many do not even
realize that that is the essence of our Baptist faith. We have
some who insist on immersion in a purely legal and ritualistic
spirit. We have others who would be only too glad if we had an
iron-clad Baptist creed with a thousand points that they might

insist on it. I know, too, that "experience" with very many is a very shallow emotion, copied often from others and passing away again without changing life and conduct at all, unless it be to add religious conceit to all other faults. This is the smallness and pettiness that is inseparable from human life. But our Baptist faith, like our American political constitution, is founded on great principles, and even if some misuse it or misunderstand it, or are inwardly traitors to it, its greatness lifts others up to it. Baptists uphold Baptist principles; and Baptist principles in turn lift up Baptists.

MY SECOND REASON

. . . But religion is not a purely individual matter. Nothing in human life is. We are social beings, and all elements of our life come to their full development only through social interchange and cooperation. A man working alone is an inefficient producer; by division of labor and cooperation the productive efficiency of all is multiplied. A person educating himself is at a great disadvantage compared with a student who has teachers and fellow-students to stimulate him. . . . We never realize all our powers and enthusiasms until we shout with others in a public meeting, or keep step with others to the drum-beat, and see the flag, which is the symbol of our common life, leading us forward.

It stands to reason that religion, too, demands social expression, and will come to its full strength and richness only when it is shared with others. And so in fact we find it. There is a sweetness in private prayer, but there is an additional thrill when we join in a heartfelt hymn and are swept on the wave-crest of a common emotion. Most of us have come to the great religious decision in life only under the influence of social emotion. With most of us the flame of religious longing and determination would flicker lower and lower in the course of the years, if it were not fanned afresh by contact with the experiences and the religious will-power of others. When Jesus said that where two or three are gathered in his name, he is in the midst of them, he expressed the profound truth that his presence is fully realized only in a Christian society; it may be a very small group, but it needs at least one other human heart next to ours to be fully sensible of the Christ. . . .

Christians have had no end of controversy about the proper organization of the church. The Roman Catholic church holds that there is no true church apart from the bishops and the Roman pope. Pope Boniface VIII in 1302 solemnly asserted: "The one and unique church has one body, and one head, namely Christ, and the vicar of Christ, Peter, and the successor of Peter. Further we declare, assert and define that for every human being it is absolutely essential for salvation that he be subject to the Roman Pontiff." Pope Pius IX in 1854 reiterated that "it is part of faith that outside of the apostolic Roman church no one can be saved." The Episcopal church holds that all ministerial authority is derived through the ordination coming down through the historic episcopate, and that Presbyterian and Baptist ministers, while they may be very good men and blessed of God in saving souls, are not ministers of the Christian church in the proper sense. Thus the one church makes salvation and the other makes ministerial authority depend on connection with the right church organization. There are Baptists, too, who are ready to assert that none but a Baptist church is a true church at all.

To my mind the essential matter is not that a church body is very ancient, or that it has a continuous history, but that it embodies the Christian spirit in the method of its organization, and by its very constitution offers the largest possible opportunity to its members to live a truly Christian life together. The fundamental question is not even whether a certain church order is Biblical, but whether it is Christian. The Bible merely helps us to see if it is Christian.

Now I think our Baptist church organization, though it is faulty in many ways and though it creaks and groans as it works along, just as all other human organizations do, is built on very noble Christian lines and therefore it is dear to me.

1. It tries to create an organization of really Christian people. It admits to membership only those who deliberately apply for it and who can assert that they have met Christ and love him and want to follow him. It scrutinizes their statements to save them

from self-deception and votes to receive them only if it feels confident that there is a real beginning of conscious spiritual life. It also eliminates from its membership those who are manifestly not living a Christian life. It may make many mistakes in receiving too quickly and in excluding too slowly, but at least it tries to keep its membership clean and homogeneous. Churches may become so worldly that it is hard to see any line dividing them from the world, but still the principle is embedded in the very constitution of our church life, and that always offers a ready possibility of reformation. On the other hand with other churches their very constitution works the other way. Individual pastors in such churches may strive to create a really Christian fellowship, but their churches neutralize these efforts by admitting everybody through the gate of infant baptism.

2. Our churches are Christian democracies. The people are sovereign in them. All power wielded by its ministers and officers is conferred by the church. It makes ample room for those who have God-given powers for leadership, but it holds them down to the service of the people by making them responsible to the church for their actions. That democracy of the Baptist churches is something to be proud of. . . . It also corresponds more completely to primitive Christianity. The farther we get back to apostolic Christianity the completer is the democracy we encounter.

The Roman Catholic church is a benevolent despotism. All power flows from the pope downward. That type of church organization originated under the despotism of imperial Rome and has perpetuated the political ideas and customs of that epoch. Government by bishops also has strong affinities for a monarchy. As James I said: "No bishop, no king." He saw in the bishops the best props against Puritan democracy. Our congregational government originated in a great wave of popular democracy in England, and has embodied and perpetuated the democratic ideals of the Puritan Revolution. I am proud to think that our church life is in harmony with the great ideal of government of the people, by the people and for the people, which mankind is slowly toiling to realize.

3. Our Baptist churches recognize no priestly class. Our ministers are not essentially different from the laity. According to Catholic and high church views a priest receives an indelible character in ordination which enables him to do things which no other man can do. We take no such view of our ministry and I thank God we do not. The havoc which priestly assumption of power has wrought in the history of the church is incalculable. The priest is an inheritance from heathenism. He is needed only if there are magical sacraments to be offered or administered. Jesus was not a priest, not the creator of priests. Other churches have only a vague line of demarcation between the ministry and the laity. We reverse that. We have a sharp line of demarcation between church and world, but only a vague line between ministry and laity. Which is most Christian?

4. We have no hierarchy within our ministry. We have no rector above the vicar, no bishop above the rector, no archbishop above the bishop, no pope above them all. Jesus bids us call no man father or master, but all of us are to be brethren, and the only greatness is to be by pre-eminent service (Matt. 23:1-12). That settles all hierarchies for me. Some have greater natural gifts than others, and that inequality should be frankly recognized. Some have a holier character and deeper spiritual insight, and they should have honor and leadership accordingly. But fraternity in the ministry must prevail.

5. Our churches have home-rule. Each church is sovereign in its own affairs. In that respect we follow the same principle on which our country is built up. . . . The self-government of our churches does not hinder them from joining with others in fraternal cooperation, in associations and State conventions, in city mission societies and national missionary organizations. I do think, however, that our Baptist churches have lagged in this voluntary cooperation, and have too generally allowed each church to struggle along as best it could. In Rochester, for instance, we have no adequate organic expression of our unity.

6. Our Baptist churches decline all alliances with the State. They accept no dictation from the State in their spiritual affairs. They ask no favors from the State, except that they accept such

exemptions from taxation as the State grants to all institutions which labor for common good and not for private profit. Baptists insisted on this separation between church and State at a time when the principle was novel and revolutionary.

Some Baptists seem to think that this separation is based on the idea that the spiritual life has nothing to do with the secular life. I utterly deny that assertion and think it a calamitous heresy. Our Baptist forefathers insisted on that separation because they saw that it brought mischief when unspiritual men, actuated by political or covetous motives, tried to interfere with the centers of religious and moral life. To let the churches alone meant to let the religious and moral life of the nation work out its own problems unhampered and unthwarted by baser considerations and forces. But in turn it was also found that the political life of the nation is freed from a warping and disturbing influence when ecclesiastical questions are removed from politics. Other churches have had to be wrenched loose forcibly from their hold on public income and political power. Baptists have the far nobler and prouder position of declining these things voluntarily and of being pioneers in that principle toward which the civilized nations are slowly drifting.

. . . I know well that Baptist churches have not lived up to these magnificent principles. Churches, like individuals, are in perpetual danger of backsliding. There are churches that admit almost anybody and exclude scarcely anybody. There are Baptist churches in which a small junto of men rule and democracy has become a mere name. There are Baptist ministers who are more priestly in spirit and temper than the present pope. But it is a great thing for a nation to have adopted a constitution guaranteeing freedom, even if that nation is ridden by bosses and sold out to those who pay; it is a great thing for a young man to have committed himself definitely to a life of unselfish service, even if he is often led away by selfish impulses; and it is a great thing for a body of churches to have embodied such advanced Christian principles in their very constitution, even if individually or collectively they drop below them.

MY THIRD REASON

. . . My third reason deals with the conception of worship.

I can best make this clear by going back a little into the history of religion. In the rude and primitive forms of religion, worship is mainly an attempt to "get on the right side" of the gods. Men are afraid of the terrible powers of nature, of thunder, disease, blight, flood and drought, and they try to placate and conciliate the supernatural beings who show their displeasure by sending these terrors on helpless mortals. So they offer sacrifices and piteous prayers, just as they would bring gifts and wail before the angry human despots with whose ferocity and whims they were well acquainted. Men want good harvests, health, offspring, revenge and protection, and they tell the gods of their wants and bring them presents to win their help and favor. To ward off evil and to secure favors is the main object of worship in these lower stages of religion.

But each god has his peculiar tastes and disposition which must be consulted. One god likes rice and flowers; another wants the smell of burning mutton or beef; another insists on human blood. They have their sacred places where they have appeared and where they can best be approached. They have their sacred names and formulas by which they can be summoned. And they have their priests, who are experts on all these matters, and are allowed to draw near the god and offer sacrifices on behalf of the ignorant and unclean folk—for a consideration. These forms of worship are handed down from generation to generation, and are carefully preserved in the memory of the experts, for their effectiveness depends on the very wording of a prayer or on a prostration to right or left. In heathen Rome the priests muttered ancient prayers which they no longer understood. Religion is marvelously conservative about the form of worship. All old religions are full of petrified usages.

In a higher stage of religious development men want personal contact with the deity. They have a sense of impurity and de-filement. They are told that by being bathed with water or anointed with oil, or touched with hot blood—all, of course, with the proper magic formula—they will be supernaturally cleansed and made holy and freed from the power of the evil forces. Men now have a deep sense of the frail and perishable nature of mortal life; they long for immortality and the assurance of it. They are told that if they pass through certain mysterious rites they will come under the protection of the gods who rule the hereafter and will be saved from death; or something of the divine life will enter into them and survive death. Thus in this higher stage of religion men seek expiation of guilt, freedom from impurity, victory over death, direct and concrete contact with the deity. In this stage, too, the forms of worship are supposed to be of the utmost importance. If they are not performed exactly, they lose their power.

To anyone who knows the dense pall of superstition that has hung over mankind, it is a wonderful relief to pass from this smoke of incense and burnt-offering to the outdoor air and sunlight in which Jesus walked with his Father. The crew of supernatural despots who want sacrifices and who love to see men cringe and implore, has vanished away, and the Best Being in the universe bows down with fatherly love. Holy places, holy times, holy formulas, holy experts are all left behind, and the only thing God asks for is love for himself and love for our fellowmen. The old cowering fear of the slave is gone, and instead we see the free love and obedience of the son and child of God. Jesus did not pray because he had to or because he wanted to get something from God, but because he loved to pray and speak to his Father. To become a disciple of Jesus means to learn to think of God and live with him as Jesus did, and to let all life be transformed by that new knowledge and faith.

Paul understood Jesus. His contest against the Law was a mighty effort to cut away the old forms of religion that cramped and gagged the spirit of religion, and to set Christians free to look at Christ before them and to listen to the spirit within them. Read Romans 8, or Galatians from that point of view.

But the old religious habits of mind were very strong in men. It took hard work to emancipate the Jewish Christians from their old Jewish forms of religion, and the people who had lived in heathenism very soon created a new system of ceremonialism, which had a Christian face but a pagan spirit. Christianity had only two religious acts in which form counted for anything, baptism and the Lord's Supper; one was a bath, the other a meal. These two simple acts of daily life were used to express great spiritual thoughts.

But men with pagan habits of mind seized on these and saw in them just what they were looking for. Baptism was to them a mystic cleansing which washed away guilt and defilement, a magic bath from which a man rose regenerate as new man with the past all cleaned away. When they heard the words "This is my body, this is my blood," they felt that in some mysterious way Christ was really present in the bread and wine, and when they swallowed the elements, his divine life entered into them and gave them the assurance and power of immortality.

These superstitious ideas became ever more powerful and concrete as time passed; they were adopted by theologians and defended as part of the essence of Christianity. Gradually it was believed that Christ was not merely present in the sacrament; the bread and wine were actually changed into his body and blood and chewed with the teeth, and this new body of Christ, which was created under the magic formula of the priest, was offered anew to God in the sacrifice of the mass. A new priesthood early grew up, equipped with mysterious powers to consecrate the sacraments and to forgive sins. Additional sacraments were developed. Christianity once more had its holy places, holy times, holy formulas, its sacrifices and incense, its set prayers and all the apparatus of worship, just like the heathen religions, only more so.

Through it all still breathed the spirit of Jesus with pitying and saving power, but the saving power was largely in spite of what was called Christian worship, and not by means of it. And this established religion was exceedingly conservative and anxious to keep things just as they had been, and refused to let the spirit of Jesus educate it up to better things. Just as the ancient heathen priest in Rome muttered formulas in a dead language, so the Christian priest in Rome chants his formulas in Latin, which was a living language when Christianity began and is now a dead language. The Greek Church, too, uses a ritual language which has become unintelligible to the people. This is merely a trifling indication of the petrifying conservatism in religion.

The Reformation was a rising of the religious and democratic and national spirit against this dead inheritance of the past. Among other things the Reformation simplified worship and swept out a great mass of superstitious ceremonial. In some countries the break from Catholic forms of worship was far more thorough than in others. The Calvinistic churches in Switzerland, France, Holland, and parts of Germany were very thorough; the Lutheran churches in Germany and Scandinavia not quite so thorough; and the Church of England least of all.

The Baptists, and all those bodies with whom we are historically connected, marched in the vanguard of Protestantism. That is one reason I am a Baptist, because by being a Baptist I am a radical Protestant. I can help to cleanse Christianity of the mass of heathen influence which leaked in during the early centuries and was afterward so religiously preserved and cherished. I can help to bring humanity to that simple, ethical, spiritual worship which Jesus taught and which has been so sadly overlaid by the gilded and jeweled worship of a paganized church.

Baptists are, in fact, more Protestant than the great Reformers on some points. The Reformers all retained infant baptism. But infant baptism was part and parcel of that very paganizing tendency which I have tried to describe. It grew out of a double root: the belief that original sin damns even infants to hell; and the belief that baptism regenerates. If baptism saves and if children need salvation, of course human love wanted the children to be baptized in order to save them from the risk of hell.

There was widespread doubt about infant baptism at the beginning of the Reformation, but to reject it would have meant churches of baptized believers and would have unchurched the great mass of men. The reformers recoiled from so sweeping a change, largely for political reasons, and infant baptism was maintained, defended and extolled. It was an alien element in Protestantism, and has been most subtly influential in opening the door to other alien elements in worship, organization and doctrine. It is now slowly dying out.

Modern Protestant Christians no longer believe that unbaptized infants go to hell through their original sin, nor do they believe that baptism regenerates. And if a baby does not need baptism and if baptism does not do it any good, why should the baby be baptized? Other sentimental reasons are now used to prop the custom, but the number of infant baptisms is constantly decreasing. People are sensibly concluding to give their children a chance to be baptized when it will mean something to them. Of course Baptists have largely helped to bring this result about. They made a cleaner sweep of the old pagan leaven at the outset, and the slow development of the purified Christian spirit in modern Protestantism is swinging their way.

. . . The life of Jesus was as full of religion as a nightingale is full of song or a rose full of fragrance, but the bent of his life was away from the inherited forms of worship, and he can scarcely be said to have taught new forms. He taught a prayer when his disciples asked for it, but that prayer was meant to teach utter simplicity. In our common worship we shall come closest to the spirit of true Christianity if every act is full of joy in God and his fellowship, love for one another, hatred for all evil, and an honest desire to live a right life in the sight of Christ.

Our worship should eliminate as far as possible all selfish greed, all superstition, and all untrue and unworthy ideas about God. It should clear our conception of the right life by instructing our moral nature; it should give our will strong, steady, lasting impulses toward righteous action; and it should breed and foster habits of reverence and the faculty of adoration. . . .

Just how much spirituality and essential religion there is in a given Baptist church service, is another question. That depends entirely on the men and women who engage in it. It may be utterly barren and dead. But even then there is an advantage in our simplicity of form, for the deadness will not be hidden and masked by the borrowed life of mere ceremonial. An unspiritual priest may sing the mass more beautifully than the sweetest saint, but a Baptist minister or church can not be dead long with-

out having men know it, and then there is a fair chance for repentance. . . .

It is of the utmost importance that the individual and the race
should retain the capacity for growth in religious thought. It is
fatal to make the religious thought of one age binding for a later
age. It is equally fatal for a grown man not to put away childish
things, but still to think and talk like a child.

Yet that is what religion has very commonly done. After
Christianity had become the State religion of the Roman Empire
under Constantine the Great, it was a matter of great concern
to the emperors that the Church should remain united and not
be broken up by bitter doctrinal fights. So, if some doctrinal
question was giving trouble, they summoned a great council of
bishops and had them decide by a mere majority vote on the
profoundest questions. Moreover, these councils were usually
packed and engineered by wire-pulling exactly like modern political conventions, and the result was usually reached by com-
promise or intimidation. Yet when the result was reached, it
became the binding law of orthodoxy, and men believed that the
Holy Ghost, who had promised to lead the Church into all truth,
had guided the decisions.

Such a general council could not err, and its decisions were
binding on all Christian thinkers. Such infallible decisions increased as the centuries went on, and each was riveted around
the intellect of the Church like an iron hoop around a barrel.
Hoops are good around barrels, but I should not advise putting
nice, tightly fitting hoops around the body of a growing child.
It is hard to overstate the damage that was done to the intellectual and moral and religious growing power of humanity by this
incubus of dead authority. For instance, the doctrine of transubstantiation, that is, the belief that the bread and wine of the
Lord's Supper are actually changed into the flesh and blood of
Christ, was the product of the Dark Ages. When education and
science were at their lowest state, when the civilization of the
ancient world lay buried under the raw barbarism of the Teu-
tonic tribes, when superstition sprouted like toadstools in the
dark, this belief was evolved which laughs at common sense and

reason. But the Catholic Church solemnly adopted it, and now American Catholic scholars of the twentieth century have to believe it. And they do. But they can not without crippling their intellect in other ways.

. . . It is very hard, almost impossible, to get rid of a creed again after it is once adopted. Our Presbyterian brethren have long been restless under the straight Calvinism of their Westminster Confession, and it has cost them a long struggle to secure some modification of it. The great church historian Harnack, knowing how tenaciously creeds cling to a church, was lost in admiration when our American Presbyterians first began to make the effort.

Now we Baptists have no authoritative creed. Our ministers and professors are not required solemnly to declare that they adopt some obsolete statement as their belief and will always teach that. We have a couple of summaries, called the New Hampshire and the Philadelphia Confession, which are often adopted by newly organized churches, but no one is compelled to use them. So far as I remember I never read either of them until I had been several years a Baptist minister, and when I did read them, I was not interested in them. This freedom from creeds has left Baptists free to grow without jars and struggles. We used to be strict Calvinists, just like our Presbyterian brethren, and we, too, have insensibly grown away from rigid Calvinism, but we have had no creed to tinker with and therefore no conflict about it. Like Topsy, we just "growed."

Yet Baptists have been remarkably free from doctrinal vagaries. They have not moved zig-zag, but in a fairly straight line. There was enough conservative instinct to balance their thinking without carrying a big stick of timber on their shoulders to balance them.

Baptists have always insisted that they recognize the Bible alone as their sufficient authority for faith and practice. There are, indeed, many Baptists who have tried to use the Bible just as other denominations use their creeds. They have turned the Bible into one huge creed, and practically that meant: "You must believe everything which we think the Bible means and says." They have tried to impose on us their little interpretation of the great Book as the creed to which all good Baptists must cleave.

But fortunately the Bible is totally different from a creed. A creed contains sharply defined and abstract theology; the Bible contains a record of concrete and glowing religious life. A creed addresses itself to the intellect; the Bible appeals to the whole soul and edifies it. A creed tells you what you must believe; the Bible tells you what holy men have believed. A creed is religious philosophy, the Bible is religious history. A creed gives the truth as it looked to one set of clever men at one particular stage of human history; the Bible gives the truth as it looked to a great number of God-filled men running through many hundreds of years. The strength of a creed is in its uniformity and its tight fit; the beauty of the Bible is in its marvelous variety and richness. A creed imposes a law and binds thought; the Bible imparts a spirit and awakens thought.

Any collection of historical documents, growing right out of human life, would be more useful and instructive to after-times than the cleverest piece of abstract thinking done by a single man or group of men. The epoch-making treaties of the past grow obsolete with fearful rapidity; human nature with its love and hate and fear and hope and sin and passion is always the same, and what was true in the days of Rameses II under the shadow of the pyramids is true in the days of Roosevelt I under the shadow of the skyscrapers. Hence creeds are dead and the Bible is alive. And such a life in it! A unique and gifted nation, with a lofty conception of God and a thrilling faith in him, preserves the thoughts of its most daring thinkers, its prophets and revolutionists, its poets and religious historians, and the whole collection throbs with the living breath of God—if only we have a mind to respond. And then comes the Highest One of all, the Son of God and the King of Humanity, and his life and thought are preserved in artless books, and the powerful impulse which he gives to human souls records itself in a series of letters and tracts, and these are added to the Old Bible of the Jewish people as the New Bible of the Christian people.

These books are the deposit of the purest and freshest form of Christianity. It is the mountain-brook before it has grown muddy in the plain by the inflow of other waters. The New Testament has been the conscience in the heart of the Church, always warning and recalling it from its sinful wanderings. It is still calling us up higher today, beyond traditional Christianity to the religion of Christ. In the New Testament lies the power of perpetual reformation for the Church. Baptists, in tying to the New Testament, have hitched to their chariot to a star, and they will have to keep moving.

It seems to me a great thing that Baptists are not chained by creeds, but have taken the Bible as their authority. The full significance of that principle has never yet appeared among us. We have paralyzed the Bible by turning it into a law-book and a collection of proof-texts. We have often refused to take it in its own plain meaning and to comprehend the larger sweep of history in it. We have fussed about trifles in it and have missed the greatest things. We have reduced it all to a single level, as if Esther was equal to Isaiah, and the Old Testament to the New, and Zephaniah or Jude to our Lord Jesus Christ. But my faith is that the old veil of Moses will be taken away from the Bible and its full light will break forth.

POSTLUDE

. . . Sometimes while writing these articles I felt in doubt whether I was doing good or harm. I should do harm if I gave Baptists the impression that "we are the people and there are no others." We are not a perfect denomination. We are capable of being just as narrow and small as anybody. There are fine qualities in which other denominations surpass us. I do not want to foster Baptist self-conceit, because thereby I should grieve the spirit of Christ. I do not want to make Baptists shut themselves up in their little clam-shells and be indifferent to the ocean outside of them. I am a Baptist, but I am more than a Baptist. All things are mine; whether Francis of Assisi, or Luther, or Knox, or Wesley; all are mine because I am Christ's. The old Adam is a strict denominationalist; the new Adam is just a Christian.

H. WHEELER ROBINSON (1872-1945)

H. WHEELER ROBINSON *won a foremost place among the theological teachers and writers of his generation. He was for fourteen years on the staff of Rawdon Baptist College and then from 1920 to 1942 was principal of Regent's Park College, first in London and then in Oxford. Many present-day English scholars were his students. He wrote many noteworthy books. The following selection is Chapter VII from his little book* The Life and Faith of the Baptists, *revised edition of 1946.*

"The Strength and the Weakness of the Baptists"

The great majority of religious men are what they are ecclesiastically because of the way they have grown up. This is as it should be, since nothing atones for the absence of those memories of childhood and youth which are progressively hallowed by the faith of the grown man and gain a richer interpretation by the experience of life. The familiar walls of the church, the familiar phrases of prayer and praise, even the familiar tones of voice of him who first opened to us the way of the Spirit, gain a sacramental quality, so as to be inseparable in memory from the experience they mediated. They have helped to bring us into a living tradition that we might discover "how great a thing it is to live at the end of so many ages, heirs to the thoughts of the wise, the labours of the good, the prayers of the devout." [1]

---

[1] James Martineau, *Home Prayers*, p. 6.

Yet it is also true that each of us enters this living stream with his own unique life, his own capacities for emotion ready to be stirred, his own thoughts striving to become articulate, his own will claiming its free exercise. The truth—at least, the truth for me—lies in, and is tested by, a personal reaction to this tradition. "Tradition and conscience are the two wings given to the human soul to reach to truth. . . . Where you find the general permanent voice of humanity agreeing with the voice of your conscience, be sure that you hold in your grasp something with absolute truth—gained and forever yours." [2] This, of course, implies the right and the duty of each to criticize the religious tradition in and through which he lives. Such criticism is the essential condition not only of progress, individual and corporate, but even of clear conviction and intelligent faith. This is true for all religion; it ought to be especially true for those forms of it which emphasize voluntary choice and personal faith as primary duties.

We may often gain much help in the process of examining our own religious faith and practice by learning how it looks to one who stands outside our own communion, provided he be sympathetic, well-informed, and able to give expression to his thinking. Some years before this book was planned, I asked three such competent observers to give me their frank opinions on "The Strength and the Weakness of the Baptists." I summarize their answers, for the sake of brevity.

The Congregationalist answered: "Your strength is your correspondence with the original practice of the New Testament and the fact that you make the moral meaning of baptism unmistakable. Your weakness is that all matters of ceremony are secondary to the truths of the Gospel, that your special emphasis is a bar to Christian reunion, and that you lay stress on one side only of the meaning of baptism, i.e., individual faith, whereas it also symbolizes divine grace."

The Wesleyan answered: "Your strength is your devotion to evangelical truth, and rich Christian experience, and your willingness to bear criticism about baptism. Your weakness is theo-

---

[2] Giuseppe Mazzini, quoted by Bolton King, *Mazzini*, pp. 240, 244.

logical narrowness and excessive individualism, the lack of a connexional system, so that the ministers of smaller churches suffer, and too little use is made of lay preachers, and the undue emphasis implied in the name 'Baptist,' for which, of course, you are not to blame."

The Quaker said: "Your strength is your evangelical emphasis, your open and public confession of faith, with definite and dramatic entrance into the Church, the stress on personal decision, and the stand for supremacy of conscience. Your weakness is your theological narrowness, your Scriptural literalism, the making baptism essential to Church membership, the want of a circuit system which would bring in more lay ministry, and the lack of sufficiently definite Christian teaching to young people."

The general justice of these criticisms would be admitted by many Baptists, and the practical agreement is significant. The strength of Baptists lies in their Scriptural individualism, their weakness chiefly in the defects of their quality. We cannot emphasize one word in a sentence without running the risk of slurring over other words; we cannot emphasize one truth without the risk of inadequate attention to other truths, as history has repeatedly taught.

The direct appeal to the authority of Scripture is common to all the Protestant Churches, but there is a special motive for the Baptist use of it. Baptists are continually thrown back on the Bible to justify what seems to many a strange and arbitrary idiosyncrasy. But intelligent use of the Bible to justify the baptism of believers trains men in the intelligent use of the Bible for other purposes, teaches them to look up things for themselves, and to trust no reports at second-hand—a habit which is always one mark of a good student. Such direct use of the Bible serves to bring men into touch with the experience it records, and often into that intuitive experience in which God and man are face to face. The value of such Bible reading is great; there can be hardly any more serious feature of the religious life of today than the very marked decline in it—a decline which, unfortunately, Baptists also exhibit.

On the other hand, the very simplicity and directness of this use of Scripture brings its own perils. The individual believer

is encouraged to interpret it for himself, but he often lacks the
most elementary training for this. The prejudice of ignorance
borrows the strength of genuine religious conviction, and sometimes issues in a papal dogmatism. Baptists as a whole are often
wanting in any sense of history, whether the history of the thousand years in which the experience behind the Bible slowly de-
posited itself in the literary record, or those intervening centuries
of the history of the Church which have added so much to the
interpretation of the Bible. It may be admitted that this is a defect in some degree common to many Churches, but other
Churches have silent correctives of overweening confidence
which Baptists lack—such as the respect for education amongst
the Presbyterians, or the long and rich perspective of the parish
church and the prayer book amongst the Anglicans. Whilst
"Fundamentalism" as a belligerent movement has relatively little
hold amongst Baptists of this country, there is still a good deal
of suspicion of even the moderate amount of Biblical scholarship
which has been more or less assimilated by most other Churches.
Yet Baptists, of all people, ought to welcome that criticism which
takes men back beyond the letter to the living spirit, and un-
bares the experience which was first creative of the literature.
Fortunately, the Baptist love of liberty comes in to correct the
tendencies of assertive literalism and eschatological vagary, and
heresy hunters are not popular with a Baptist Union Assembly.

The real strength of the emphasis on individual experience has
already been exhibited, and need not be further developed, except to say that it brings men face to face with God in Christ.
This makes the intrinsic nature of His Gospel, as known in experience, the ultimate authority—indeed, the only authority in
the real sense, for "God is love" and the Gospel of His love is
the revelation of His nature, and what further testimonial does
God ever need? But the connected weakness found alongside of
this strength amongst Baptists needs careful thought, for it affects the whole conception of the Church and the life of the
Church. It does not seem to me too much to say that Baptists as
Churchmen are still largely dominated by an eighteenth-century
philosophy of society, disguised under their traditional interpre-

tation of Scripture. That pronounced individualist, Jean Jacques Rousseau, discussed the social forms of life as if they were the arbitrary and voluntary creation of a number of unitary individuals, instead of being the cradle in which the individual life is nurtured and the breast at which it sucks. Similarly, it is possible to talk of conversion and the work of the Holy Spirit as if it occurred in a social vacuum, in order that a number of unitary products might subsequently be brought together to form a Church. But this ignores the fact that in personality there are the two elements of individuality and sociality growing side by side from the very beginning, and not less in religious than in biological and cultural and moral developments. The family is already a social environment, and without it there could be no individual life, yet it is possible for a Baptist to write, "Fatherhood and sonship are relations expressive of individual and not of corporate experiences." [3]

How can there be a father before there is a son, or a son before there is a father? The truth is rather that the social relation implied in fatherhood and sonship is just as much a capacity of personality as the individual consciousness. If it were not for such relationship as the family and the clan and the state imply there could be no development of the individual consciousness at all. These things are, of course, the commonplaces of sociology today, but they are singularly ignored in many discussions of the "separated" Church. The only difference is that the application in this case is to man's highest interests. The Church is not an arbitrary "extra," a sort of religious club he may choose to join; it is the crowning religious expression of that sociality which is part of his very constitution. Because it is that, it becomes the temple of the Holy Spirit in larger ways than the individual temple of a single life can offer. It is unreasonable to contrast the work of the Holy Spirit in the individual life and in the social group as if there could be any rivalry; these realms are complementary and closely—indeed inseparably—interwoven.

---

[3] Edgar Young Mullins, *The Axioms of Religion,* p. 39.

Baptists must and will continue to stand for the truth of a regenerated Church membership expressed in believers' baptism;
but they will never make that testimony as effective as it ought
to be till they have added to it a nobler Church-consciousness,
and a profounder sense of the whole group, as well as of individual life, as the arena of the Spirit's activity.[4]

It belonged to them in the earlier days, when the Church was
identified with the narrow group of "true" believers, and the
world lay without; it has gradually grown dim—except for a few
old-fashioned Churches—through the increasing relation of the
"believer" with that outside world and his recognition that the
old distinction of "saved" and "lost" is *not* longer possible—at any
rate, in its old sense and scope. A nobler Church-consciousness
can come only through a new conception of the Church—such
a conception, for example, as that which runs through the Epistle to the Ephesians. At the risk of saying something that may
be misunderstood by those within and those without, I would
say quite deliberately that Baptists need an "Oxford Movement"
of *their own order*, so as to give their truth of an individual relation to God its complementary truth of a social relation to
Him. Such a movement would doubtless bring some changes in
worship and in polity, not those changes which are like new
patches on an old garment, but those true changes of a living
development in which the unity is not lost.

The third point in which both the strength and weakness of
the Baptists may be discerned relates to believers' baptism itself,
and brings to a focus what has just been said about the relation
to the Bible and to the Church. The first and foremost contribution of Baptists to the Church Catholic is like that of the Hebrew prophets—the essential and primary place of the moral
within the religious. The moral change wrought in genuine conversion, the personal repentance and faith which are the religious

---

[4] This must not be taken to ignore the fine achievements of Baptists in
voluntary giving, for work at home and abroad, to which reference is
made elsewhere—the more remarkable because this has been done in the
absence of any "connexional" system.

features of that conversion, the open confession which commits the life to a new purpose—these great truths are admirably and forcibly expressed in believers' baptism by immersion, and expressed as no other Church expresses them. All this is New Testament faith and practice. But it is not the whole faith of the New Testament.

Does not baptism express much more than a personal act? Is it not, by virtue of being that, the New Testament door of entrance into a life of supernatural energies, the surrender to that "Law of the Spirit" which the Apostle set in strongest contrast to the common life of men? Let any Baptist, with an open mind, set himself to study the New Testament references to baptism, and he will perhaps be surprised to find how closely it is related to the gift of the Holy Spirit. The baptism of John expressed a moral decision; the baptism of Christ is sharply contrasted with this, as a baptism with or in the Holy Spirit. There is the same contrast in the conversation of Christ with Nicodemus, when entrance into the Kingdom is made conditional of being "born of water and the Spirit."

That Paul closely related water baptism and that which it symbolized is evident, for "in one Spirit were we all baptized into one body . . . and were all made to drink of one Spirit." If the descent into the waters of baptism meant death and burial with Christ, in that mystical union with Him which carries with it death unto sin, not less did it mean to Paul the ascent into new life, defined by him as newness of "Spirit." The Colossians are reminded not only that they were buried with Christ in their baptism, but that they were raised with Christ in the same baptism, the power of the new life working through their faith. It is not without significance that when Paul speaks of the one Body and the one Spirit, he should straightway pass on to speak of the one baptism expressing the one faith which unites to the one Lord, "The Lord the Spirit," as he elsewhere says. Thus to be baptized into Christ is to put on Christ, i.e., to enter that realm of the Spirit over which Christ is Lord.

It needs to be said, of course, that the connection between

water baptism and the baptism of the Spirit is of no mechanical kind, such as quasi-magical ideas of the ceremony would suggest. The Spirit baptism of Cornelius and his friends preceded their water baptism; in fact, the water baptism was administered to these Gentiles (without precedent) on the ground that they had already received the gift which it expressed. The group of disciples at Ephesus who had not received the Holy Spirit at the time of their "Johannine" baptism were baptized again into the name of the Lord Jesus, and after Paul had laid his hands upon them, the gift hitherto withheld was given.

But these are mentioned as exceptional cases. The recipient of baptism in the New Testament times normally expected to be the recipient of the spiritual powers of the new life which he entered by baptism. There could be no risk of encouraging the idea of "baptismal regeneration" (in the modern sense), because all who were baptized were already believers, i.e., the moral and spiritual conditions of their personal faith became the real channel of the Spirit's highest energies. Indeed, it was the very divorce of baptism from personal faith which has made "sacramentarianism" possible.

Let us try to enter into the experience of a believer baptized in those first days, using the interpretative reconstruction of a scholar who stands outside the present issue:

"In baptism (of course, adult) something happened. Faith had been there before, receptiveness toward the good news of Christ. The Divine Spirit had been already present, taking of the things of Christ and showing them to the believer. But now, once for all, the convert made his own the movings of the Divine love in his heart. And thus there would come to him in his baptism a wonderful spiritual quickening, a new enhancing of the power and grasp of faith, a fresh realization of communion with the once crucified and now risen Lord. Hence, there is good ground for the statement of von Dobschutz that "according to the early Christian view we may speak of real effects of baptism in the sense that here the person does not give himself something by his activity, but God gives him what he has only to receive." [5]

Baptists have been reluctant to recognize this "baptismal grace," just because, in their judgment, it is utterly misrepresented and distorted when ascribed to unconscious infants. The reaction from a false doctrine of divine grace in baptism has made them suspicious even of the genuine sacramentalism of the New Testament. We have been saying *believers'* baptism so emphatically that we have failed, or at least are failing now, to say with anything like equal emphasis, believers' *baptism*, i.e., the entrance of believers into a life of supernatural powers.

Here, then, is the present Baptist opportunity, and it is a great one. No other Church has been loyal to the New Testament connection of baptism with personal faith. No other Church, therefore, could give so forcible a testimony to the work of the Spirit on the believer, which is not less emphatically linked with baptism in the New Testament.

If any Baptist reader is afraid that this may mean a sacramentalism of the lower kind, with consecrated water rather than the evangelical truth in the heart of the believer as the primary medium of the Spirit, let it be said quite distinctly that I am pleading for the connection of water baptism with the Spirit in exactly the sense in which all Baptists plead for its connection with personal faith. If the New Testament teaches the latter, it assuredly also teaches the former, and Baptists are really committed to both. If appeal be made to such a word as the Apostle's "Received ye the Spirit by the works of the law, or by the hearing of faith?" the answer is that undoubtedly personal faith is the realm of the Spirit's activity, but the confession of that faith in believers' baptism brought a new opportunity for divine grace, because it was itself an act of personal faith.

Though this book is not a history of the Baptists, enough has been said of the different types of life within the three centuries to show the great changes that have taken place. Doubtless

---

[5] H. A. A. Kennedy, *St. Paul and the Mystery Religions*, p. 249.

other changes equally great will mark our further development, and no man can foresee them. But at the present time, and in this country, the Baptist future seems to depend on the relation to the distinctive feature of believers' baptism. Baptists must make either more or less of it. If they make less of it, they will be absorbed into Congregationalism, and their distinctive testimony and consciousness will be lost—a result I should greatly deplore. If they make more of it, it must be along the line indicated of a greater spiritual content, and not simply of a literalistic appeal to the Bible. Believers will not be deterred from baptism by immersion if they are taught the rich and full meaning given to it by the New Testament.

Apart from this characteristic feature (and all it implies) the future of the Baptists is bound up with the future of the evangelical faith. The presentation of that faith, in order to be successful, has always to be in terms of contemporary thought and life. This is true even when the presentation is antithetical, or perhaps we should say that its especial truth is then seen. Thus, at the present time, the fundamental need is for a clear assertion of the reality of religion over against the modern challenge that religion is a subjective allusion. Here the primary Baptist emphasis should be on the appeal to experience, that experience of obedience to the will of God which brings the proof of the teaching that it is of God. The central truth of the evangelical faith is the sacrificial love of God realized in the grace of Christ.

Over against the idea of a passive or absent God, or a God fettered by the "laws" of His universe, we have to teach that God is active, present, redeeming, and that man, by His grace, may have a direct relation of fellowship with Him. All revivals of religion are in essence due to the realization that God is much nearer than we thought. Further, the Baptist emphasis on conversion asserts moral responsibility and human freedom over against the naturalism and determinism of the past generation (themselves profoundly shaken by the new physics). Most of all there is needed a new and clear teaching of the doctrine of the Holy Spirit, as against the rationalism that rejects all mystery, and the externalism which materializes mystery into manageable forms. The true emphasis is that of the New Testament—on personal faith as the human condition of divine activity, which is the truth supremely expressed in believers' baptism.[6]

---

[6] See A. C. Underwood, *Conversion: Christian and Non-Christian*, for an excellent account of baptism as "The Dramatic Representation of Regeneration" (chap. IX).

V

SERMONS AND ADDRESSES

———◦◦◦◦———

WILLIAM R. WILLIAMS (1804-1885)

This son of a New York City Baptist pastor was one of the most able and brilliant leaders American Baptists have had. He received highest honors when he graduated from Columbia College in 1822. He then studied and practiced law, showing tremendous talent, until 1830. In 1832 he became pastor of Amity (Street) Baptist Church in New York and remained there the rest of his life. He was quiet in manner but exerted great influence through the recognized powers of his mind and pen. He helped to found Rochester Theological Seminary. Our selection is a good example of his beautiful literary style, his clear thought, and of an effective way to meet Roman Catholicism on theoretical and historical grounds.

"The Jesuits as a Missionary Order"
. . . . . .

The Jesuits, as a missionary order, furnish then a theme in which we have a national interest; and the subject may well employ for a passing hour the thoughts of an assembly of American Christians. Odious as the society justly became for its acts and its crimes, it had its purer era, when its emissaries were men, not only of singular talent, but of burning zeal, and in some cases even of true piety. If it has had its Escobars, it has also been honored by its Xaviers, its Riccis, and its Nobregas. Nor is it just, in denouncing its shameless casuistry, its mendacious miracles, its remorseless ambition, and its crooked policy, to overlook the usefulness, or deny the virtues that have adorned some among the sons of Loyola. Its eight hundred martyrs prove that its zeal has been of no ordinary kind.

Man is but too prone to pour over the checkered good and evil of human character the sweeping flood of indiscriminate praise, or censure as unmitigated. So does not the Judge of all the earth. His tribunal metes out a more exact sentence. And, in his Scriptures, with what impartiality does he detect some good thing to be found towards the Lord God, even in the house of Jeroboam, the corrupter of Israel. Dark as was the depravity of Ahab, "who sold himself to work wickedness," inspiration draws no veil over the brief interval of light in his history, that shot, like a moment of unnatural sunshine, across the depth of midnight darkness. And Christ himself, the chiefest missionary of the church, taught his disciples to learn wisdom from the policy of the fraudulent steward, and the fears of the unjust judge.

Truth, then, may well afford to be just even to error, and to glean even from such fields lessons of wisdom. No missionary undertakings have embodied a greater array of talent, been arranged with more masterly skill, displayed more illustrious proofs of courage and of patience, or wielded a wider influence, than those of the Society of Loyola. Baxter confessed that their labors moved him to emulation, and the Protestant Leibnitz, the scholar, the jurist, and the philosopher, the rival of Newton, has been their fervent eulogist.

The character of Loyola, the founder, was deeply impressed on this order. On deserting the military life, he had spent a year in the most revolting austerities, and during this period composed his celebrated treatise. (Spiritual Exercises.) His attention now became turned to the salvation of his neighbor; before, it had been engrossed by care for his own soul. To profit others, he must relinquish the squalid dress and some of the austere penances of his former course, and he felt also that he must remedy the defects of a neglected education.

Now in the prime of manhood, he set himself down, nothing daunted or ashamed, among children, to learn his Latin grammar. His progress was slow and painful. At the University of Paris he gathered around him his first associates. Their early design was a mission to Palestine. War frustrated this. They offered themselves for the service of the supreme pontiff, at their own charge, in whatever part of the world he might command. This offer won the reluctant consent of the Romish see to their establishment in 1540. They were thus missionaries from their first constitution. Long a soldier, Loyola had felt both the need of discipline and its power. Reminiscences of his military course appear in the whole structure, as in the very title, of his Spiritual Exercises. It seems, from the description given of it, to be but the drill-book of a spiritual regiment.

The treatise is said to represent the world as divided into two hosts, the one arrayed under the banners of Christ, and the other uplifting the standard of Satan; and, inviting the reader to enlist with his Redeemer, furnishes marks by which he may judge of the work appointed him, and rules for its accomplishment. Obedience, incessant and implicit, such as is elsewhere scarce found out of a camp, was Loyola's favorite lesson. It was in his order the subject of a special vow. They swore it to the pope and to their superior, called their general, who was elected for life, and clothed with absolute power.

Ignatius was accustomed to term such obedience the most sublime of virtues, the daughter of humility, and the nurse of charity, a guide that never wandered, and the mark that was to distinguish his order from all others. Exacting it most rigidly from others, he displayed it himself, in an implicit deference to his physicians and his confessor; while to the Roman pontiff so profound was his submission, that he was accustomed to say, at the command of the pope he would embark on a mission for any shore in a vessel without rudder, or sails, or mast, or stores. When the objection was made, that such conduct would be inconsistent with ordinary prudence, his reply was that prudence was the virtue of the ruler, not of the ruled. His last will, as he termed it, was but an unfinished homily on obedience.

Yet in all this, the object of Ignatius does not seem to have been consciously his own personal aggrandizement. Wealth, fame, and even power he seems to have sought less than usefulness. The first year of his religious course had been one of stormy fanaticism; the rest of his career breathed a high, sustained enthusiasm. He dreaded, as he often said, worldly prosperity for his order, excluded its members from episcopal preferment, and by earnest remonstrances prevented the elevation of two of his early associates, Lainez and Borgia, to the cardinalate.

He spent much time in prayer, and laid more stress than many Roman religionists on the prayer of the heart, while Thomas à Kempis was his favorite book of devotion. Simple and severe in his own personal habits, his labors never remitted. Lodging in hospitals, tending their sick, catechizing children, seeking the restoration of the profligate, wherever he went, he gave himself to the toils of benevolence.

Seeing that the emergencies of the time required not the retired life—the contemplative one, as it was called, of the monastic orders—he desired for his institute a life of active piety. The three great duties of the order from the beginning were announced as being the education of youth, controversy with heretics, and the conversion of the heathen. They were to be men of the world, and not of the cloister. Hence he procured them exemption from the chants and choral services customary with many Romish fraternities.

"They do not sing," said the enemies of the Jesuits, "birds of prey never do." Yet to maintain their devotional feelings, there were many provisions. One especially was, that, for a space of eight days in each year, every member of the order should make "a retreat," as it was called, retiring from the world, and devoting himself to the study of his heart and way, by the help of the Spiritual Exercises. With the zeal of Loyola was mingled much knowledge of the world. With the merchant he spoke of traffic, and with the scholar of books, that he might attract both to religion; entering, as he described it, at their door, that he might leave at his own. What in him, however, seems to have been little more than skillful courtesy not inconsistent with real principle, became in the latter members of the order, a supple and lithe pliability, alike unprincipled and selfish.

To exercise and perfect their great principle of obedience, the rules of the society were most skillfully framed. Their colleges gave them facilities for the selection of the most brilliant talents. A long novitiate and varied trials preceded admission to the full privileges of the order. Every one on entering it was required to make a full manifestation, as it was termed, of his conscience, giving the minutest and most private details of his past history and feelings. This was repeated each half year. Each member was constituted a spy upon his fellow. Regular reports of every incident of moment, and of the character and deportment of each member, were made to the provincial, and from the provincial were transmitted to the general at Rome, to be transcribed into the archives at the order. From the will of this general there lay no appeal; complaint was sin, and resistance ruin. In the whole society, there was but one will, but one conscience, and it was in the bosom of the general.

So true a despotism Tiberius never attempted, and Machiavelli himself could not have imagined. Superstition only could have made men its willing subjects. The individual being was lost in one vast machine, all the parts of which were intelligent to observe, the eyes of one soul, and strong to obey, the hands of one will. Limited at first to sixty members, but soon left without such restriction, the order increased in sixty years from ten to 10,000 members, and in 1710 the Jesuits numbered about 20,000 in their widespread association. These, scattered through all countries, men of the finest talents and most finished education, wearing every garb, and speaking every language, formed a body that could outwatch Argus with his hundred eyes, and outwork Briareus with his hundred hands.

It is readily seen what tremendous energies such a system wielded. In every other combination of human effort, much of power is lost, not only by the resistance to be overcome in the world without, but by the discord and internal weakness of the combined parties within themselves, and the lumbering weight of the machinery upon which the motive power acts. . . . One soul swayed the vast mass; and every cog and pin in the machinery consented with its whole power to every movement of the one central conscience. The world never had seen so perfect a despotism; yet never was any government so ardently loved by its earlier members. "If I forget thee, O Society of Jesus," exclaimed Xavier in India, "may my right hand forget its cunning."

The man who thus spoke is their greatest name; and he would not have felt this affection, had the order been originally as corrupt as it afterwards became. Gladly, did our limits permit, would we dwell on his history. A man of higher talent than Loyola, a ripe scholar, and of that commanding courage which nothing could daunt, there were also in him a fervent piety, and boundless self-sacrificing benevolence, that all the errors of his faith could not obscure. On the Malabar coast, in the kingdom of Travancore, where he gave baptism to 10,000 in one month with his own hand, in the Moluccas, and in Ceylon, he labored in perils imminent, and amid great privations and difficulties, but never without fruit. His chief triumphs were, however, in Japan.

Having seen the principles of his religion spreading rapidly through that empire, he longed next to enter China. With the assurance that it was at the risk of his life, he bargained but to be put ashore on its inhospitable coast. They who were to have done this failed him; and in sight of the empire which he was not allowed to enter, on the small rocky island of Sancian, he breathed his last. Dying thus, with his last and greatest enterprise unachieved, he yet laid his body thus as on the counterscarp, leaving to the ranks behind, a name and example that never lost their rallying power, until these ramparts of heathenism were scaled, and China too was entered and won.

In Japan, the order followed up his plans, until their converts had reached the number of 200,000. The Jesuit fathers who succeeded in forcing the barriers of China—Ricci, Scholl, and Verbiest—were men distinguished in science and talent. The manuscripts left by some of them are said to show too—written evidently but for their own use—that they were men of piety. Of some of them at least, Milne, and Morrison, and other Protestant missionaries have thought highly, as men of real devotedness and mistaken piety.

. . . . .

On our own shores, their missionaries were found at an early day. They followed the red man to his haunts, paddled with him the rude canoe, reared beside his their hut, and displayed a patient and winning sweetness that disarmed his ferocity. The tribes beside our great inland seas claimed more than a century ago the care of the Jesuit fathers. Sault Sainte Marie and Mackinaw were sites of their missions; and yet beyond these places there were points where the wandering son of Loyola reared his wooden crucifix, and built his bark chapel, in regions that even in our own late day the westward wave of emigration has not yet reached. To other parts of North America the same fraternity had expanded their establishments. In the peninsula of California, they gathered villages of converted Indians that still exist, although in a declining state and under the charge since of other religious orders.

In Mexico, also, they labored for the conversion of the Aborigines. In the southern portion of our continent were, however, the scenes of their greatest toils and their most glorious triumphs. They labored in Peru and in Chili. Far more repulsive was the field chosen, however, by those of the Jesuit fathers who, like Ortega and Nobregas, labored among the cannibals of Brazil. Tribes with whom the flesh of their captives was the choicest of dainties, and whose older women bore to the battlefield the vessels in which the horrid banquet of victory was to be prepared, were compelled at length to yield to the dauntless zeal of the intrepid missionary; and, relinquishing their cannibalism, learned gentleness and piety. . . . Yet, beneficent as was the Jesuit rule over these their subjects, it was so absolute, that their converts might be said never to have outgrown the state of nonage. Theirs was a filial servitude.

In all these their missions, the order displayed an indomitable energy, and a spirit of most adventurous enterprise. As dauntless as they were versatile, and as unwearied as they were dauntless, the door closed against them was undermined, if it could not be opened, and stormed where it could not be undermined. Martyrdom for them had no terrors. Did the news return to their colleges in Europe of a missionary falling riddled by the arrows of the Brazilian savage, at the foot of the crucifix he had planted, or of scores sent into the depths of ocean by heretic captors, the names of the fallen were inserted on the rubrics of Jesuit martyrs; and not the students only, but the professors of their institutions rushed to fill the ranks that had been thus thinned. And, turning from their fields of missionary enterprise in the far East, and in the remotest West, to what they had accomplished in Europe, there was much at this time to stir the Jesuit of self-gratulation.

Their science, and address, and renunciation of ecclesiastical preferment had made members of their order confessors to some of the most powerful monarchs. In controversy, they had given to the Romish church Bellarmine, the ablest of her defenders, and though a Jesuit, perhaps also the most candid of Romish controversialists. To the French pulpit they had furnished Bourdaloue, among its great names no weaker luminary, and perhaps its first reasoner. Their divines, orators, poets, historians and critics were well nigh numberless, the order claiming to have produced more distinguished scholars than all the other Romish communities together.

In education, they had been the benefactors of the world. Their institutions are proposed by Bacon as the best of models, and Mackintosh has pronounced the strides made by the society in the work of instruction the greatest ever witnessed. But in missions was the beginning of their strength, and the excellency of their glory. The character of Xavier gave to the cause of evangelization an impulse such as it had not received for seven centuries; and to this day, his church looks in vain for one, who, to his dauntless zeal and his untiring patience, has united the splendor of his talents, and his wide influence, that went overrunning a nation like some great conflagration. . . .

From East to West, from North to South, the sons of Ignatius were pursuing one object through a thousand mazy channels. The motto and device in one of their earlier histories was well illustrated in their conduct. That device was a mirror, and the superscription was "Omnia omnibus," *All things to all men*. But what in Paul was Christian courtesy, leaning on inflexible principle; and what in Loyola himself was probably wisdom, but slightly tinged with unwarrantable policy, became, in some of his disciples, the laxest casuistry, chameleon-like, shifting its hues to every varying shade of interest or fashion. . . .

Yet from this height of success, and influence, and honors they were doomed to fall, and for a time the world seemed to shake with their far-resounding ruin. In Japan, their 200,000 converts, exciting, justly or unjustly, apprehension of political intrigue in the mind of a native prince, who was consolidating the kingdoms of Japan into one empire, they were exterminated by one of the fiercest persecutions that Christianity has ever experienced. Multitudes perished in prison; some were buried in ditches, others, immersed in freezing water, died a death of lingering agony; some were crucified, others were beheaded; and large numbers were thrown into one of the volcanic craters of the country, while the crosses of the Jesuit pastors studded the edges of the fearful cavity into which their flocks were hurried. That country has been thenceforward sealed against the gospel more closely than any other heathen land on the earth.

It was, perhaps, one instance of those fearful retributions, that, in the language of Bacon, are occasionally written by the hand of Nemesis along the highway of nations, in characters which he that runneth may read, that the Japanese were instigated, in this extinction of the Jesuit churches, by the Dutch, a people who had never forgotten the butcheries of the ferocious Alva, and thus requited on the rising Romanism of the East the wrongs that religion had wrought them in the West. In China, contentions with other Romish orders thwarted their labors; their political power was soon lost, and their converts were driven into concealment. But though denounced by edicts of the empire, and on pain of death expelled from its territories, they have never ceased laboring there, and the Catholic Christians at this hour secreted in the bosom of that nation, are calculated by Medhurst at 200,000.

In Paraguay and California, their settlements have been transferred to the charge of other orders, and themselves were exiled, as was also the case in the Philippine Islands. Their expulsion from the fields in South America, watered so freely with the wealth, and talents, and best blood of the order, grew out of their disgrace in Europe.

In France, they had denounced and suppressed Jansenism; but received in their conflict with that body of most able and holy men, the Port Royalists, a deathful arrow they could never extricate. We need not say we allude to the Provincial Letters of Pascal, a work whose mingling powers of wit, and argument, and eloquence, well nigh unrivaled apart, and in their union unequaled, fixed the ultimate fate of the Jesuit order. They stood up, too, in the same country, in the days of their own intellectual decrepitude, to wrestle against the young skepticism of the Regency and of the days of Louis XV. Voltaire, and Diderot, and D'Holbach, and Helvetius, men educated in their own colleges, overwhelmed their old teachers with sarcasm, and irony, and wit, the more burning in its severity often, because it was the language of truth.

To every state they had made themselves odious by intermingling themselves with political affairs. In their own church they found the bitterest enemies, in the worldly who envied their power, and in the zealous, who detested their lax casuistry and their erroneous doctrine. By principles, which if not their own invention, were at least their favorite implements, they explained away all obligation; and some of their doctors seemed scarce to have left faith on the earth, or justice in the heavens. In short, they threw conscience into the alembic, and drew from the retort a mixture, like the aqua Tofana of Italian poisons, clear as the water that streams from the rock, but to drink of which was lingering, inevitable death.

This laxity of moral teaching was felt to be the more inexcusable, in a body who had constituted themselves the jealous guardians of what they called orthodoxy in doctrine: "a sort of men," as said the Abbe Boileau, brother of the poet, "who set themselves to lengthen the creed, and abridge the commandments." Casuistry became in their hands, as Bayle has well called it, "the art of cavilling with God." But men, even the vilest, cannot long respect those who pander to their corruptions, and the order soon fell under the ban of the human race. Their principles in morals, too, reacted upon themselves. Like the French poisoner, who perished by the fall of his mask, inhaling unexpectedly the fumes of the poison he was compounding for others, the order could not retain its old zeal, and the life of its early fanaticism, while propagating such sentiments. Some, even, of the Jesuit missionaries to heathenism were, it is said, in secret, infidels. At Rome itself, they had become tools more convenient than reputable. . . .

Never slow, in the day of their power, to use the arm of the civil government for the purpose of persecution, they now felt its weight upon themselves. They had instigated in France the bloody massacre of St. Bartholomew, it is said, and had most certainly shared largely in the perfidy, the frauds, and the revolting dragonnades that procured and followed the Revocation of the Edict of Nantz. The recompense long accumulating now descended. Reluctantly, but necessarily, the Roman Court itself withdrew in terror from these its stanchest servants, and pronounced with faltering lips the dissolution of the order.

They had forgotten, in their abuse of power, and talent and influence, that there was on high One mightier than all the mighty of earth, whom they had subsidized, or flattered, or corrupted. Providence, an element upon which in their latter days they had forgotten to calculate, was now meeting them at every turn. If they had lost sight of it, never had it lost sight of them. It used no confessors, and they could not guide it; nor did it wait in its movements for the shuffling of the pieces on the checkerboards of earthly cabinets, which Jesuitism watched so narrowly. But when its fullness of times was come, it called, and every stormy passion of human nature rushed at its bidding, eager to do the work of retribution; while, unpitied, Jesuitism stood to bear, in its loneliness, the meeting vengeance of earth and heaven.

Never had Romanism progeny that bore more perfectly its own image, or embodied its grand principles so faithfully as did the Jesuit system. The principle of the order was but a reduction to its simplest essence of that one master idea of the Romish creed—implicit faith—unlimited obedience. These are, in justice, due only to a Being of infinite truth, and underived, and unending sovereignty. Nothing less able or less wise, nothing short of the divine wisdom, that cannot mistake, and that will not deceive, is entitled to demand such subjection and confidence. . . . They destroyed, also, by this same process the higher order of talents, which act only in a state of comparative freedom. Splendid as were their scholars in every walk, yet, as Mackintosh has remarked, through two centuries of power and fame, they gave to Europe no genius to be named with Racine and Pascal, men who sprung from the Port Royalists, in the career, both far more brief and far more stormy, of that persecuted community.

In this, his distinctive trait of character, the Jesuit stood as the moral antipodes of the Puritan. In the latter, the Reformation presented its principle, the right of private judgment, as displayed in its barest, broadest shape. While, in the Jesuit, the man was nought, and the community was every thing, with the Puritan, on the contrary, the society was comparatively nothing, and the individual all. With him religion was, in its highest privileges and its profoundest mysteries, a personal matter. He studied his Bible for himself; to aid in turning its pages and loosening its seal, God the Son, the Lion of the tribe of Judah, stooped over him as he read; and to reveal its inner lessons, God the Spirit whispered in his heart, and brooded over the depths of his soul.

He profited by the prayers and teachings of his pastor, gave liberally for his support, and received reverently at his hands the sacramental symbols; but he believed even this his beloved guide, companion and friend, but a fellow-servant, whose help could not supersede his own private studies, and his individual faith. He valued his fellow-Christians, communed with them, prayed with them, shared with them his last loaf, and falling into their ranks, raised with them the battle-cry, "The sword of the Lord and of Gideon!" But, away from pastor and from fellow-Christian, the Puritan turned in the trying hour to his God.

It was the genius of this system to develop the individual; and in every emergency, to throw him in the last resort upon the lonely communings of his own soul with its Creator. It taught him to make religion, in the affecting language of one of the later Platonists, "the flight of one alone to the only One." To the place of audience the petitioner went by no deputy; but the individual man was brought to confront for himself the one Mediator, and to hear for himself the response of Heaven to the prayer of faith. When mind was thus thrown upon its individual responsibility, and came forth from its solitary meditations to the place of conference and action, there was frequent dissonance in opinion; and a collision in action, often more apparent than real, threatened at times to rend the social bonds, to break up all concert, and to destroy all power.

Yet conscientious men were not likely to differ widely or long. And, on the other hand, take from such a community its spiritual guides, and how soon were they replaced. Persecute them, and how indomitable was their faith. Scatter them, and how rapidly were they propagated. Jesuitism gathered more numerous and united societies; but they were societies of men without consciences and without a will, whose judgments and souls were under the lock of the confessional, or were carried about under the frock of their Jesuit pastor. Kind he might be and faithful, but did death remove him, or persecution exile the shepherd and disperse the flock, they had no rallying power. Like the seeds from which the industrious ant has removed the germinating principle, the largest hoard, when scattered, brought no harvest.

It were a curious employment, to trace the unwitting adoption, at times in our own land, of this great principle of Romanism, of which the Jesuit order was the embodiment and incarnation, as if it were one of the radical truths of democracy —we mean, the principle of the absorption of the individual conscience into that of the mass. It is to some an essential law of democracy, that the many have unlimited power over the will and conscience of the few. Yet it would require little of time or of labor to show, how fatal is such a principle to the rights of conscience and the interests of truth.

God made man apart. Apart he is regenerated. Apart he dies. Apart he is judged. To each of us his Maker gave a conscience, but to none of us did He assign a conscience-keeper. Man was not made for society, but society was made for man. Back of its first institution, lie some of his inalienable rights, and his first and most sacred duties.

Communities of men, then, cannot receive, and should not ask, any transfer of conscience. Between a man's own spirit and his God, neither king, nor kaiser, nor congress, synod, nor pontiff, voluntary societies, nor compulsory societies, if such there be, may lay sceptre or crosier, edict or vote. The thing is a grand impertinence. When personal duty is involved, to his own Master the man stands or falls. We mean not these remarks for those duties which man owes to society, and where their laws may rightfully control and punish him. We speak of the far wider field over which some would extend those laws, and where they do not justly come, where a man walks accountable to his God only, and where, if human legislation follow him, it is usurpation upon the rights of man, and impiety against his Maker.

We know how irksome to many is all noise of dissent and all free expression of private judgment. To remedy and reform all this dangerous independence, this ominous revolt against parental care, was the high attempt of Jesuitism. Let those who envy to that society their fame and their fate tread in their steps, breaking down the individual man to build up the man social.

Another remarkable feature in the Jesuit order, illustrated in the history of all their missions, was their fatal principle of accommodation—one in the use of which they alternately triumphed and fell. The gospel is to be presented with no needless offense given to the prejudices and habits of the heathen, but the gospel itself is never to be mutilated or disguised; nor is the ministry ever to stoop to compliances in themselves sinful. The Jesuit mistook or forgot this. From a very early period, the order were famed for the art with which they studied to accommodate themselves and their religion to the tastes of the nation they would evangelize. Ricci, on entering China, found the bonzes, the priests of the nation; and to secure respect, himself and his associates adopted the habits and dress of the bonzes. But a short acquaintance with the empire taught him that the whole class of the priesthood was in China a despised one, and that he had been only attracting gratuitous odium in assuming their garb. He therefore relinquished it again, to take that of the men of letters.

In India, some of their number adopted the Braminical dress, and others conformed to the disgusting habits of the Fakeer and the Yogee, the hermits and penitents of the Mohammedan and Hindoo superstition. Swartz met a Catholic missionary, arrayed in the style of the Pagan priests, wearing their yellow robe, and having like them a drum beaten before him. It would seem upon such principles of action, as if their next step ought to have been the creation of a Christian Juggernaut; or to have arranged the Christian suttee, where the widow might burn according to the forms of the Romish breviary; or to have organized a band of Romanist Thugs, strangling in the name of the Virgin, as did their Hindoo brethren for the honor of Kalee.

In South America, one of the zealous Jesuit fathers, finding that the Payernes, as the sorcerers and priests of the tribe were called, were accustomed to dance and sing in giving their religious instructions, put his preachments into meter, and copied the movements of these Pagan priests, that he might win the savage by the forms to which he had been accustomed.

In China, again, they found the worship of deceased ancestors generally prevailing. Failing to supplant the practice, they proceeded to legitimate it. They even allowed worship to be paid to Confucius, the atheistical philosopher of China, provided their converts would, in offering the worship, conceal upon the altar a crucifix to which their homage should be secretly directed. Finding the adoration of a crucified Saviour unpopular among that self-sufficient people, they are accused by their own Romanist brethren of having suppressed in their teachings the mystery of the cross, and preached Christ glorified, but not Christ in his humiliation, his agony and his death. A more arrogant act than this the wisdom of this world has seldom perpetrated, when it has undertaken to modify and adorn the gospel of the crucified Nazarene.

But to Robert de Nobilibus, the nephew of Bellarmine, and the near kinsman of one of the pontiffs, a man of distinguished talent and zeal, laboring in India, it was reserved to exhibit one of the worst instances of this fatal spirit. Finding the Bramins in possession of the spiritual power, he published abroad that the Bramins of Rome were the kindred, but the seniors and the superiors of those of India. Enmity may have charged him falsely, in declaring that he forced deeds, in which a direct descent was claimed for these Western Bramins from Brama himself, the chief god of Hindoo idolatry; but it is certain, that in this or some other mode he made the new faith so popular, that twelve, or as some accounts state, seventy of the Indian Bramins became his coadjutors; and after his death, with the collusion of the Portuguese priests, the new sect went on still triumphing. But even the Romish see repudiated such conversions as these; and a bull from the Vatican extinguished the new communion.

To this same able but treacherous laborer belongs the fame of another kindred achievement. He composed in the language of the country a treatise in favor of Christianity. The work had the title of the *Ezour Vedam*. It was intended to sap the skepticism of the East; but so covertly, though with much ability, did it undertake the task, that having been translated and reaching France, where it fell into the hands of Voltaire, he pounced upon it as an ancient Braminical treatise, full of Oriental wisdom, and proving that Christianity had borrowed its chief doctrines from Eastern sources. Thus, while laboring to destroy unbelief in India, he became in the next century instrumental in aiding its progress in Europe. The Jesuit, caught in his own snare, was made from his grave to lend weapons to the scoffer; while the arch-mocker, the patriarch of French infidelity, entangled in the toils of that willful credulity which has distinguished so many eminent unbelievers, quoted the work of modern Jesuitism as an undoubted monument of ancient Braminism. Thus are the wise taken in their own craftiness, when in their self-confidence they undertake either to patronize or to impugn the gospel of the Nazarene.

We need scarcely to name another defect of the Jesuit missions, which must have occurred to all—their fatal neglect of the Scriptures. Even Xavier translated into Japanese but the creed, the Lord's prayer, and a brief catechism, and afterwards a *Life of the Saviour*, compiled from the Gospels. *The Lives of the Saints*, afterwards appeared in that language. In the tongue of China the Jesuits acquired such proficiency as to become voluminous authors, writing, it is said, hundreds of books; but although they translated the ponderous *Sum of Theology* of Thomas Aquinas into Chinese, the Scriptures seem to have been thought a needless or dangerous book, and a compend of the gospel history was, we believe, their chief work in the form of scriptural translation.

With no religious light but that emanating from the altar and pulpit, their churches were, when persecution veiled these, left in thick darkness. The Jesuits, anxious to shut up their converts into a safe and orthodox submission, seem to have preferred this fearful risk, to the peril of leaving the lively oracles to beam forth their living brightness upon the minds of their people. Hence the Catholics, lingering still in the Celestial Empire, and their Indian neophytes in Paraguay and California, have probably never known, scarce even by name, those Scriptures which are the rightful heritage of every Christian. Nor for their own use, even, did their missionaries prize the Bible aright. . . .

The institution, on whose history we have dwelt, shows what a few resolute hearts may accomplish. When Ignatius with his first companions bound themselves, by a midnight vow, at Montmartre, near Paris, on the 15th of August, 1534, some three centuries ago, to renounce the world for the purpose of preaching the gospel, wherever the supreme pontiff might send them, the engagement, thus ratified in darkness and secrecy beside the slumbering capital of France, was one most momentous to the interests of our entire race. . . . In the shadows of that subterranean chapel, where these first Jesuits thus bound themselves, fancy sees Africa, and Asia, and our own America, watching intently a transaction that was to affect so deeply their subsequent history. It remains for those rejoicing in the principles of the Reformation, to bring the devotedness and intrepidity of the Jesuit to bear upon their own purer system, in the missionary field. With the incorruptible word of our God for our chosen weapon, victories impossible to them may become easy to us; and what was but too often a forgotten motto, on the surface of Jesuitism, may become a principle at the heart of the Protestant missionary, "All for the greater glory of God." [1]

In the missionary toils, that are to aid in ushering in this day, do we expect too much from the youthful scholars of our country? Are not its colleges already sheltering those who are destined to become the heralds of Christianity to the far heathen? On this theme, we would quote yet again from one on whose own history we should gladly have lingered longer, Francis Xavier. From one of his missions in Cochin China, this apostolic man wrote to the university of the Sorbonne, then the focus of theological science to Catholic Europe, in language much of which we doubt not a Carey or a Martyn would not have hesitated to adopt. "I have often thought to run over all the universities of Europe, and especially that of Paris, and to cry aloud to those who abound more in learning than in charity, O how many souls are lost to heaven through your neglect! Many would be moved. They would say, Behold me in readiness, O Lord! How much more happily would these learned men then live—with how much more assurance die. Millions of idolaters might be easily converted, if there were more preachers who would sincerely mind the interests of Jesus Christ and not their own."

The letter was read, admired and copied. We may suppose there were those who applauded and transcribed that letter, but failed to obey its summons; to whose dying pillow that appeal came back, and sounded through the depths of the soul as the voice of neglected duty. May no such regrets disturb the hour of our dismission. May a life, instinct with zeal for God and

---

[1] "Ad majorem Dei gloriam," the motto of Loyola.

love to man, and crowded with effort, make death, whether it come late or soon, the welcome discharge of a laborer found toiling at his post.

JESSE MERCER (1769-1841)

The influence of Jesse Mercer is still felt in the South, particularly in the field of education. Mercer University, which bears his name, is a memorial to one of the many enterprises of this remarkable and gifted man. Much of the work for which he is remembered was done in connection with the Georgia Baptist Association, which he served as clerk for twenty-one years and as moderator for twenty-three years. The Circular Letters of this association were, in many instances, the product of Jesse Mercer's pen. The selections that follow are: first, an extract from the Circular Letter of 1821; and second, parts of a sermon entitled "Knowledge Indispensable to a Minister of God," delivered before the Georgia Baptist Convention in 1834.

Selections from the Circular Letter of 1821

We pray you to walk charitably towards those, who, in Christian profession, differ from you in faith or practice. And though you cannot reasonably hold communion with them at the Lord's Table, . . . yet, dear brethren, we exhort and admonish you to carry yourselves towards them as Christian professors; engage with them, and invite them to engage with you, in exercises of devotion and enterprises of usefulness; go with them freely as far as you can preserve a good conscience and the fellowship of your brethren, and stop where you must according to the Scriptures; evince to them that the reason why you do not yield

an entire and cheerful compliance with their wishes in communion, is not founded in prejudice or ill-will, but in a conscientious regard to the views you entertain of truth and propriety;
extend to them your brotherly watch-care, and invite theirs over
you; reprove and admonish them in love when you overtake them
in a fault, and endeavor to reclaim in the spirit of meekness; and
thus, by an affectionate intercourse, and a dispassionate, free, and
candid interchange of sentiments, combined with a friendly use
of Christian discipline, lessen, if you cannot annihilate, the un-
happy differences which are between you and them. This course,
accompanied by the blessing of God, we think is the only anchor
of hope for the union and communion of the present contending
religious denominations.

Furthermore, brethren, we exhort you carefully to cultivate
in yourselves views of extended and general usefulness. Dismiss,
for ever banish from your hearts, that God-dishonoring and soul-
starving sentiment, that your Christian obligations are restricted
to the church to which you in particular belong. Recollect that
"what the Spirit saith to the churches," is bound on the observance of "him that hath an ear." Feel as you ought to feel, as
"members in particular" of the whole body of Christ, and bound
by his authority in the same ties of brotherly love to all and to
each member of that body "as you have opportunity to do
good," and "always abound in the work of the Lord, knowing
that your labor shall not be in vain in the Lord."

And we also admonish you to esteem very highly, as your
most gospel attitude, the medium of your highest privileges, and
the source of your most extended usefulness on earth, your associated union. Here you are "like a company of horses in Pharaoh's chariots," and "terrible as an army with banners," prepared
for united and powerful effort. What cannot be done in your
individual capacity, may receive its highest accomplishment in
your associated union. Divided strength is weak, but united
strength is powerful.

Do not treat the resolutions and advices of the association with
neglect and indifference, as the counsels of a mere "advisory
body," with which you have no connection, but as decisions and

advices of your own body, composed of your "messengers, who are the glory of Christ." If the counsels of the association are consonant with the word of God, you are bound to observe and obey them on Divine authority, as well as from the bond of union which holds you together "in one."

Study agreement, and endeavor through your associated connection, to come at a uniform practice in the order of your religious affairs. Be ready, not as a matter of constraint, "but of ready mind," to act in concert, like the churches of Macedonia, of whom the apostle bears this honorable testimony, that "they are willing of themselves" even "beyond their power," in any matter of general utility, whether benevolent, charitable, or religious. Attempt whatsoever God in his word has instituted to be done through the instrumentality of his church on earth, and fear not.

Keep in mind you are not alone: even in your associated body you are but one detachment of the thousands of Israel's hosts. The strength of opposition against you is "an arm of flesh"; but with you is the Lord your God to help you and to fight your battles. And what may be done by united and vigorous effort of all the churches of Christ in his name, will never be known until the experiment is made; but when that experiment is made, the result will be, that the whole earth will be full of the glory of God. Let each heart hail the day in adding a double Amen.

Finally, dear brethren, "whatsoever things are true, are honest, are just, are pure, are lovely, are of good report,—if there be any virtue, if there be any praise, think on these things."

And may "the God of all grace, who hath called us unto his eternal glory, by Jesus Christ, after that ye suffer awhile, make you perfect, establish, strengthen, settle you to do his will; to whom be glory and dominion now and for ever.—Amen."

Selections from "Knowledge Indispensable to a Minister of God"

1. *What knowledge is necessary to a minister of God?*
2. *How is it attainable?*

· · · · ·

As to what knowledge is necessary to a minister of God, the author remarks, "To this inquiry we unhesitatingly answer—THE KNOWLEDGE OF THE TRUTH. For we know of *no truth*, the knowledge of which would be *unimportant* to a minister of God. We should like, dear friends, you would now throw your thoughts over the universe, and see if you can discover *any truth* which would be unnecessary to be known by a gospel minister. If it should be said by any, that it ought to be restricted to the knowledge of the truth *as it is in Jesus;* then we answer again, that we know of no truth which is not in Christ Jesus. The Scriptures declare, "It pleased the Father that in him all fullness should dwell." He it is "that filleth *all in all*." "He is head over all things to the church." And "by him all things consist."—Then we ask, what truth is not in Christ Jesus? But the whole may be summed up in *the knowledge of God and his works.*—Nay, God is only to be known through his works of nature, grace, and providence. . . .

· · · · ·

We conceive a thorough knowledge of God in his natural and moral perfections (on which the Scripture places the highest value), is of the utmost importance to the minister, to fill him with a holy reverence, and to guard him against fanciful constructions of Scripture, and the forming of false systems of theology. The standard of truth is in the God of truth. The most fruitful source of error is ignorance, or vague notions of God. But if God be truly known and kept in view, it regulates all the thoughts of the heart, and fixes the sentiments of the soul accordingly. Whatever, therefore, is in strict accordance with

God's nature and perfections, must be truth; and whatever is inconsistent therewith, *however plausible*, must be false. . . .

. . . . .

But objection is made to schools for the education of young ministers, on the ground that the instruction afforded is *human* learning. To see the weight of this objection, it is requisite to know what the objectors intend by *human* learning. If they mean instruction in *human* inventions, in which the knowledge of God and his works *are not taught*, then we join heart and hand with them to put it down: but if they intend to object to all learning, which is received by *human* instrumentality, then we most sincerely pity them as ignorantly opposing the institution of God; for we think no man can read the Scriptures, and not see that God requires knowledge to be imparted from the parents to the children, and from the wise to the simple. But we presume the objection proceeds altogether from a mistaken notion of the nature and design of the instructions given in those schools. They have heard of geography, geology, chemistry, history, astronomy, philosophy, and theology; . . . but what is the study of these, but the study of the works of God, in creation, and providence, and grace? For instance: Is the *earth* the Lord's? *Geography* describes it, in its extent, with its different soils, climates, and productions—its inhabitants, with their various religions, laws, and customs.

Geology gives a view of its state, and teaches the nature of its pebbles and mighty rocks, stupendous mountains and majestic seas: where the wonders of God are seen.

Chemistry enables us to discover and separate the peculiar properties of all natural bodies, and learn their various uses.

History teaches us the events of time—the rise and downfall of nations and kingdoms, together with a minute account of those facts which have transpired under the providence of God, in the successive generations of the earth; so indispensable to a right understanding of Scripture.

Astronomy teaches us of the heavenly bodies—the sun, moon, and stars—their distances, magnitudes, and velocities—wherein is declared the glory of God, and shown his handiwork.

Philosophy teaches the nature and reason of things. It is the system in which general causes and effects are explained; and mind, both human and divine, with all its natural properties and moral powers, is examined and exhibited in its dignity, beauty, and moral excellence.

Theology teaches of divine things. It is the study of the Bible —a critical examination into its language—the modes and figures of speech employed in it—the manners and customs of the times in which it was written—and the best rules of construction, in order to come at the truth, taught in that sacred volume.

Thus you see, brethren, the instruction given, under these and such like heads, in the schools, are not about the inventions and theories of men of corrupt minds, but of the truth of God as displayed in his works of nature and grace; and *as such* proper, that the mind of a minister of God should be deeply imbued with it.

Again, objection is made to the Convention, as opposing *a call* to the ministry, and designing *to rear up* a set of *graceless* preachers. In reply to the first cause of complaint, we say the Convention believes that no man ought to attempt, or be encouraged to preach the gospel, until he has a full satisfaction in his own conscience, that God requires it of him, and can afford his brethren the same satisfaction in regard to it. And as to the second, we say, that one of the first requirements for admission is, that the applicant must be licensed to preach by the church of which he is a member, and be approved by surrounding churches—so that if the Convention should unfortunately contribute to raise up a set of graceless ministers, the churches shall share in the first blame.

And now, dear brethren in the ministry, let us enjoin on you the acquisition of knowledge; by the right use of which you may approve yourselves *as the ministers of God*. We urge this on you, that you may understand the Bible—the Bible is a learned book, and cannot be understood well without much pious knowledge and learning. He who now addresses you regrets that he knows *so little* of the Bible. After reading and studying it for near half a century in some sort, he has to make this humbling confession, that he knows *to his shame*, comparatively but little of the Bible. This he does not say for his own sake, but for yours, *young* brethren, that you may devote your youthful days to the acquisition of all possible useful knowledge. Give yourselves to reading and study, that you may be approved unto God, and that your profiting may appear to all; to the honor of God and the advancement of the kingdom of Christ. Amen.

JAMES B. TAYLOR (1804-1871)

JAMES BARNETT TAYLOR *began his ministry as a pastor in Richmond, Virginia. When the Foreign Mission Board of the Southern Baptist Convention was established, he was invited to become its secretary. After some hesitation he agreed to undertake this work and continued in it for twenty-six years. One of his first duties as secretary was to deliver a charge to newly appointed missionaries to China, on June 15, 1846. The following selection is that charge.*

"A Charge to Missionaries"

BELOVED BRETHREN: As you are about to go forth under the direction of the Board of Foreign Missions, you will doubtless expect to receive from them special instructions as to the course you are to pursue. In performing this duty on their behalf, permit me to remind you of the importance of the position you are to occupy. The great empire of China is to be the field of your labors. You go out, not as ambassadors from an earthly government, but as ministers of the kingdom of Christ—not to treat with secular powers on great national questions, but to *bear communications of divine love*, beseeching the heathen to be reconciled to God.

Yours is an office unequaled in dignity by any within the gift of man. It has relation to the soul and eternity. The responsibilities involved are of the most solemn character. Upon the manner in which this vocation is filled will very much depend your success. I will call your attention to the following suggestions, which you will doubtless perceive to be appropriate, and endeavor to carry out in your future course:

1. It will be important to maintain a free and fraternal intercourse with the Board. We are your friends, your brethren in Christ. It is ours to regard the will of the denomination in all plans which may be adopted, but this will not be incompatible with special concern for your welfare. We shall sympathize with you in your sorrows and joys, and extend to you whatever means may be in our power to promote your happiness. You may, therefore, safely confide in the Board. Whatever measures they may propose to carry out, you may consider as demanded by the sentiment of the churches and the circumstances in which they are placed. You will not hesitate freely to communicate with them on all matters pertaining to yourselves and to the mission. A regular journal should be kept by you and transmitted to us, or such reports of your labors as will furnish a distinct view of the manner in which your time is employed. It will be important that the Board hear from you frequently. Scenes and circumstances connected with your operations it will be proper to describe with as much vividness and point as possible. This will enable us to present the information requisite to animate the friends of missions in their sacrifices and contributions.

2. Allow me to enforce the cultivation of fraternal feelings among yourselves. You would be more than human not to find occasions when differences of judgment respecting plans of action would be entertained. By reason of constitutional infirmities, too, you will be in danger of saying or doing that which may tempt to alienation of heart. Beware of strife among yourselves. Cautiously avoid all evil surmisings and jealousies—cul-

tivate that charity which "suffereth long and is kind, which envieth not, is not easily provoked, thinketh no evil." Love as brethren, pray for each other regularly, bear each other's burdens, and provoke each other only to love and good works.

3. In the pursuance of your work you should cultivate habits of economy. It must not be presumed that the Christian missionary is altogether exempted from the temptation to extravagance in his pecuniary expenditures. In some instances the temptation is stronger than even in a Christian land. In Eastern cities, where a small circle of Europeans and Americans are collected for purposes of gain or national dipomacy, their circumstances allowing them to indulge in an expensive style of living, the missionary will be in danger of aiming to move in the same sphere. But, my brethren, you should remember that you are the servants of him who in his mission to earth "endured the cross, despising the shame." You will be everywhere regarded as specimens of self-denial—as those who in an eminent measure walk even as Christ walked. Let this peculiar glory of the Christian missionary be yours. In your dress and style of living study simplicity. Be conscientiously and rigidly economical in your habits. The Board is not, indeed, willing that you should suffer; the churches owe to you a competent support, and this we will endeavor to secure. But let it be constantly borne in mind that funds are with difficulty obtained, and that an economical disbursement will enable the Board to increase the number of its missionaries.

4. In respect to your intercourse with the people for whom you labor it may not be improper to say a word. You should, as far as practicable, mingle with them. Our religion encourages the exercise of the social principle. The great Redeemer, as he went about doing good, was found in the dwellings of all classes of society. You will find it contributing essentially to your success to visit from house to house in the prosecution of your ministry. The idiom of the language will be more readily acquired, while the ascertainment of the habits and customs of the people, their modes of thought and expressions, will prepare you clearly and forcibly to commend the truth in the great congregation.

You will also by the manifestation of a generous spirit and a courteous manner find a way to the affections of the people. They will be ready to listen to the word because they respect and love you. In your associations it will be necessary to avoid all interference with political questions. "My kingdom is not of this world," said the divine Prince, and while the tendency of the gospel is to uproot every unholy influence in the social and political world, it is inconsistent with the vocation of the Christian minister to mingle in worldly strife. He has a higher and holier duty to perform. You will therefore, my dear brethren, as far as may be consistent with your obligations to Jesus Christ and your usefulness, conform yourselves to the circumstances by which you are surrounded.

5. Permit me to say a word with respect to your public ministrations. As soon as you shall sufficiently acquire the language to make yourselves clearly understood, you are to engage in preaching the gospel. This is your appropriate work. For this you are distinctly sent forth; you go from this land not to engage in scientific research or pecuniary speculations, not to represent the best form of government or to exhibit the various stores of human knowledge, but to preach the gospel.

You can, indeed, show to them the purest system of ethics the world has ever seen, but this would only still more embitter the cup of their misery were it not that you can point to the Lamb of God that taketh away the sin of the world. Hold up, then, the cross—know nothing among them but Jesus Christ, and him crucified. You may almost endlessly diversify your methods of teaching. Your arguments and illustrations may vary according to the character and circumstances of those you address, but in all places and at all times the love of God to a lost race is to be the great theme of your addresses.

6. Allow us, my dear brethren, in this brief directory, to caution you against the spirit of despondency. To this fell influence you will be exposed. Now you are in the presence of your friends; every eye directed to you is moistened with the tear of sympathy, every hand extended to you is nerved with the strength of affection. Here you are surrounded with the sweet

and hallowed associations of our holy religion. You listen to supplications from many kindred spirits and praises from a thousand raptured tongues. There is, too, thrown around the enterprise in which you engage something of the romantic, which tends to animate the soul.

But presently all will be changed; you will brave the dangers of the deep, and soon be found in the midst of idolaters. Beyond your own little circle you will not hear mentioned the revered names of the great Jehovah and his Son Jesus Christ, but be familiar only with gods made by human hands—gods that can neither see nor hear nor save. You will sit down to acquire, by slow degrees, an unknown language; and then, when you begin to publish the salvation of the gospel, they may not receive your message—you may be treated with scorn by some and with opposition by others.

Under such circumstances you will be in danger of yielding to discouragement. But you need not despond. By whose command do you go forth? Is it not the glorified Redeemer's? On whose promise do you rely for support? Is it not that of the immutable God? He who sends you to preach the gospel has said, "Lo, I am with you alway, even to the end of the world." The very word which impels you to this service contains the foundation on which you may rest for consolation.

7. That you may be prepared, cheerfully and successfully, to prosecute these labors, I will lastly beg to impress upon your minds the importance of cherishing habitual spirituality of mind. Let your aims be simple, your heart right in the sight of God. Cultivate communion with God. Familiarize yourself with the realities of eternity and the worth of the soul. Contemplate the objects in which you are engaged as accordant with the predictions and commands of God's word and identified with his glory.

Be much engaged in prayer, and let the precious promises of the gospel be the ground of your support and comfort. If it be your supreme desire to please God in all things, you will not be without most cheering indications of his favor.

If the honor of Christ shall be the great object at which you aim, he will be near to defend and bless. He that toucheth you will touch the apple of his eye. His smile will rest upon your endeavors, and though you go forth weeping, bearing precious seed, you shall return again with rejoicing, bringing your sheaves with you. And in the day when he cometh to make up his jewels he will recognize you as his own, and save you with an everlasting salvation.

———————··❦··———————

FRANCIS WAYLAND (1796-1865)

For a short biography of Francis Wayland, see page 135.

From "The Moral Dignity of the Missionary Enterprise."

Philosophers have speculated much concerning a process of sensation, which has commonly been denominated the emotion of sublimity. Aware that, like any other simple feeling, it must be incapable of definition, they have seldom attempted to define it, but, content with remarking the occasions on which it is excited, have told us that it arises in general from the contemplation of whatever is vast in nature, splendid in intellect, or lofty in morals. Or, to express the same idea somewhat varied, in the language of a critic of antiquity, "that alone is truly sublime of which the conception is vast, the effect irresistible, and the remembrance scarcely if ever to be erased."

But although philosophers alone have written about this emotion, they are far from being the only men who have felt it. The untutored peasant, when he has seen the autumnal tempest collecting between the hills, and as it advanced, enveloping in misty obscurity village and hamlet, forest and meadow, has tasted the sublime in all its reality; and whilst the thunder has rolled and the lightning flashed around him, has exulted in the view of nature moving forth in her majesty. The untaught sailor boy, listlessly hearkening to the idle ripple of the midnight wave, when on a sudden he has thought upon the unfathomable abyss beneath him and the wide waste of waters around him and the infinite expanse above him, has enjoyed to the full the emotion of sublimity, whilst his inmost soul has trembled at the vastness of its own conceptions. But why need I multiply illustrations from nature? Who does not recollect the emotion he has felt whilst surveying aught in the material world of terror or of vastness?

. . . . .

It will not be doubted that in such actions as these, there is much which may truly be called the moral sublime. If, then, we should attentively consider them, we might perhaps ascertain what must be the elements of that enterprise, which may lay claim to this high appellation. It cannot be expected that on this occasion we should analyze them critically. It will, however, we think be found, upon examination, that to that enterprise alone has been awarded the need of sublimity, of which the conception was vast, the execution arduous, and the means to be employed simple but efficient.

Were not the object vast, it could not arrest our attention. Were not its accomplishment arduous, none of the nobler energies of man being tasked in its execution, we should see nothing to admire. Were not the means to that accomplishment simple, our whole conception being vague, the impression would be feeble. Were they not efficient, the intensest exertion could only terminate in failure and disgrace.

And here we may remark, that wherever these elements have combined in any undertaking, public sentiment has generally united in pronouncing it sublime, and history has recorded its achievements among the noblest proofs of the dignity of man. Malice may for a while have frowned, and interest opposed; men who could neither grasp what was vast, nor feel what was morally great, may have ridiculed. But all this has soon passed away. Human nature is not to be changed by the opposition of interest or the laugh of folly. There is still enough of dignity in man to respect what is great, and to venerate what is benevolent.

The cause of man has at last gained the suffrages of man. It has advanced steadily onward, and left ridicule to wonder at the impotence of its shaft, and malice to weep over the inefficacy of its hate.

And we bless God that it is so. It is cheering to observe, that amidst so much that is debasing, there is still something that is ennobling in the character of man. It is delightful to know that there are times when his morally bedimmed eye "beams keen with honour;" that there is yet a redeeming spirit within him, which exults in enterprises of great pith and moment. We love our race the better for every such fact we discover concerning it, and bow with more reverence to the dignity of human nature. We rejoice that, shattered as has been the edifice, there yet may be discovered now and then a massive pillar, and here and there a well turned arch, which remind us of the symmetry of its former proportions, and the perfection of its original structure.

Having paid this our honest tribute to the dignity of man, we must pause, and shed a tear over somewhat which reminds us of any thing other than his dignity. Whilst the general assertion is true, that he is awake to all that is sublime in nature, and much that is sublime in morals, there is reason to believe that there is a single class of objects, whose contemplation thrills all heaven with rapture, at which he can gaze unmelted and unmoved. The pen of inspiration has recorded, that the cross of Christ, whose mysteries the angels desire to look into, was to the tasteful and erudite Greek, foolishness. And we fear that cases very analogous to this may be witnessed at the present day.

But why, my hearers, should it be so? Why should so vast a dissimilarity of moral taste exist between seraphs who bow before the throne, and men who dwell upon the footstool? Why is it that the man, whose soul swells with ecstasy whilst viewing the innumerable suns of midnight, feels no emotion of sublimity when thinking of their Creator? Why is it that an enterprise of patriotism presents itself to his imagination beaming with celestial beauty, whilst the enterprise of redeeming love is without form or comeliness? Why should the noblest undertaking of mercy, if it only combine among its essential elements the distinctive principles of the gospel, become at once stale, flat, and unprofitable?

When there is joy in heaven over one sinner that repenteth, why is it that the enterprise of proclaiming peace on earth, and good will to man, fraught, as it would seem, with more than angelic benignity, should to many of our fellow men appear worthy of nothing better than neglect or obloquy?

The reason for all this we shall not on this occasion pretend to assign. We have only time to express our regret that such should be the fact. Confining ourselves therefore to the bearing which this moral bias has upon the missionary cause, it is with pain we are obliged to believe, that there is a large and most respectable portion of our fellow citizens, for many of whom we entertain every sentiment of personal esteem, and to whose opinions on most other subjects we bow with unfeigned deference, who look with perfect apathy upon the present system of exertions for evangelizing the heathen; and we have been greatly misinformed, if there be not another, though a very different class, who consider these exertions a subject for ridicule.

Perhaps it may tend somewhat to arouse the apathy of the one party, as well as to moderate the contempt of the other, if we can show that this very missionary cause combines within itself the elements of all that is sublime in human purpose, nay, combines them in a loftier perfection than any other enterprise, which was ever linked with the destinies of man. To show this will be our design; and in prosecuting it, we shall direct your attention to the grandeur of the object; the arduousness of its execution; and the nature of the means on which we rely for success.

1st. THE GRANDEUR OF THE OBJECT. In the most enlarged sense of the terms, *The Field is the World*. Our design is radically to affect the temporal and eternal interests of the whole race of man. We have surveyed this field *statistically*, and find, that of the eight hundred millions who inhabit our globe, but two hundred millions have any knowledge of the religion of Jesus Christ. Of these, we are willing to allow that but one half are his real disciples, and that therefore there are seven of the eight hundred millions to whom the gospel must be sent.

We have surveyed this field *geographically*. We have looked upon our own continent, and have seen that, with the exception of a narrow strip of thinly settled country, from the Gulf of St. Lawrence to the mouth of the Mississippi, the whole of this new world lieth in wickedness. Hordes of ruthless savages roam the wilderness of the West, and men almost as ignorant of the spirit of the gospel, are struggling for independence in the South.

We have looked over Europe, and behold there one nation putting forth her energies in the cause of evangelizing the world. We have looked for another such nation; but it is not to be found. A few others are beginning to awake. Most of them, however, yet slumber. Many are themselves in need of missionaries. Nay, we know not but the movement of the cause of man in Europe is at present retrograde. There seems too evidently a coalition formed of the powers that be, to check the progress of moral and intellectual improvement, and to rivet again on the human mind the manacles of papal superstition. God only knows how soon the reaction will commence, which shall shake the continent to its center, scatter thrones and sceptres and all the insignia of prescriptive authority, like the dust of the summer's threshing floor, and establish throughout the Christian world representative governments, on the broad basis of common sense and inalienable right.

We have looked over Africa, and have seen that upon one little portion, reclaimed from brutal idolatry by missionaries, the Sun of Righteousness has shined. It is a land of Goshen, where they have light in their dwellings. Upon all the remainder of this vast continent, there broods a moral darkness, impervious as that which once veiled her own Egypt, on that prolonged and fearful night when no man knew his brother.

We have looked upon Asia, and have seen its northern nations, though under the government of a Christian prince, scarcely nominally Christian. On the West, it is spellbound by Mohammedan delusion. To the South, from the Persian gulf, to the sea of Kamchatka, including also its numberless islands, except where here and there, a Syrian church, or a missionary station twinkles amidst the gloom; the whole of this immense portion of the human race is sitting in the region and shadow of death. Such then is the field for our exertion. It encircles the whole family of man, it includes every unevangelized being of the species to which we belong. We have thus surveyed the missionary field, that we may know how great is the undertaking to which we stand committed.

We have also made an estimate of the *miseries* of this world. We have seen how in many places the human mind, shackled by ignorance and enfeebled by vice, has dwindled almost to the standard of a brute. Our indignation has kindled at hearing of men immortal as ourselves, bowing down and worshiping a wandering beggar, or paying adoration to reptiles and to stones.

Not only is intellect everywhere under the dominion of idolatry prostrated; beyond the boundaries of Christendom, on every side the dark places of the earth are filled with the habitations of cruelty. We have mourned over the savage ferocity of the Indians of our western wilderness. We have turned to Africa, and seen almost the whole continent a prey to lawless banditti, or else bowing down in the most revolting idolatry. We have descended along her coast, and beheld villages burnt or depopulated, fields laid waste, and her people, who have escaped destruction, naked and famishing, flee to their forests at the sight of a stranger.

We have asked, What fearful visitation of Heaven has laid these settlements in ruins? What destroying pestilence has swept over this land, consigning to oblivion almost its entire population? What mean the smoking ruins of so many habitations? And why is yon fresh sod crimsoned and slippery with the traces of recent murder? We have been pointed to the dark slave-ship hovering over her coast, and have been told that two hundred thousand defenseless beings are annually stolen away, to be murdered on their passage, or consigned for life to a captivity more terrible than death!

We have turned to Asia, and beheld how the demon of her idolatry has worse than debased, has brutalized the mind of man.

Everywhere his despotism has been grievous; here, with merciless tyranny, he has exulted in the misery of his victims. He has rent from the human heart all that was endearing in the charities of life. He has taught the mother to tear away the infant as it smiled in her bosom, and cast it, the shrieking prey, to contending alligators. He has taught the son to light the funeral pile, and to witness unmoved, the dying agonies of his widowed, murdered mother!

We have looked upon all this; and our object is, to purify the whole earth from these abominations. Our object will not have been accomplished till the tomahawk shall be buried forever, and the tree of peace spread its broad branches from the Atlantic to the Pacific; until a thousand smiling villages shall be reflected from the waves of the Missouri, and the distant valleys of the West echo with the song of the reaper; till the wilderness and the solitary place shall have been glad for us, and the desert has rejoiced and blossomed as the rose.

Our labors are not to cease, until the last slave-ship shall have visited the coast of Africa, and, the nations of Europe and America having long since redressed her aggravated wrongs, Ethiopia, from the Mediterranean to the Cape, shall have stretched forth her hand unto God.

How changed will then be the face of Asia! Brahmins and Sudra and castes and shastra will have passed away, like the mist which rolls up the mountain's side before the rising glories of a summer's morning, while the land on which it rested, shining forth in all its loveliness, shall, from its numberless habitations, send forth the high praises of God and the Lamb. The Hindoo mother will gaze upon her infant with the same tenderness which throbs in the breast of any one of you who now hears me, and the Hindoo son will pour into the wounded bosom of his widowed parent, the oil of peace and consolation.

In a word, point us to the loveliest village that smiles upon a Scottish or New England landscape, and compare it with the filthiness and brutality of a Kaffir kraal, and we tell you that our object is to render that Kaffir kraal as happy and as gladsome as that Scottish or New England village. Point us to the spot on the face of the earth, where liberty is best understood and most perfectly enjoyed, where intellect shoots forth in its richest luxuriance, and where all the kindlier feelings of the heart are constantly seen in their most graceful exercise; point us to the loveliest and happiest neighborhood in the world on which we dwell; and we tell you that our object is to render this whole earth, with all its nations and kindreds and tongues and people, as happy, nay, happier than that neighborhood.

. . . . .

But all this is not to be accomplished without laborious exertion. Hence we remark,

2d. THE MISSIONARY UNDERTAKING IS ARDUOUS ENOUGH TO CALL INTO ACTION THE NOBLEST ENERGIES OF MAN.

Its arduousness is explained in one word, our *Field is the World.* Our object is to effect an entire moral revolution in the whole human race. Its arduousness then results of necessity from its magnitude.

I need not say to an audience acquainted with the nature of the human mind, that a large moral mass is not easily and permanently affected. A little leaven does not soon leaven the whole lump. To produce a change even of speculative opinion upon a single nation, is an undertaking not easily accomplished. In the case before us, not a nation, but a world is to be *regenerated:* therefore the change which we would effect is far from being merely speculative.

If any man be in Christ, he is a new creature. Nothing short of this new creation will answer our purpose. We go forth not to persuade men to turn from one idol to another, but to turn universally from idols to serve the living God. We call upon those who are earthly, sensual, devilish, to set their affections on things above. We go forth exhorting men to forsake every cherished lust, and present themselves a living sacrifice, holy and acceptable unto God. And this mighty moral revolution is to be effected, not in a family, a tribe, or a nation, but in a world which lieth in wickedness.

We have to operate upon a race divided into different nations, speaking a thousand different languages, under every different form of government from absolute inertness to unbridled tyranny, and inhabiting every district of country, salubrious or deadly, from the equator to the poles. To all these nations must the gospel be sent, into all these languages must the Bible be translated, to all these climes, salubrious or deadly, must the missionary penetrate, and under all these forms of government, mild or despotic, must he preach Christ and him crucified.

Besides, we shall frequently interfere with the more sordid interests of men; and we expect them to increase the difficulties of our undertaking. If we can turn the heathen to God, many a source of unholy traffic will be dried up, and many a convenience of unhallowed gratification taken away. And hence we may expect that the traffickers in human flesh, the disciples of mammon, and the devotees of pleasure, will be against us. From the heathen themselves we have the blackest darkness of ignorance to dispel. We have to assault systems venerable for their antiquity, and interwoven with every thing that is proud in a nation's history. Above all, we have to oppose the depravity of the human heart, grown still more inveterate by ages of continuance in unrestrained iniquity. In a word, we go forth to urge upon a world dead in trespasses and sins, a thorough renewal of heart, and a universal reformation of practice.

Brief as is this view of the difficulties which surround us, and time will not allow us to state them more in detail, you see that our undertaking is, as we said, arduous enough to task to the uttermost the noblest energies of man.

This enterprise requires consummate wisdom in the missionary who goes abroad, as well as in those who manage the concerns of a society at home. He who goes forth unprotected, to preach Christ to despotic or badly governed nations, must be wise as a serpent, and harmless as a dove. With undeviating firmness upon every thing essential, he must combine the most yielding facility upon all that is unimportant. And thus while he goes forth in the spirit and power of Elias, he must at the same time become all things to all men, that by all means he may gain some.

Great abilities are also required in him who conducts the mission at home. He must awaken, animate, and direct the sentiments of a very large portion of the community in which he resides, whilst at the same time, through a hundred different agents, he is exerting a powerful influence upon half as many nations a thousand or ten thousand miles off. Indeed it is hazarding nothing to predict, that if efforts for the extension of the gospel continue to multiply with their present ratio of increase, as great abilities will, in a few years, be required for transacting the business of a missionary society, as for conducting the affairs of a political cabinet.

The missionary undertaking calls for perseverance; a perseverance of that character, which, having once formed its purpose, never wavers from it till death. And if ever this attribute has been so exhibited as to challenge the respect of every man of feeling, it has been in such instances as are recorded in the history of the missions to Greenland and to the South Sea Islands, where we beheld men, for fifteen or twenty years, suffer every thing but martyrdom, and then, seeing no fruit from their labor, resolve to labor on till death, if so be they might at last, save one benighted heathen from the error of his ways.

This undertaking calls for self-denial of the highest and holiest character. He who engages in it must, at the very outset, dismiss every wish to stipulate for any thing but the mere favor of God. His first act is a voluntary exile from all that a refined education loves; and every other act must be in unison with this. The salvation of the heathen is the object for which he sacrifices, and is willing to sacrifice, every thing that the heart clings to on earth. For this object he would live; for this he would die; nay, he would live any where, and die any how, if so be he might rescue one soul from everlasting woe.

Hence you see that this undertaking requires courage. It is not the courage which, wrought up by the stimulus of popular applause, can rush now and then upon the cannon's mouth; it is the courage which, alone and unapplauded, will, year after year, look death, every moment, in the face, and never shrink from its purpose. It is a principle which will "make a man intrepidly dare every thing which can attack or oppose him within the whole sphere of mortality, retain his purpose unshaken amidst the ruins of the world, and press toward his object while death is impending over him." Such was the spirit which spake by the mouth of an Apostle when he said, And now I go bound in the spirit unto Jerusalem, not knowing the thing which shall befall me there; save that the Holy Ghost witnesseth in every city, saying that bonds and afflictions abide me. Yet none of these things move me; neither count I my life dear unto myself, so that I may finish my course with joy, and the ministry which I have received of the Lord Jesus.

But above all, the missionary undertaking requires faith, in its holiest and sublimest exercise. And let it not be supposed that we speak at random, when we mention the sublimity of faith. "Whatever," says the British moralist, "withdraws us from the power of the senses; whatever makes the past, the distant, or the future predominate over the present, advances us in the dignity of thinking beings." And when we speak of faith, we refer to a principle which gives substance to things hoped for, and evidence to things not seen; which, bending her keen glance on the eternal weight of glory, makes it a constant motive to holy enterprise; which, fixing her eagle eye upon the infinite of future, makes it bear right well upon the purposes of today; a principle which enables a poor feeble tenant of the dust to take strong hold upon the perfections of Jehovah; and, fastening his hopes to the very throne of the Eternal, "bid earth roll, nor feel its idle whirl."

This principle is the unfailing support of the missionary through the long years of his toilsome pilgrimage; and, when he is compared with the heroes of this world, it is peculiar to him. By as much then as the Christian enterprise calls into being this one principle, the noblest that can attach to the character of a creature, by so much does its execution surpass in sublimity every other.

3d. Let us consider THE MEANS BY WHICH THIS MORAL REVOLUTION IS TO BE EFFECTED. It is, in a word, by the preaching of Jesus Christ and him crucified. It is by going forth and telling the lost children of men, that God so loved the world, that he gave his only begotten Son to die for them; and by all the eloquence of such an appeal, to entreat them, for Christ's sake, to be reconciled unto God. This is the lever by which, we believe, the moral universe is to be raised; this is the instrument by which a sinful world is to be regenerated.

And consider the commanding simplicity of this means, devised by Omniscience to effect a purpose so glorious. This world is to be restored to more than it lost by the fall, by the simple annunciation of the love of God in Christ Jesus. Here we behold means apparently the weakest, employed to effect the most magnificent of purposes. And how plainly does this bespeak the agency of the omnipotent God. The means which effect his greatest purposes in the kingdom of nature, are simple and unostentatious; while those which man employs are complicated and tumultuous.

How many intellects are tasked, how many hands are wearied, how many arts exhausted in preparing for the event of a single battle; and how great is the tumult of the moment of decision. In all this, man only imitates the inferior agents of nature. The autumnal tempest, whose sphere of action is limited to a little spot upon our little world, comes forth attended by the roar of thunder and the flash of lightning; while the attraction of gravitation, that stupendous force which binds together the mighty masses of the material universe, acts silently. In the sublimest of natural transactions, the greatest result is ascribed to the simplest, the most unique of causes. He spake and it was done; he commanded and it stood fast.

Contemplate the benevolence of these means. In practice, the precepts of the gospel may be summed up in the single command, Thou shalt love the Lord thy God with all thy heart, and thy neighbor as thyself. We expect to teach one man obedience to this command, and that he will feel obliged to teach his neighbor, who will feel obliged to teach others, who are again to become teachers, until the whole world shall be peopled with one family of brethren. Animosity is to be done away by inculcating universally the obligation of love. In this manner we expect to teach rulers justice, and subjects submission; to open the heart of the miser, and unloose the grasp of the oppressor. It is thus we expect the time to be hastened onward when men shall beat their swords into plowshares, and their spears into pruning hooks; when nation shall no more lift up sword against nation, neither shall they learn war any more.

With this process, compare the means by which men, on the principles of this world, effect a melioration in the condition of their species. Their almost universal agent is threatened or inflicted misery. And, from the nature of the case, it cannot be otherwise. Without altering the disposition of the heart, they only attempt to control its exercise. And they must control it by showing their power to make the indulgence of that disposition the source of more misery than happiness.

Hence when men confer a benefit upon a portion of their brethren, it is generally preceded by a protracted struggle to decide which can inflict most, or which can suffer longest. Hence the arm of the patriot is generally and of necessity bathed in blood. Hence with the shouts of victory from the nation he has delivered, there arises also the sigh of the widow, and the weeping of the orphan. Man produces good by the apprehension or the infliction of evil. The gospel produces good by the universal diffusion of the principles of benevolence. In the former case, one party must generally suffer; in the latter, all parties are certainly more happy. The one, like the mountain torrent, may fertilize now and then a valley beneath, but not until it has wildly swept away the forest above, and disfigured the lovely landscape with many an unseemly scar. Not so the other;

> It droppeth as the gentle rain from heaven
> Upon the place beneath; it is twice bless'd,
> It blesseth him that gives, and him that takes.

· · · · ·

This enterprise of mercy the Son of God came down from heaven to commence, and in commencing it, he laid down his life. To us has he granted the high privilege of carrying it forward. The legacy which he left us, as he was ascending to his Father and our Father, and to his God and to our God, was, Go ye into all the world, and preach the gospel to every creature;

and, lo, I am with you always, even unto the end of the world. With such an object before us, under such a Leader, and supported by such promises, other motives to exertion are unnecessary. Each one of you will anxiously inquire, how he may become a co-worker with the Son of God, in the glorious design of rescuing a world from the miseries of the fall!

Blessed be God, this is a work in which every one of us is permitted to do something. None so poor, none so weak, none so insignificant, but a place of action is assigned him; and the cause expects every man to do his duty. We answer, then,

1. You may assist in it by your prayers. After all that we have said about means, we know that every thing will be in vain without the influences of the Holy Spirit. Paul may plant, and Apollos water, it is God who giveth the increase. And these influences are promised, and promised alone, in answer to prayer. Ye then who love the Lord, keep not silence, and give him no rest, until he establish and make Jerusalem a praise in the whole earth.

2. You may assist by your personal exertions. This cause requires a vigorous, persevering, universal and systematic effort. It requires that a spirit should pervade every one of us, which shall prompt him to ask himself every morning, What can I do for Christ today? and which should make him feel humbled and ashamed, if at evening, he were obliged to confess he had done nothing. Each one of us is as much obligated as the missionaries themselves, to do all in his power to advance the common cause of Christianity. We, equally with them, have embraced that gospel, of which the fundamental principle is, *None of us liveth to himself*. And not only is every one bound to exert himself to the uttermost, the same obligation rests upon us so to direct our exertions, that each of them may produce the greatest effect.

Each one of us may influence others to embark in the undertaking. Each one whom we have influenced, may be induced to enlist that circle of which he is the center, until a self-extending system of intense and reverberated action shall embody into one invincible phalanx, "the sacramental host of God's elect." Awake, then, brethren, from your slumbers. Seek first the kingdom of God and his righteousness. And recollect that what you would do, must be done quickly. The day is far spent; the night is at hand. Whatsoever thy hand findeth to do, do it with thy might; for there is no work, nor device, nor knowledge, nor wisdom in the grave whither thou goest.

3. You may assist by your pecuniary contributions. An opportunity of this kind will be presented this evening. And here, I trust, it is unnecessary to say that in such a cause we consider it a privilege to give. How so worthily can you appropriate a portion of that substance which Providence has given you, as in sending to your fellow men, who sit in the region and shadow of death, a knowledge of the God who made them, and of Jesus Christ whom he hath sent? We pray you, so use the mammon of unrighteousness, that when ye fail, they may receive you into everlasting habitations.

But I doubt not you already burn with desire to testify your love to the crucified Redeemer. Enthroned in the high and holy place, He looks down at this moment upon the heart of every one of us, and will accept of your offering, though it be but the widow's mite, if it be given with the widow's feeling. In the last day of solemn account, he will acknowledge it before an assembled universe, saying, In as much as ye did it unto one of the least of these my brethren, ye did it unto me!

May God of his grace enable us so to act, that on that day, we may meet with joy the record of the doings of this evening; and to his name shall be the glory in Christ. Amen.

AUGUSTUS HOPKINS STRONG (1836-1921)

Augustus Hopkins Strong, great American theologian, received his training at Yale and at Rochester Theological Seminary. After eleven years' service in the pastorate in Massachusetts and Ohio, in 1872 he became president and professor of theology at Roch-

*ester Theological Seminary. He retired from this position in
1912. It was his custom to deliver a brief address to the graduat-
ing classes of the seminary. The first of these, delivered in 1873,
is entitled "The Three Onlies." It is reproduced below.*

"The Three Onlies"

DEAR BRETHREN: It is my pleasant duty to declare your prelim-
inary work in the Rochester Theological Seminary as at length
completed, to congratulate you upon the good measure of success with which that work has been performed, and to commend
you to the guidance and blessing of the great Head of the Church
in that larger work to which you go and which I trust He has
called you to do.

There is an element of sadness in this occasion. We shall see
your faces, and you will see each other's faces, no more for many
a year—perhaps never again until we all come to lay the fruits of
our labors at the Master's feet. Yet the dominant feeling in your
hearts as well as in ours tonight is one of rejoicing,—in yours,
because you break through the last obstacle that holds you back
from the wider life and broader influences to which you have
been so long aspiring,—in ours, because your going out from us
gives us new faith that Christ is making the Institution from
which you graduate a power for the building up of His kingdom
in the world.

Not because you are so many or because you add so greatly
to the *number* of His ministers do we rejoice, but rather because
we trust that under God you will improve the *quality* of ministerial work in the land and the world. In one sense there are
ministers enough,—but of men thoroughly furnished, men who
know the times, men who know the truth of God as the only
and all-sufficient remedy for the evils of these times and of all
times, men who have learned from God the secret of divine wisdom and power in bringing this truth to bear upon the living
hearts of men, men who believe in a personal God, a present
Savior, an old but everlasting gospel, and who are willing to give
themselves body and soul for life and death to the preaching of

it—of these, though thank God we have many, we have not enough. If you be such men, my brethren, the world is waiting and longing for your coming; God calls you forward to your work, assuring your success and your reward; and all the churches of our Lord cry: "How beautiful upon the mountains are the feet of him that bringeth good tidings, that publisheth peace, that bringeth good tidings of good, that publisheth salvation, that saith unto Zion, Thy God reigneth."

The German poet said: "Respect the dreams of thy youth!" There is a loftiness of aspiration and an enthusiasm of self-sacrifice which belong to the youth of Christ's servants. Now, if ever in life, noble voices speak within you, urging you to the highest consecration, and the most absolute and faithful following of the path marked out by God. I would be the mouthpiece of the Spirit tonight. I would stir up those familiar but central thoughts which are the inspiration and power of every successful ministry. I would commend to you anew those old and tried ideas and powers, which have proved their strength by leading the march of the kingdom until now.

There are three of them,—and the first of them is the word of God. In the personality of that word, as I may term it, speaking as with living voice to him who reads it or hears it preached, discerning as it does the thoughts and intents of the heart, bringing the soul into contact with the living God, we have the sufficient proof of its divinity and inspiration. This Institution has sought to ground you in that word, as the norm of faith, the source of comfort, the guide of life. Preach that word, my brethren, in its due proportion, in its relation to the times, in its old and supreme authority. Remember that, if human opinion speak not according to that word, it is because there is no light in it. Remember that by that word we must be approved or condemned at the last day. Not novelties, not paradoxes, not sensations, not tricks of eloquence, not progressive views, but the old word of God that is able to make us wise unto salvation—let this be the weapon, and the only weapon, of your ministry. As you shall bring this word of God, this sword of the Spirit, to bear upon the conscience and the heart, with all its penetrating and clearing power, shall your work be judged a success or a failure.

But by this word you are to lead men to something beyond the word—to Him who speaks through the word, I mean to the living Christ. Not impersonal truth, viewless and impalpable, a breath that enters the ear and leaves it as soon, but a living personal Redeemer, who makes God known and brings the soul into relations of amity and communion with Him—this is the unspeakable gift of God—this is the hope of the ministry. Not faith in an abstract God, but in a living, present Saviour—One whose work outside of us has reconciled God to us, One whose work within us has reconciled us to God—this is the faith of the gospel.

The hope of the Church and the world is a living Christ—not a Christ stretched upon the crucifix, not a dead Christ entombed and buried but a risen and glorified Savior, exalted to give repentance and remission of sins.—No success, till you bring men to this faith in a living Jesus and to personal dealings of Jesus with their souls,—actual communication of life to life—heart beating against heart,—intercourse and communion with One whose presence and being are more real to us than the existence of the world around us. The personal knowledge of this Christ—introduction to Him, life in Him—this is the end and aim of the Christian ministry.

How can this be realized? Partly by the spirit of our own lives. Do you not remember how some unlettered man has thrilled you, and drawn you to Christ, by his simple words of love to Jesus? Do you not know how a true Christian man makes all men who meet him feel the indefinable attraction of his goodness and self-sacrifice? Believe that the presence of Christ in you will give you, even though your natural powers may not be the greatest, an attraction to all believers, and an influence to draw all men to God. The power of a life lived by faith in the Son of God—why, it is irresistible! He must succeed who sides with God. But not simply because his own spirit is a power. No! there is a divine Spirit that makes man's weakness strength, that teaches man to labor and to pray, and that supplements his efforts with divine efficiency.

They are Luther's "three onlies"—these powers of the Christian ministry—the word of God only, faith in Christ only, the power of the Spirit only. Trust these, my brethren. In the strength of these, go forth to meet this living age, and the living God shall go with you. There is no work s⌒ noble on earth to do—none that so develops mind and heart. Whether outward success may be yours or not, is little matter. God will make your work the means of developing in you the highest manhood, and your labor shall not be in vain in the Lord.

As you come back in future years to this scene of your early studies and vows, we shall greet you as soldiers who bring good news from the fight,—we shall send you out again, as we do now, laden with our prayers that God will give you a multitude of trophies in the great conflict. But whether the reward shall come on earth or not, be willing all the same to labor, with God and the angels for your witnesses, and the Judgment for the testing-day and day of triumph. But I must not detain you. The time of preparation is past. Your work calls you. Go forth to meet it. Quit you like men, and may the grace of our Lord, Jesus Christ, the love of God, and the communion and participation of the Holy Ghost, be with you both now and evermore, Amen.

CHARLES HADDON SPURGEON (1834-1892)

C. H. SPURGEON *is probably the best-known name in Baptist history. He was the son of Independent (Congregational) parents but became a Baptist through his own study of the New Testament. His natural gifts for preaching developed very early. Before he was called to John Rippon's church in London at the age of nineteen, he was approvingly 'characterized by an older friend as "the sauciest dog that ever barked in a pulpit." His*

*immediate success in London (1854), however, did not spoil his
sincerity and earnestness.* His church built the famous Metro-
politan Tabernacle (destroyed in World War II) for him in
1861 and he preached to an average of more than five thousand
people in every service there for thirty years. Self-educated, he
suffered some of the limitations to be expected but he appealed
to the common people with his direct, simple, unaffected, sincere,
vibrant, and witty style. He was a prodigious worker. He published almost 150 volumes, mostly sermons, besides his Sword and
Travel, a weekly paper. He founded a seminary, an orphanage,
an evening school, and a colportage association besides carrying
heavy pastoral and denominational responsibilities.*

*Spurgeon was particularly concerned with what he called "the
Down Grade Movement" among Baptists and, as a result, withdrew from the British Baptist Union. He was also disturbed by
the teaching of the Church of England with regard to baptismal
regeneration. It was this latter concern which caused him to deliver the sermon that is reprinted here.*

"Baptismal Regeneration"

"And He said unto them, go ye into all the world, and
preach the Gospel to every creature, he that believeth and
is baptized shall be saved; but he that believeth not shall be
damned." Mark 16:15, 16.

In the preceding verse our Lord Jesus Christ gives us some little
insight into the natural character of the apostles whom he se-
lected to be the first ministers of the Word. They were evidently men of like passions with us, and needed to be rebuked
even as we do. On the occasion when our Lord sent forth the
eleven to preach the gospel to every creature, he "appeared unto
them as they sat at meat, and upbraided them with their unbelief
and hardness of heart, because they believed not them which had
seen him after he was risen;" from which we may surely gather,
that, to preach the Word, the Lord was pleased to choose imperfect men; men, too, who of themselves were very weak in the

grace of faith in which it was most important that they should excel.

Faith is the conquering grace, and is of all things the main requisite in the preacher of the Word; and yet the honored men who were chosen to be the leaders of the divine crusade needed a rebuke concerning their unbelief. Why was this? Why, my brethren, because the Lord has ordained evermore that we should have this treasure in *earthen vessels*, that the excellency of the power may be of God, and not of us. If you should find a perfect minister, then might the praise and honor of his usefulness accrue to man; but God is frequently pleased to select for eminent usefulness men evidently honest and sincere, but who have some manifest infirmity by which all the glory is cast off from them and laid upon himself, and upon himself alone.

Let it never be supposed that we who are God's ministers either excuse our faults or pretend to perfection. We labor to walk in holiness, but we cannot claim to be all that we wish to be. We do not base the claims of God's truth upon the spotlessness of our characters, but upon the fact that it comes from him. You have believed in spite of our infirmities, and not because of our virtues. If, indeed, you had believed our word because of our supposed perfection, your faith would stand in the excellency of man and not in the power of God. We come unto you often with much trembling, sorrowing over our follies and weaknesses; but we deliver to you God's Word as God's Word, and we beseech you to receive it, not as coming from us, poor, sinful mortals, but as proceeding from the eternal and thrice-holy God; and if you so receive it, and by its own vital force are moved and stirred up towards God and his ways, then is the work of the Word sure work, which it could not and would not be if it rested in any way upon man.

Our Lord having thus given us an insight into the character of the persons whom he has chosen to proclaim his truth, then goes on to deliver to the chosen champions their commission for the holy war. I pray you mark the words with solemn care. He sums up in a few words the whole of their work, and at the same time foretells the result of it, telling them that some would doubtless believe and so be saved, and some on the other hand would not believe and would most certainly, therefore, be damned; that is, condemned forever to the penalties of God's wrath.

The lines containing the commission of our ascended Lord are certainly of the utmost importance, and demand devout attention and implicit obedience, not only from all who aspire to the work of the ministry, but also from all who hear the message of mercy. A clear understanding of these words is absolutely necessary to our success in the Master's work; for if we do not understand the commission, it is not at all likely that we shall discharge it aright. To alter these words were more than impertinence: it would involve the crime of treason against the authority of Christ and the best interests of the souls of men. Oh for grace to be very jealous here!

Wherever the apostles went they met with obstacles to the preaching of the gospel, and the more open and effectual was the door of utterance, the more numerous were the adversaries. These brave men so wielded the sword or the Spirit as to put to flight all their foes; and this they did not by craft and guile, but by making a direct cut at the error which impeded them. Never did they dream for a moment of adapting the gospel to the unhallowed tastes or prejudices of the people, but at once directly and boldly they brought down with both their hands the mighty sword of the Spirit upon the crown of the opposing error. This morning, in the name of the Lord of Hosts, my helper and defense, I shall attempt to do the same; and if I should provoke some hostility—if I should through speaking what I believe to be the truth lose the friendship of some and stir up the enmity of more—I cannot help it. The burden of the Lord is upon me, and I must deliver my soul.

I have been loath enough to undertake the work but I am forced to it by an awful and overwhelming sense of solemn duty. As I am soon to appear before my Master's bar, I will this day, if ever in my life, bear my testimony for truth, and run all risks. I am content to be cast out as evil if it must be so; but I cannot, I dare not, hold my peace. The Lord knoweth I have nothing in my heart but the purest love to the souls of those whom I feel imperatively called to rebuke sternly in the Lord's name. Among my hearers and readers, a considerable number will censure if not condemn me; but I cannot help it. If I forfeit your love for truth's sake I am grieved for you; but I cannot, I dare not, do otherwise. It is as much as my soul is worth to hold my peace any longer; and, whether you approve or not, I must speak out. Did I ever court your approbation? It is sweet to every one to be applauded; but if for the sake of the comforts of respectability and the smiles of men any Christian minister shall keep back a part of his testimony, his Master at the last shall require it at his hands. This day, standing in the immediate presence of God, I shall speak honestly what I feel, as the Holy Spirit shall enable me; and I shall leave the matter with you to judge concerning it, as you will answer for that judgment at the last, great day.

I find that the great error which we have to contend with throughout England (and it is growing more and more), is one in direct opposition to my text, well known to you as the doctrine of baptismal regeneration. We will confront this dogma with the assertion that *baptism without faith saves no one.* The text says, "He *that believeth* and is baptized shall be saved"; but whether a man be baptized or no, it asserts that *"he that believeth not* shall be damned"*: so that baptism does not save the unbeliever; nay, it does not in any degree exempt him from the common doom of all the ungodly. He may have baptism, or he may not have baptism; but if he believeth not, he shall be in any case most surely damned. Let him be baptized by immersion or sprinkling, in his infancy or in his adult age: if he be not led to put his trust in Jesus Christ—if he remaineth an unbeliever—then this terrible doom is pronounced upon him, "He that believeth not shall be damned."

I am not aware that any Protestant church in England teaches the doctrine of baptismal regeneration, except one, and that happens to be the corporation which with none too much humility calls itself *the* Church of England. This very powerful sect does not teach this doctrine merely through a section of its ministers, who might charitably be considered as evil branches of the vine, but it openly, boldly, and plainly declares this doctrine in her own appointed standard, the Book of Common Prayer, and that in words so express, that, while language is the channel of conveying intelligible sense, no process short of violent wresting from their plain meaning can ever make them say anything else.

Here are the words—we quote them from the Catechism which is intended for the instruction of youth, and is naturally very plain and simple, since it would be foolish to trouble the youth with metaphysical refinements. The child is asked its name, and then questioned, "Who gave you this name?" *"My godfathers and godmothers in my baptism; wherein I was made a member of Christ, the child of God, and an inheritor of the kingdom of heaven."* Is not this definite and plain enough? I prize the words for their candor: they could not speak more plainly. Three times over the thing is put, lest there should be any doubt in it.

The word *regeneration* may, by some sort of juggling, be made to mean something else; but here there can be no misunderstanding. The child is not only made "a member of Christ"—union to Jesus is no mean spiritual gift—but he is made in baptism "the child of God" also; and, since the rule is, "if children, then heirs," he is also made "an inheritor of the kingdom of heaven." Nothing can be more plain. I venture to say, that, while honesty remains on earth the meaning of these words will not admit of dispute. It is clear as noonday that, as the Rubric hath it, "Fathers, mothers, masters, and dames are to cause their children, servants, and apprentices," no matter how idle, giddy, or wicked they may be, to learn the Catechism, and to say that in baptism they were made members of Christ and children of God.

The form for the administration of this baptism is scarcely less plain and outspoken, seeing that thanks are expressly returned unto Almighty God because the person baptized is regenerated: *"Then shall the priest say, 'Seeing, now, dearly beloved brethren, that this child is regenerate and grafted into the body of Christ's church, let us give thanks unto Almighty God for these benefits; and with one accord make our prayers unto him, that this child may lead the rest of his life according to this beginning.' "* Nor is this all; for, to leave no mistake, we have the words of the thanksgiving prescribed: "*Then shall the priest say, 'We yield thee hearty thanks, most merciful Father, that it hath pleased thee to regenerate this infant with thy Holy Spirit, to receive him for thine own child by adoption, and to incorporate him into thy holy church.*' "

This, then, is the clear and unmistakable teaching of a church calling itself Protestant. I am not now dealing at all with the question of infant baptism: I have nothing to do with that this morning. I am now considering the question of baptismal regeneration, whether in adults or infants, or ascribed to sprinkling, pouring, or immersion. Here is a church which teaches every Lord's Day in the Sunday-school, and should, according to the Rubric, teach openly in the church, all children that they were made members of Christ, children of God, and inheritors of the kingdom of heaven when they were baptized! Here is a professedly Protestant church, which, every time its minister goes to the font, declares that every person there receiving baptism is there and then "regenerated and grafted into the body of Christ's church."

"But," I hear many good people exclaim, "there are many good clergymen in the church who do not believe in baptismal regeneration!" To this my answer is prompt:—Why, then, do they belong to a church which teaches that doctrine, in the plainest terms? I am told that many in the Church of England preach against her own teaching. I know they do, and herein I rejoice in their enlightenment, but I question, gravely question, their morality. To take oath that I sincerely assent and consent to a doctrine which I do not believe, would to my conscience appear little short of perjury, if not absolute, downright perjury; but those who do so must be judged by their Lord. For me to take money for defending what I do not believe—for me to take the money of a church, and then to preach against what are most evidently its doctrines—I say *for me* to do this (I shall not judge the peculiar views of other men), for me or for any other simple, honest man to do so, were an atrocity so great that, if I had perpetrated the deed, I should consider myself out of the pale of truthfulness, honesty, and common morality.

Sirs, when I accepted the office of minister of this congregation, I looked to see what were your articles of faith. If I had not believed them I should not have accepted your call; and when I change my opinions, rest assured that, as an honest man, I shall resign the office; for how could I profess one thing in your declaration of faith, and quite another thing in my own preaching? Would I accept your pay, and then stand up every Sabbath day and talk against the doctrines of your standards? For clergymen to swear or say that they give their solemn assent and consent to what they do not believe, is one of the grossest pieces of immorality perpetrated in England, and is most pestilential in its influence since it directly teaches men to lie whenever it seems necessary to do so in order to get a living or increase their supposed usefulness: it is in fact an open testimony from priestly lips that, at least in ecclesiastical matters, falsehood may express truth, and truth itself is a mere unimportant nonentity.

I know of nothing more calculated to debauch the public mind than a want of straightforwardness in ministers; and when worldly men hear ministers denouncing the very things which their own Prayer Book teaches, they imagine that words have no meaning among ecclesiastics, and that vital differences in religion are merely a matter of tweedle-dee and tweedle-dum, and that it does not much matter what a man does believe so long as he is charitable towards other people. If baptism does regenerate people, let the fact be preached with a trumpet tongue, and let no man be ashamed of his belief in it. If this be really their creed, by all means let them have full liberty for its propagation. My brethren, those are honest Churchmen in this matter who, subscribing to the Prayer Book, believe in baptismal regeneration, and preach it plainly. God forbid that we should censure those who believe that baptism saves the soul, because they adhere to a church which teaches the same doctrine. So far they are honest men; and in England, wherever else, let them never lack a full toleration. Let us oppose their teaching by all scriptural and intelligent means, but let us respect their courage in plainly giving us their views. I hate their doctrine, but I love their honesty; and as they speak but what they believe to be true, let them speak it out, and the more clearly the better. Out with it, sirs, be it what it may, but do let us know what you mean.

For my part, I love to stand foot to foot with an honest foeman. To open warfare, bold and true hearts raise no objections but the ground of quarrel; it is covert enmity which we have most cause to fear and best reason to loathe. That crafty kindness which inveigles me to sacrifice principle, is the serpent in the grass—deadly to the incautious wayfarer. Where union and friendship are not cemented by truth, they are an unhallowed confederacy. It is time that there should be an end put to the flirtations of honest men with those who believe one way and swear another. If men believe baptism works regeneration, let them say so; but if they do not so believe it in their hearts, and yet subscribe, and yet more, get their livings by subscribing to words asserting it, let them find congenial associates among men who can equivocate and shuffle, for honest men will neither ask nor accept their friendship.

We ourselves are not dubious on this point: we protest that persons are not saved by being baptized. In such an audience as this, I am almost ashamed to go into the matter, because you surely know better than to be misled. Nevertheless, for the good of others we will drive at it. We hold that persons are not saved by baptism; for we think, first of all, that *it seems out of character with the spiritual religion which Christ came to teach,* that he should make salvation depend upon mere ceremony. Judaism might possibly absorb the ceremony by way of type into her ordinances essential to eternal life; for it was a religion of types and shadows. The false religions of the heathen might inculcate salvation by a physical process; but Jesus Christ claims for his faith that it is purely spiritual, and how could he connect regeneration with a peculiar application of aqueous fluid? I cannot see how it would be a spiritual gospel, but I can see how it would be mechanical, if I were sent forth to teach that the mere dropping of so many drops upon the brow, or even the plunging a person in water, could save the soul. This seems to me to be the most mechanical religion now existing, and to be on a par with the praying windmills of Thibet, or the climbing up and down of Pilate's staircase to which Luther subjected himself in the days of his darkness.

The operation of water baptism does not appear even to my faith to touch the point involved in the regeneration of the soul. What is the necessary connection between water and the overcoming of sin? I cannot see any connection which can exist between sprinkling, or immersion, and regeneration, so that the one shall necessarily be tied to the other in the absence of faith. Used by faith, had God commanded it, miracles might be wrought; but without faith or even consciousness, as in the case of babes, how can spiritual benefits be connected necessarily with the sprinkling of water? If this be your teaching, that regeneration goes with baptism, I say that it looks like the teaching of a spurious church, which has craftily invented a mechanical salvation to deceive ignorant, sensual, and groveling minds, rather than the teaching of the most profoundly spiritual of all teachers, who rebuked Scribes and Pharisees for regarding outward rites as more important than inward grace. . . .

Here let me bring in another point. It is a most fearful fact, that, *in no age since the Reformation, has Popery made such fearful strides in England as during the last few years.* I had comfortably believed that Popery was only feeding itself upon foreign subscriptions, upon a few titled perverts, and imported monks and nuns. I dreamed that its progress was not real. In fact, I have often smiled at the alarm of many of my brethren at the progress of Popery. But, my dear friends, we have been mistaken, grievously mistaken. If you will read a valuable paper in the magazine called *Christian Work*, those of you who are acquainted with it will be perfectly startled at its revelations.

This great city is now covered with a network of monks and priests and sisters of mercy, and the conversions made are not by ones or twos but by scores, till England is being regarded as the most hopeful spot for Romish missionary enterprise in the whole world; and at the present moment there is not a mission which is succeeding to anything like the extent which the English mission is. I covet not their money, I despise their sophistries, but I marvel at the way in which they gain their funds for the erection of their ecclesiastical buildings. It really is an alarming matter to see so many of our countrymen going off to that superstition which as a nation we once rejected, and which it was supposed we should never again receive. Popery is making advances such as you would never believe, though a spectator should tell it to you. Close to your very doors, perhaps even in your own houses, you may have evidence ere long of what a march Romanism is making.

And to what is it to be ascribed? I say, with every ground of probability, that there is no marvel that Popery should increase when you have two things to make it grow: first of all, the falsehood of those who profess a faith which they do not believe, which is quite contrary to the honesty of the Romanist, who does through evil report and good report hold his faith; and then you have, secondly, this form of error known as baptismal regeneration, and commonly called Puseyism, which is not only Puseyism, but Church-of-Englandism, because it is in the Prayer Book, as plainly as words can express it,—you have this baptismal regeneration, preparing stepping-stones to make it easy for men to go to Rome. I have but to open my eyes a little to foresee Romanism rampant everywhere in the future, since its germs are spreading everywhere in the present.

In one of our courts of legislature, but last Tuesday, the Lord Chief Justice showed his superstition, by speaking of "the risk of the calamity of children dying unbaptized!" Among Dissenters you see a veneration for structures, a modified belief in the sacredness of places, which is all idolatry; for to believe in the sacredness of anything but of God and of his own Word, is to idolize, whether it is to believe in the sacredness of the men, the priests, or in the sacredness of the bricks and mortar, or of the fine linen, or what not, which you may use in the worship of God. I see this coming up everywhere—a belief in ceremony, a resting in ceremony, a veneration for altars, fonts, and churches —a veneration so profound that we must not venture upon a remark, or straightway of sinners we are chief. Here is the essence and soul of Popery, peeping up under the garb of a decent respect for sacred things. It is impossible but that the Church of

Rome must spread, when we who are the watchdogs of the fold are silent, and others are gently and smoothly turfing the road, and making it as soft and smooth as possible, that converts may travel down to the nethermost hell of Popery.

We want John Knox back again. Do not talk to me of mild and gentle men, of soft manners and squeamish words: we want the fiery Knox; and even though his vehemence should "ding our pulpits into blads," it were well if he did but rouse our hearts to action. We want Luther, to tell men the truth unmistakably, in homely phrase. The velvet has got into our ministers' mouths of late, but we must unrobe ourselves of soft raiment, and truth must be spoken, and nothing but truth; for of all lies which have dragged millions down to hell, I look upon this as being one of the most atrocious—that in a Protestant church there should be found those who swear that baptism saves the soul. Call a man a Baptist, or a Presbyterian, or a Dissenter, or a Churchman—that is nothing to me: if he says that baptism saves the soul, out upon him, out upon him: he states what God never taught, what the Bible never laid down, and what ought never to be maintained by men who profess that the Bible, and the whole Bible, is the religion of Protestants.

I have spoken thus much, and there will be some who will say, spoken thus much bitterly. Very well; be it so. Physic is often bitter, but it shall work well, and the physician is not bitter because his medicine is so; or if he be accounted so, it will not matter, so long as the patient is cured; at all events, it is no business of the patient whether the physician is better or not; his business is with his own soul's health. There is the truth, and I have told it to you; and if there should be one among you, or if there should be one among the readers of this sermon when it is printed, who is resting on baptism, or resting upon ceremonies of any sort, I do beseech you, shake off this venomous faith into the fire as Paul did the viper which fastened on his hand. I pray you do not rest on baptism.

> "No outward forms can make you clean:
> The leprosy lies deep within."

I do beseech you to remember that you must have a new heart and a right spirit, and baptism cannot give you these. You must turn from your sins and follow after Christ; you must have such a faith as shall make your life holy and your speech devout, or else you have not the faith of God's elect, and into God's kingdom you shall never come. I pray you never rest upon this wretched and rotten foundation, this deceitful intention of antichrist. Oh! may God save you from it, and bring you to seek the true rock of refuge for weary souls. . . .

THE BAPTISM IN THE TEXT IS ONE EVIDENTLY CONNECTED WITH FAITH. "He that believeth and is baptized shall be saved." It strikes me, there is no supposition here that anybody would be baptized who did not believe; or if there be such a supposition, it is very clearly laid down that his baptism will be of no use to him, for he will be damned, baptized or not, unless he believes. The baptism of the text seems to me, my brethren—if you differ from me I am sorry for it, but I must hold my opinion, and out with it—it seems to me that baptism is connected with, nay, directly follows belief. I would not insist too much upon the order of the words; but, for other reasons, I think that baptism should follow believing. At any rate, it effectually avoids the error we have been combating.

A man who knows that he is saved by believing in Christ does not, when he is baptized, lift his baptism into a saving ordinance. In fact, he is the very best protester against that mistake, because he holds that he has no right to be baptized until he is saved. He bears a testimony against baptismal regeneration in his being baptized as professedly an already regenerate person. Brethren, the baptism here meant is a baptism connected with faith, and to this baptism I will admit there is very much ascribed in Scripture. Into that question I am not going; but I do find some very remarkable passages in which baptism is spoken of very strongly. I find this: "Arise, and be baptized, and wash away thy sins, calling on the name of the Lord." I find as much as this elsewhere. I know that believer's baptism itself does not wash away sin, yet it is so the outward sign and emblem of it to the believer, that the thing visible may be described as the thing signified. Just as our Saviour said, "This is my body," when it was not his body, but bread; yet, inasmuch as it represented his body, it was fair and right according to the usage of language to say, "Take, eat, this is my body." And so, inasmuch as baptism to the believer representeth the washing of sin—it may be called the washing of sin; not that it is so, but that it is to saved souls the outward symbol and representation of what is done by the power of the Holy Spirit in the man who believes in Christ.

What connection has this baptism with faith? I think it has just this, *baptism is the avowal of faith;* the man was Christ's soldier, but now in baptism he puts on his regimentals. The man believed in Christ, but his faith remained between God and his own soul. In baptism he says to the baptizer, "I believe in Jesus Christ"; he says to the church, "I unite with you as a believer in the common truths of Christianity"; he saith to the onlooker, "Whatever you may do, as for me, I will serve the Lord." It is the avowal of his faith.

Next, we think baptism is also to the believer a *testimony of his faith;* he does in baptism tell the world what he believes. "I am about," saith he, "to be buried in water. I believe that the Son of God was metaphorically baptized in suffering; I believe he was literally dead and buried." To rise again out of the water sets forth to all men that he believes in the resurrection of Christ. There is a showing forth in the Lord's Supper of Christ's death, and there is a showing forth in baptism of Christ's burial and resurrection. It is a type, a sign, a symbol, a mirror to the world— a looking-glass, in which religion is as it were reflected. We say to the onlooker, when he asks what is the meaning of ordinance, "We mean to set forth our faith that Christ was buried, and that he rose again from the dead; and we avow this death and resurrection to be the ground of our trust."

Again, baptism is also *Faith's taking her proper place*. It is, or should be, one of her first acts of obedience. Reason looks at baptism, and says, "Perhaps there is nothing in it; it cannot do me any good." "True," says Faith, "and therefore I will observe it. If it did me some good, my selfishness would make me do it; but inasmuch as to my sense there is no good in it, since

I am bidden by my Lord thus to fulfil all righteousness, it is my first public declaration that a thing which looks to be unreasonable and seems to be unprofitable, being commanded by God, is law to me."

If my Master had told me to pick up six stones and lay them in a row I would do it, without demanding of him, "What good will it do?" *Cui bono?* is no fit question for soldiers of Jesus. The very simplicity and apparent uselessness of the ordinance should make the believer say, "Therefore I do it because it becomes the better test to me of my obedience to my Master." When you tell your servant to do something, and he cannot comprehend it, if he turns round and says, "Please, sir, what for?" you are quite clear that he hardly understands the relation between master and servant. So when God tells me to do a thing, if I say, "What for?" I cannot have taken the place which Faith ought to occupy, which is that of simple obedience to whatever the Lord hath said. Baptism is commanded, and Faith obeys because it is commanded, and thus takes her proper place.

Once more, *baptism is a refreshment to faith.* While we are made up of body and soul as we are, we shall need some means by which the body shall sometimes be stirred up to co-work with the soul. In the Lord's Supper my faith is assisted by the outward and visible sign. In the bread and in the wine I see no superstitious mystery: I see nothing but bread and wine; but in that bread and wine I do see to my faith an assistant. Through the sign my faith sees the thing signified. So in baptism there is no mysterious efficacy in the baptistry or in the water. We attach no reverence to the one or to the other; but we do see in the water and in the baptism such an assistance as brings home to our faith most manifestly our being buried with Christ, and our rising again in newness of life with him.

Explain baptism thus, dear friends, and there is no fear of Popery rising out of it. Explain it thus, and we cannot suppose any soul will be led to trust to it; but it takes proper place among the ordinances of God's house. To lift it up in the other way, and say men are saved by it—ah! my friends, how much of mischief that one falsehood has done and may do, eternity alone will disclose. Would to God another George Fox would spring up, in all his quaint simplicity and rude honesty, to rebuke the idol-worship of this age; to rail at their holy bricks and mortar, holy lecterns, holy altars, holy surplices, right reverend fathers, and I know not what. These things are not holy. God is holy; his truth is holy: holiness belongs not to the carnal and the material, but to the spiritual. Oh what a trumpet tongue would cry out against the superstition of the age! I cannot, as George Fox did, give up baptism and the Lord's Supper; but I would infinitely sooner do it, counting it the smaller mistake of the two, than perpetrate and assist in perpetrating the uplifting of baptism and the Lord's Supper out of their proper place.

O my beloved friends, the comrades of my struggles and witnessings, cling to the salvation of faith, and abhor the salvation of priests. If I am not mistaken, the day will come when we shall have to fight for a simple spiritual religion far more than we do now. We have been cultivating friendship with those who are either unscriptural in creed or else dishonest; who either believe baptismal regeneration, or profess that they do, and swear before God that they do when they do not. The time is come when there shall be no more truce or parley between God's servants and time-servers. . . .

EDGAR YOUNG MULLINS (1860-1928)

EDGAR YOUNG MULLINS, *after some years in pastorates, including Harrisburg, Kentucky, and Newton Center, Massachusetts, in 1899 became president of the Southern Baptist Theological Seminary, Louisville, Kentucky, where he also served as professor of theology. He was president of the Southern Baptist Convention from 1921 to 1924, and was elected president of the Baptist World Alliance in 1928. The following passage is taken from an address delivered on July 14, 1905, in the first meeting of the Baptist World Congress in London, England. The address is entitled "The Theological Trend."*

"The Axioms of Religion"

The critical questions which remain in the theology of today are concerned with the following: the basis and nature of religious authority, the deity of Christ and His atoning work, the nature of sin, and the general relations of theology to social questions.

Behind these questions lie the philosophic issues between Christian theism and antitheistic theories, and, most fundamental of all, the question of the reality and nature of knowledge.

I must now forecast briefly the probable course of theological reconstruction in the light of the above considerations. Theology, then, in future will not adopt rationalism as its constructive principle, because rationalism is not always compatible with the interests of life. Naturalism also, which fails altogether to yield a theology in the proper sense, will be avoided, for the reason that it is incapable of coping with the situation created by sin. Evolution, while containing a relative truth as to physical nature, breaks down in the attempt to explain the phenomena and facts of the personal and social realm. A merely deistic conception of God is, of course, to be discarded as inadequate. The doctrine of the Divine immanence alone cannot serve as a sufficient principle of theological reconstruction, because it inevitably merges God in nature and in man, and tends to pull the entire structure down to the level of naturalism.

Positively stated, the best theology of the future will continue to accept the authority of the Scriptures, but it will take as its starting point, for the interpretation and illumination of Scripture, the facts of Christian experience, not in a single aspect, but in their totality.

First, because Christian experience, thus employed, conforms to the scientific ideal which above all things seeks to know the

facts of nature, life and religion, and resents theoretical constructions apart from experience in the realm of facts.

It conforms, second, to the true philosophical ideal, which
also demands a fact basis for all the speculative attempts of the
intellect.

Thirdly, experience will also restore with greatly increased
power the older arguments from the cosmos for the existence of
God, transferred in part, however, from the cosmos of nature
to the cosmos of the inner life.

Fourthly, experience will sustain the cause of the supernatural
in its collision with naturalism, because it brings contact with
the supernatural in consciousness the most indubitable of all the
spheres of reality.

In the fifth place, experience will in increasing measure establish the validity of the vicarious atonement of Christ, and its corresponding doctrines of sin and of Christ's deity and present
action upon men. Thus it will indirectly add an important contribution to the doctrine of the Trinity. It will also affirm, and
at the same time limit and define, the reality of knowledge of
transcendental objects in the religious sphere, and indirectly re-
juvenate the weakened convictions of an agnostic science in the
realm of material research.

Sixth, theological dogma will increasingly become the dogma
of conviction, as opposed to the dogma of mere authority.

Thus the confusions and contradictions in recent writers on
authority, as of Sabatier, for example, will be dispelled. The ex-
ternalists and internalists on authority will discover a larger truth
than either theory. Christ's authority will be seen to be real, but
incapable of adequate statement save as a paradox. Christ is man's
final authority in religion, because He imparts spiritual autonomy
to man. Man, who is made in God's image, finds in the truth of
Christ the ideal of his own higher moral self. Man realizes in
and through Christ his own ideal independence. He is thus
eternally a subject and eternally free. Authority in religion will
remain external so long as there is a reserve of life and truth in
Christ, but that authority is forever in process of becoming internal, as men appropriate Christ. Experience will vindicate the

authority of the Scriptures, for the experience of God through Christ and the Spirit is seen to be the real inner bond of unity in all the course of revelation.

Scripture as a record of original experience cannot be transcended, nor can it lose its authority; for the sufficient reason that to discard Scripture is to discard the only means of understanding the historic Christ who emancipates man and imparts to him spiritual autonomy. Faith expires in a vacuum without contact with the historic Christ of Scripture as well as the risen and ascended and living Christ.

Again, experience will guide in the final construction of the doctrine of God, for the reason that experience reaches its conception of God, not through nature, but through man, nature's crown; and not merely through the natural man, but through the supernatural and Divine Man, Jesus Christ. It will also appear, as experience grows, that in its Christian form it gathers together as in. a focus all that is valid and universal in man's quest for God. It will at once thus discredit and fulfill the ethnic types of experience, by showing their inadequacy to man's needs on the one hand, and on the other that it is the answer of God in Christ to man's age-long endeavor to find God. Christian experience, then, will appear as the universal religious and moral ultimate for man, short of which it is impossible for religious experience to halt, and beyond which it is impossible to proceed.

Now, the relation of Baptists to this great theological movement has not been adequately recognized and needs defining afresh. Behind our contentions as to baptism and communion and related topics lie a group of great and elemental principles. These principles are religious ultimates, nay, they are axioms, which the instructed religious consciousness of man cannot repudiate. I sum them up and submit them as a statement of the basis at once for a new Baptist apologetic and a platform for universal adoption.

1. The theological axiom: THE HOLY AND LOVING GOD HAS A RIGHT TO BE SOVEREIGN. Time forbids that I elaborate this statement in its implications as to the incarnation, and as to Christianity as the religion of the Divine initiative.

2. The religious axiom: ALL MEN HAVE AN EQUAL RIGHT TO DI-
RECT ACCESS TO GOD. This principle is fatal to the practice of infant baptism and to the idea of a human priesthood.

3. The ecclesiastical axiom: ALL BELIEVERS HAVE EQUAL PRIVI-
LEGES IN THE CHURCH. Hierarchies and centralized authorities dis-
appear under the operation of this principle.

4. The moral axiom: TO BE RESPONSIBLE MAN MUST BE FREE.
This is an elemental truth which cannot receive thoroughgoing
application save where ecclesiastical bonds of mere authority are
absent.

5. The social axiom: LOVE YOUR NEIGHBOR AS YOURSELF. This
makes the Kingdom of God the goal of the social movement.

6. The religio-civic axiom: A FREE CHURCH IN A FREE STATE.
For this principle Baptists have ever stood. Without it the future of theology and of the Church is fraught with extreme peril.

These axioms are the predestined goal of man's religious thinking. They spring out of Scripture teaching, they meet a deep
response in Christian experience. When understood they commend themselves as the universal and necessary and self-evident
forms of man's religious life. They are deep like the ocean,
elastic and free as the life-giving atmosphere which enswathes
the earth, and expansive and comprehensive as the overarching
sky. For them the Baptists stand. Planting ourselves upon them
our position cannot be successfully assailed. By means of them
Baptists will make fruitful the course of theological development
in the ages to come.

GEORGE W. TRUETT (1867-1944)

DR. TRUETT *was pastor of the First Baptist Church, Dallas, Texas,
from 1897 to 1944. Loved as a pastor, famed as a preacher, he*

was honored as a Christian statesman by Baptists and others, being elected to serve two years as president of the Southern Baptist Convention and five years as president of the Baptist World Alliance. Following is his famous address delivered from the east steps of the National Capitol, May 16, 1920.

From "Baptists and Religious Liberty"

• • • • •

THE DOCTRINE OF RELIGIOUS LIBERTY

We shall do well, both as citizens and as Christians, if we will hark back to the chief actors and lessons in the early and epoch-making struggles of this great Western democracy, for the full establishment of civil and religious liberty—back to the days of Washington and Jefferson and Madison, and back to the days of our Baptist fathers, who have paid such a great price, through the long generations, that liberty, both religious and civil, might have free course and be glorified everywhere.

Years ago, at a notable dinner in London, that world-famed statesman John Bright, asked an American statesman, himself a Baptist, the noble Dr. J. L. M. Curry, "What distinct contribution has your America made to the science of government?" To that question Dr. Curry replied: "The doctrine of religious liberty." After a moment's reflection, Mr. Bright made the worthy reply: "It was a tremendous contribution."

SUPREME CONTRIBUTION OF THE NEW WORLD

Indeed, the supreme contribution of the new world to the old is the contribution of religious liberty. This is the chief contribution that America has thus far made to civilization. And historic justice compels me to say that it was pre-eminently a Baptist contribution. The impartial historian, whether in the past, present or future, will ever agree with our American historian Mr. Bancroft, when he says: "Freedom of conscience, unlimited freedom of mind, was from the first the trophy of the Baptists." And such a historian will concur with the noble John Locke, who said: "The Baptists were the first propounders of absolute liberty, just and true liberty, equal and impartial liberty." Ringing testimonies like these might be multiplied indefinitely.

NOT TOLERATION, BUT RIGHT

Baptists have one consistent record concerning liberty throughout all their long and eventful history. They have never been a party to oppression of conscience. They have forever been the unwavering champions of liberty, both religious and civil. Their contention now is, and has been, and, please God, must ever be, that it is the natural and fundamental and indefeasible right of every human being to worship God or not, according to the dictates of his conscience; and, as long as he does not infringe upon the rights of others, he is to be held accountable alone to God for all religious beliefs and practices. Our contention is not for mere toleration, but for absolute liberty.

There is a wide difference between toleration and liberty. Toleration implies that somebody falsely claims the right to tolerate. Toleration is a concession, while liberty is a right. Toleration is a matter of expediency, while liberty is a matter of principle. Toleration is a gift from man, while liberty is a gift from God. It is the consistent and insistent contention of our Baptist people, always and everywhere, that religion must be forever voluntary and uncoerced, and that it is not the prerogative of any power, whether civil or ecclesiastical, to compel men to conform to any religious creed or form of worship, or to pay taxes for the support of a religious organization to which they do not belong and in whose creed they do not believe. God wants free worshipers and no other kind.

A FUNDAMENTAL PRINCIPLE

What is the explanation of this consistent and notably praiseworthy record of our plain Baptist people in the realm of religious liberty? The answer is at hand. It is not because Baptists are inherently better than their neighbors—we would make no such arrogant claim. Happy are our Baptist people to live side by side with their neighbors of other Christian communions, and to have glorious Christian fellowship with such neighbors, and to honor such servants of God for their inspiring lives and their noble deeds.

From our deepest hearts we pray: "Grace be with all them that love our Lord Jesus Christ in sincerity." The spiritual union of all true believers in Christ is now and ever will be a blessed reality, and such union is deeper and higher and more enduring than any and all forms and rituals and organizations. Whoever believes in Christ as his personal Saviour is our brother in the common salvation, whether he be a member of one communion or of another, or of no communion at all.

How is it, then, that Baptists, more than any other people in the world, have forever been the protagonists of religious liberty, and its compatriot, civil liberty? They did not stumble upon this principle. Their uniform, unyielding and sacrificial advocacy of such principle was not and is not an accident. It is, in a word, because of our essential and fundamental principles. Ideas rule the world. A denomination is molded by its ruling principles, just as a nation is thus molded and just as individual life is thus molded. Our fundamental essential principles have made our Baptist people, of all ages and countries, to be the unyielding protagonists of religious liberty, not only for themselves, but as well for everybody else.

THE FUNDAMENTAL BAPTIST PRINCIPLES

Such fact at once provokes the inquiry: What are these fundamental Baptist principles which compel Baptists in Europe, in America, in some far-off seagirt island, to be forever contending for unrestricted religious liberty? First of all, and explaining all the rest, is the doctrine of the absolute Lordship of Jesus Christ. That doctrine is for Baptists the dominant fact in all their Christian experience, the nerve center of all their Christian life, the bedrock of all their church polity, the sheet anchor of all their hopes, the climax and crown of all their rejoicings. They say with Paul: "For to this end Christ both died and rose again, that he might be Lord both of the dead and the living."

THE ABSOLUTE LORDSHIP OF CHRIST

From that germinal conception of the absolute Lordship of Christ, all our Baptist principles emerge. Just as yonder oak came from the acorn, so our many-branched Baptist life came from the cardinal principle of the absolute Lordship of Christ. The Christianity of our Baptist people, from alpha to omega, lives and moves and has its whole being in the realm of the doctrine of the Lordship of Christ. "One is your Master, even Christ, and all ye are brethren." Christ is the one head of the church. All authority has been committed unto Him, in heaven and on earth, and He must be given the absolute pre-eminence in all things. One clear note is ever to be sounded concerning Him, even this, "Whatsoever He saith unto you, do it."

THE BIBLE OUR RULE OF FAITH AND PRACTICE

How shall we find out Christ's will for us? He has revealed it in His Holy Word. The Bible and the Bible alone is the rule of faith and practice for Baptists. To them the one standard by which all creeds and conduct and character must be tried is the Word of God. They ask only one question concerning all religious faith and practice, and that question is, "What saith the Word of God?" Not traditions, nor customs, nor councils, nor confessions, nor ecclesiastical formularies, however venerable and pretentious, guide Baptists, but simply and solely the will of Christ as they find it revealed in the New Testament. The immortal B. H. Carroll has thus stated it for us: "The New Testament is the law of Christianity. All the New Testament is the law of Christianity. The New Testament is the law of Christianity. The New Testament always will be all the law of Christianity."

Baptists hold that this law of Christianity, the Word of God, is the unchangeable and only law of Christ's reign, and that whatever is not found in the law cannot be bound on the conciences of men, and that this law is a sacred deposit, an inviolable trust, which Christ's friends are commissioned to guard and perpetuate wherever it may lead and whatever may be the cost of such trusteeship.

EXACT OPPOSITE OF CATHOLICISM

The Baptist message and the Roman Catholic message are the very antipodes of each other. The Roman Catholic message is sacerdotal, sacramentarian and ecclesiastical. In its scheme of salvation it magnifies the church, the priest and the sacraments.

The Baptist message is non-sacerdotal, non-sacramentarian and non-ecclesiastical. Its teaching is that the one High Priest for sinful humanity has entered into the holy place for all, that the veil is forever rent in twain, that the mercy seat is uncovered and open to all, and that the humblest soul in all the world, if only he be penitent, may enter with all boldness and cast himself upon God.

The Catholic doctrine of baptismal regeneration and transubstantiation are to the Baptist mind fundamentally subversive of the spiritual realities of the gospel of Christ. Likewise, the Catholic conception of the church, thrusting all its complex and cumbrous machinery between the soul and God, prescribing beliefs, claiming to exercise the power of the keys, and to control the channels of grace—all such lording it over the consciences of men is to the Baptist mind a ghastly tyranny in the realm of the soul and tends to frustrate the grace of God, to destroy freedom of conscience, and terribly to hinder the coming of the Kingdom of God. . . .

DIRECT INDIVIDUAL APPROACH TO GOD

When we turn to this New Testament, which is Christ's guide-book and law for His people, we find that supreme emphasis is everywhere put upon the individual. The individual is segregated from family, from church, from state and from society, from dearest earthly friends or institutions and brought into direct, personal dealings with God. Everyone must give account of himself to God. There can be no sponsors or deputies or proxies in such vital matter. Each one must repent for himself, and believe for himself, and be baptized for himself, and answer to God for himself, both in time and in eternity. The clarion cry of John the Baptist is to the individual, "Think not to say within yourselves, we have Abraham to our father: For I say unto you that God is able of these stones to raise up children unto Abraham. And now also the axe is laid upon the root of the trees; therefore, every tree that bringeth not forth good fruit is hewn down and cast into the fire."

One man can no more repent and believe and obey Christ for another than he can take the other's place at God's judgment bar. Neither persons nor institutions, however dear and powerful, may dare to come between the individual soul and God. "There is one mediator between God and men, the man Christ Jesus." Let the state and the church, let the institution, however dear, and the person, however near, stand aside, and let the individual soul make its own direct and immediate response to God. One is our pontiff, and His name is Jesus. The undelegated sovereignty of Christ makes it forever impossible for His saving grace to be manipulated by any system of human mediation whatsoever.

The right to private judgment is the crown jewel of humanity, and for any person or institution to dare to come between the soul and God is a blasphemous impertinence and a defamation of the crown rights of the Son of God.

Out of these two fundamental principles, the supreme authority of the Scriptures and the right of private judgment, have come all the historic protests in Europe and England and America against unscriptural creeds, polity and rites, and against the unwarranted and impertinent assumption of religious authority over men's consciences, whether by church or by state. Baptists regard as an enormity any attempt to force the conscience, or to constrain men, by outward penalties, to this or that form or religious belief. Persecution may make men hypocrites, but it will not make them Christians.

INFANT BAPTISM UNTHINKABLE

It follows, inevitably, that Baptists are unalterably opposed to every form of sponsorial religion. If I have fellow Christians in this presence today who are the protagonists of infant baptism, they will allow me frankly to say, and certainly I would say it in the most fraternal, Christian spirit, that to Baptists infant baptism is unthinkable from every viewpoint. First of all, Baptists do not find the slightest sanction for infant baptism in the Word of God. That fact, to Baptists, makes infant baptism a most serious question for the consideration of the whole Christian world. Nor is that all. As Baptists see it, infant baptism tends to ritualize Christianity and reduce it to lifeless forms. It tends also and inevitably, as Baptists see it, to the secularizing of the church and to the blurring and blotting out of the line of demarcation between the church and the unsaved world.

And since I have thus spoken with unreserved frankness, my honored pedobaptist friends in the audience will allow me to say that Baptists solemnly believe that infant baptism, with its implications, has flooded the world and floods it now with untold evils.

They believe also that it perverts the Scriptural symbolism of baptism; that it attempts the impossible task of performing an act of religious obedience by proxy, and that since it forestalls the individual initiative of the child, it carries within it the germ of persecution, and lays the predicate for the union of church and state, and it is a Romish tradition and a cornerstone for the whole system of popery throughout the world.

I will speak yet another frank word for my beloved Baptist

people, to our cherished fellow Christians who are not Baptists, and that word is that our Baptist people believe that if all the Protestant denominations would once for all put away infant baptism, and come to the full acceptance and faithful practice of New Testament baptism, that the unity of all the non-Catholic Christians in the world would be consummated, and that there would not be left one Roman Catholic church on the face of the earth at the expiration of the comparatively short period of another century.

Surely, in the face of these frank statements, our non-Baptist neighbors may apprehend something of the difficulties compelling Baptists when they are asked to enter into official alliances with those who hold such fundamentally different views from those just indicated. We call God to witness that our Baptist people have an unutterable longing for Christian union, and believe Christian union will come, but we are compelled to insist that if this union is to be real and effective, it must be based upon a better understanding of the Word of God and a more complete loyalty to the will of Christ as revealed in His Word.

THE ORDINANCES ARE SYMBOLS

Again, to Baptists, the New Testament teaches that salvation through Christ must precede membership in His church, and must precede the observance of the two ordinances in His church, namely, baptism and the Lord's Supper. These ordinances are for the saved and only for the saved. These two ordinances are not sacramental, but symbolic. They are teaching ordinances, portraying in symbol truths of immeasurable and everlasting moment to humanity. To trifle with these symbols, to pervert their forms and at the same time to pervert the truths they are designed to symbolize, is indeed a most serious matter.

Without ceasing and without wavering, Baptists are, in conscience, compelled to contend that these two teaching ordinances shall be maintained in the churches just as they were placed there in the wisdom and authority of Christ. To change these two meaningful symbols is to change their Scriptural intent and content, and thus pervert them and, we solemnly believe, to be the carriers of the most deadly heresies. By our loyalty to Christ, which we hold to be the supreme test of our friendship for Him, we must unyieldingly contend for these two ordinances as they were originally given to Christ's churches.

THE CHURCH A PURE DEMOCRACY

To Baptists, the New Testament also clearly teaches that Christ's church is not only a spiritual body but it is also a pure democracy, all its members being equal, a local congregation, and cannot subject itself to any outside control. Such terms, therefore, as "The American Church," or "The bishop of this city or state," sound strangely incongruous to Baptist ears. In the very nature of the case, also, there must be no union between church and state, because their nature and functions are utterly different.

Jesus stated the principle in the two sayings, "My kingdom is not of this world," and "Render unto Caesar the things that are Caesar's, and unto God the things that are God's." Never, anywhere, in any clime, has a true Baptist been willing, for one minute, for the union of church and state, never for a moment. . . .

ABSOLUTISM VERSUS INDIVIDUALISM

The student of history cannot fail to observe that through the long years two ideas have been in endless antagonism—the idea of absolutism and the idea of individualism, the idea of autocracy and the idea of democracy. The idea of autocracy is that supreme power is vested in the few, who, in turn, delegate this power to the many. That was the dominant idea of the Roman Empire, and upon that idea the Caesars built their throne. That idea has found world-wide impression in the realms both civil and ecclesiastical. Often have the two ideas, absolutism versus individualism, autocracy versus democracy, met in battle.

Autocracy dared, in the morning of the twentieth century, to crawl out of its ugly lair and propose to substitute the law of the jungles for the law of human brotherhood. For all time to come the hearts of men will stand aghast upon every thought of this incomparable death drama, and at the same time they will renew the vow that the few shall not presumptuously tyrannize over the many; that the law of human brotherhood and not the law of the jungle shall be given supremacy in all human affairs. And until the principle of democracy, rather than the principle of autocracy, shall be regnant in the realm of religion, our mission shall be commanding and unending.

THE REFORMATION INCOMPLETE

The coming of the sixteenth century was the dawning of a new hope for the world. With that century came the Protestant Reformation. Yonder goes Luther with his theses, which he nails over the old church door in Wittenberg, and the echoes of the mighty deed shake the Papacy, shake Europe, shake the whole world. Luther was joined by Melanchthon and Calvin and Zwingli and other mighty leaders. Just at this point emerges one of the most outstanding anomalies of all history. Although Luther and his compeers protested vigorously against the errors of Rome, yet when these mighty men came out of Rome—and mighty men they were—they brought with them some of the grievous errors of Rome. The Protestant Reformation of the sixteenth century was sadly incomplete—it was a case of arrested development. Although Luther and his compeers grandly sounded out the battle cry of justification by faith alone, yet they retained the doctrine of infant baptism and a state church. They shrank from the logical conclusions of their own theses.

In Zurich there stands a statue in honor of Zwingli, in which he is represented with a Bible in one hand and a sword in the other. That statue was the symbol of the union between church and state. The same statue might have been reared to Luther and his fellow reformers. Luther and Melanchthon fastened a state church upon Germany, and Zwingli fastened it upon Switzerland. Knox and his associates fastened it upon Scotland.

Henry VIII bound it upon England, where it remains even till this very hour.

These mighty reformers turned out to be persecutors like the Papacy before them. Luther unloosed the dogs of persecution against the struggling and faithful Anabaptists. Calvin burned Servetus, and to such awful deed Melancthon gave his approval. Louis XIV revoked the Edict of Nantes, shut the doors of all the Protestant churches, and outlawed the Huguenots. Germany put to death that mighty Baptist leader, Balthaser Hubmaier, while Holland killed her noblest statesman, John of Barneveldt, and condemned to life imprisonment her ablest historian, Hugo Grotius, for conscience' sake. In England, John Bunyan was kept in jail for twelve long, weary years because of his religion, and when we cross the mighty ocean separating the Old World and the New, we find the early pages of American history crimsoned with the stories of religious persecutions. The early colonies of America were the forum of the working out of the most epochal battles that earth ever knew for the triumph of religious and civil liberty.

AMERICA AND RELIGIOUS AND CIVIL LIBERTY

Just a brief glance at the struggle in those early colonies must now suffice us. Yonder in Massachusetts, Henry Dunster, the first president of Harvard, was removed from the presidency because he objected to infant baptism. Roger Williams was banished, John Clarke was put in prison, and they publicly whipped Obadiah Holmes on Boston Common. In Connecticut the lands of our Baptist fathers were confiscated and their goods sold to build a meeting house and support a preacher of another denomination.

In old Virginia, "mother of states and statesmen," the battle for religious and civil liberty was waged all over her nobly historic territory, and the final triumph recorded there was such as to write imperishable glory upon the name of Virginia until the last syllable of recorded time. Fines and imprisonments and

persecutions were everywhere in evidence in Virginia for conscience' sake. If you would see a record incomparably interesting, go read the early statutes in Virginia concerning the
Established Church and religion, and trace the epic story of the
history-making struggles of that early day. If the historic records are to be accredited, those clergymen of the Established
Church in Virginia made terrible inroads in collecting fines in
Baptist tobacco in that early day. It is quite evident, however,
that they did not get all the tobacco.

On and on was the struggle waged by our Baptist fathers for
religious liberty in Virginia, in the Carolinas, in Georgia, in
Rhode Island and Massachusetts and Connecticut, and elsewhere,
with one unyielding contention for unrestricted religious liberty
for all men, and with never one wavering note. They dared to
be odd, to stand alone, to refuse to conform, though it cost them
suffering and even life itself.

They dared to defy traditions and customs, and deliberately
chose the way of nonconformity, even though in many a case
it meant a cross. They pleaded and suffered, they offered their
protests and remonstrances and memorials, and, thank God,
mighty statesmen were won to their contention, Washington
and Jefferson and Madison and Patrick Henry, and many others,
until at last it was written into our country's Constitution that
church and state must in this land be forever separate and free,
that neither must ever trespass upon the distinctive functions of
the other. It was pre-eminently a Baptist achievement.

A LONELY STRUGGLE

Glad are our Baptist people to pay their grateful tribute to their
fellow Christians of other religious communions for all their
sympathy and help in this sublime achievement. Candor compels me to repeat that much of the sympathy of other religious
leaders in that early struggle was on the side of legalized ecclesiastical privilege. Much of the time were Baptists pitiably lonely
in their age-long struggle. We would now and always make
our most grateful acknowledgment to any and all who came to

the side of our Baptist fathers, whether early or late, in this destiny-determining struggle. But I take it that every informed man on the subject, whatever his religious faith, will be willing to pay tribute to our Baptist people as being the chief instrumentality in God's hands in winning the battle in America for religious liberty. . . .

There comes now the clarion call to us to be the right kind of citizens. Happily, the record of our Baptist people toward civil government has been a record of unfading honor. Their love and loyalty to country have not been put to shame in any land. In the long list of published Tories in connection with the Revolutionary War there was not one Baptist name. . . .

HUMANE AND RIGHTEOUS LAWS

Challenging to the highest degree is the call that comes to legislators. They are to see to it continually, in all their legislative efforts, that their supreme concern is for the highest welfare of the people. Laws humane and righteous are to be fashioned and then to be faithfully regarded. Men are playing with fire if they lightly fashion their country's laws and then trifle in their obedience to such laws. Indeed, all citizens, the humblest and the most prominent alike, are called to give their best thought to the maintenance of righteousness everywhere. Much truth is there in the widely quoted saying: "Our country is afflicted with the bad citizenship of good men." The saying points its own clear lesson. "When the righteous are in authority, the people rejoice, but when the wicked bear rule, the people mourn." The people, all the people, are inexorably responsible for the laws, the ideals, and the spirit that are necessary for the making of a great and enduring civilization. Every man of us is to remember that it is righteousness that exalteth a nation, and that it is sin that reproaches and destroys a nation.

God does not raise up a nation to go selfishly strutting and forgetful of the high interests of humanity. National selfishness leads to destruction as truly as does individual selfishness. Nations can no more live to themselves than can individuals. Humanity is bound up together in the big bundle of life. The world is now one big neighborhood. There are no longer any hermit nations.

National isolation is no longer possible in the earth. The markets of the world instantly register every commercial change. An earthquake in Asia is at once registered in Washington City. The people on one side of the world may not dare to be indifferent to the people on the other side. Every man of us is called to be a world citizen, and to think and act in world terms. The nation that insists upon asking that old murderous question of Cain, "Am I my brother's keeper?"—the question of the profiteer and the question of the slacker, is a nation marked for decay and doom and death. The parable of the good Samaritan is heaven's law for nations as well as for individuals. Some things are worth dying for, and if they are worth dying for they are worth living for. The poet was right when he sang:

> Though love repine and reason chafe,
> There comes a voice without reply,
> 'Tis man's perdition to be safe,
> When for the truth he ought to die.

THINGS WORTH DYING FOR

When this nation went into the world war a little while ago, after her long and patient and fruitless effort to find another way of conserving righteousness, the note was sounded in every nook and corner of our country that some things in this world are worth dying for, and if they are worth dying for they are worth living for. What are some of the things worth dying for? The sanctity of womanhood is worth dying for. The safety of childhood is worth dying for, and when Germany put to death that first helpless Belgian child she was marked for defeat and doom. The integrity of one's country is worth dying for. And, please God, the freedom and honor of the United States of America are worth dying for. If the great things of life are worth dying for, they are surely worth living for. Our great country may not dare to isolate herself from all the rest of the world, and selfishly say: "We propose to live and to die to ourselves, leaving all the other nations with their weaknesses and burdens and sufferings to go their ways without our help." This nation cannot pursue any such policy and expect the favor of God. Myriads of voices, both from the living and the dead, summon us to a higher and better way. Happy am I to believe that God has His prophets not only in the pulpits of the churches but also in the schoolroom, in the editor's chair, in the halls of legislation, in the marts of commerce, in the realms of literature. Tennyson was a prophet when, in *Locksley Hall,* he sang:

> Till the war drum throbbed no longer, and the battle
> flags were furled,
> In the Parliament of Man, the Federation of the world.

A LEAGUE OF NATIONS

Tennyson believed in a league of nations, and well might he so believe, because God is on His righteous throne, and inflexible are His purposes touching righteousness and peace, for a weary, sinning, suffering, dying world. Standing here today on the steps of our nation's capitol, hard by the chamber of the Senate of the United States, I dare to say as a citizen and as a Christian teacher, that the moral forces of the United States of America, without regard to political parties, will never rest until there is a worthy League of Nations. I dare to express also the unhesitating belief that the unquestioned majorities of both great political parties in this country regard the delay in the working out of a League of Nations as a national and worldwide tragedy. . . .

THE RIGHT KIND OF CHRISTIANS

This noble doctrine and heritage of religious liberty calls to us imperiously to be the right kind of Christians. Let us never forget that a democracy, whether civil or religious, has not only its perils, but has also its unescapable obligations. A democracy calls for intelligence. The sure foundations of states must be

laid, not in ignorance, but in knowledge. It is of the last importance that those who rule shall be properly trained. In a democracy, a government of the people and by the people, the people
are the rulers, and the people, all the people, are to be informed
and trained.

My fellow Christians, we must hark back to our Christian
schools, and see to it that these schools are put on worthy and
enduring foundations. A democracy needs more than intelligence, it needs Christ. He is the light of the world, nor is there
any other sufficient light for the world. He is the solution of
the world's complex questions, the one adequate Helper for its
dire needs, the one only sufficient Saviour for our sinning race.
Our schools are afresh to take note of this supreme fact, and
they are to be fundamentally and aggressively Christian. Wrong
education brought on the recent world war. Such education
will always lead to disaster.

Pungent were the recent words of Mr. Lloyd George: "The
most formidable foe that we had to fight in Germany was not
the arsenals of Krupp, but the schools of Germany." The educational center of the world will no longer be in the Old World,
but because of the great war, such center will henceforth be in
this New World of America. We must build here institutions of
learning that will be shot through and through with the principles and motives of Christ, the one Master over all mankind.

THE CHRISTIAN SCHOOL

The time has come when, as never before, our beloved denomination should worthily go out to its world task as a teaching
denomination. That means that there should be a crusade
throughout all our Christian schools. The only complete education, in the nature of the case, is Christian education, because
man is a tripartite being. By the very genius of our government,
education by the state cannot be complete. Wisdom has fled
from us if we fail to magnify, and magnify now, our Christian
schools. These schools go to the foundation of all the life of the
people. They are indispensable to the highest efficiency of the

churches. Their inspirational influences are of untold value to the schools conducted by the state, to which schools also we must ever give our best support. It matters very much, do you not agree, who shall be the leaders, and what the standards in the affairs of civil government and in the realm of business life. One recalls the pithy saying of Napoleon to Marshal Ney: "An army of deer led by a lion is better than an army of lions led by a deer." Our Christian schools are to train not only our religious leaders but hosts of our leaders in the civil and business realm as well.

The one transcending inspiring influence in civilization is the Christian religion. By all means, let the teachers and trustees and student bodies of all our Christian schools remember this supremely important fact that civilization without Christianity is doomed. Let there be no pagan ideals in our Christian schools, and no hesitation or apology for the insistence that the one hope for the individual, the one hope for society, for civilization, is in the Christian religion. If ever the drumbeat of duty sounded clearly, it is calling to us now to strengthen and magnify our Christian schools.

THE TASK OF EVANGELISM

Preceding and accompanying the task of building our Christian schools, we must keep faithfully and practically in mind our primary task of evangelism, the work of winning souls from sin unto salvation, from Satan unto God. This work takes precedence of all other work in the Christian program. Salvation for sinners is through Jesus Christ alone, nor is there any other name or way under heaven whereby they may be saved. Our churches, our schools, our religious papers, our hospitals, every organization and agency of the churches should be kept aflame with the passion of New Testament evangelism.

Our cities and towns and villages and country places are to echo continually with the sermons and songs of the gospel evangel. The people, high and low, rich and poor, the foreigners, all the people are to be faithfully told of Jesus and His great salvation, and entreated to come unto Him to be saved by Him and to become His fellow workers. The only sufficient solvent for all the questions in America, individual, social, economic, industrial, financial, political, educational, moral and religious, is to be found in the Saviourhood and Lordship of Jesus Christ. . . .

A WORLD PROGRAM

While thus caring for the homeland, we are at the same time to see to it that our program is coextensive with Christ's program for the whole world. The whole world is our field, nor may we with impunity dare to be indifferent to any section, however remote, not a whit less than that; and with our plans sweeping the whole earth, we are to go forth with believing faith and obedient service, to seek to bring all humanity, both near and far, to the faith and service of Him who came to be the propitiation for our sins, and not for ours only, but also for the sins of the whole world.

His commission covers the whole world and reaches to every human being. Souls in China, and India, and Japan, and Europe, and Africa, and the islands of the sea, are as precious to Him as souls in the United States. By the love we bear our Saviour, by the love we bear our fellows, by the greatness and preciousness of the trust committed to us, we are bound to take all the world upon our hearts and to consecrate our utmost strength to bring all humanity under the sway of Christ's redeeming love. Let us go to such task, saying with the immortal Wesley, "The world is my parish," and with him may we also be able to say, "And best of all, God is with us."

A GLORIOUS DAY

Glorious it is, my fellow Christians, to be living in such a day as this, if only we shall live as we ought to live. Irresistible is the conviction that the immediate future is packed with amazing possibilities. We can understand the cry of Rupert Brooke as he sailed from Gallipoli, "Now God be thanked who hath matched us with this hour!" The day of the reign of the common people is everywhere coming like the rising tides of the ocean. The people are everywhere breaking with feudalism. Autocracy is passing, whether it be civil or ecclesiastical. Democracy is the goal toward which all feet are traveling, whether in state or in church.

The demands upon us now are enough to make an archangel tremble. Themistocles had a way of saying that he could not sleep at night for thinking of Marathon. What was Marathon compared to a day like this? John C. Calhoun, long years ago, stood there and said to his fellow workers in the National Congress: "I beg you to lift up your eyes to the level of the conditions that now confront the American republic." Great as was that day spoken of by Mr. Calhoun, it was as a tiny babe beside a giant compared to the day that now confronts you and me. Will we be alert to see our day and faithful enough to measure up to its high demands?

THE PRICE TO BE PAID

Are we willing to pay the price that must be paid to secure for humanity the blessings they need to have? We say that we have seen God in the face of Jesus Christ, that we have been born again, that we are the true friends of Christ, and would make proof of our friendship for Him by doing His will. Well, then, what manner of people ought we to be in all holy living and godliness? Surely we should be a holy people, remembering the apostolic characterization, "Ye are a chosen generation, a royal priesthood, an holy nation, a peculiar people: That we should shew forth the praises of Him who hath called you out of darkness into His marvelous light, who in time past were not a people but are now the people of God." . . .

If in such spirit we will give ourselves to all the duties that await us, then we may go our ways, singing more vehemently than our fathers sang them, those lines of Whittier:

"Our fathers to their graves have gone,
Their strife is passed, their triumphs won;
But greater tasks await the race
Which comes to take their honored place,
A moral warfare with the crime
And folly of an evil time.

"So let it be, in God's own sight,
We gird us for the coming fight;
And strong in Him whose cause is ours,
In conflict with unholy powers,
We grasp the weapons He has given,
The light and truth and love of Heaven."

W. O. CARVER (1868-1954)

WILLIAM OWEN CARVER, *clear thinker, masterful teacher, missionary statesman, attained tremendous influence in the thinking of thousands of Baptist preachers through his long years (1896-1943) of teaching in Southern Baptist Seminary. He was emeritus professor, and very active until his death in 1954. He was a member of the American Theological Committee, a subsidiary of the World Conference on Faith and Order. Author of many books and articles. Our selection was chosen for timeliness and as illustrative of the scholarship and incisiveness of Professor Carver's mind and in hope that further study will follow this stimulating discussion, with which, of course, many may disagree.*

Introductory Chapter to *What Is the Church?*

INTRODUCTION TO DOCTRINE OF THE CHURCH

The nature of the Church is at the very center of urgent theological considerations at present. Its importance grows out of several aspects of world conditions and of their impact on, and challenge to, organized Christianity.

First of all is the fact of the unfinished task of the Christian gospel. This is pressed in on the consciousness of alert Christians by the surging tides of materialism and of revolution which are more universal and more radical than ever before in history. Any who are not blind to the confused assertiveness of peoples throughout the world are forced to recognize this fact. After eighteen centuries of gospel expansion, humanity is still largely unevangelized and still pagan in its pattern of living. One cannot escape the question of whether the churches have properly envisioned and seriously assumed the responsibilities of their meaning and message in the mind of the redeeming Christ.

As Christians face the questions that arise, they see how relatively ineffective their influence on the life of the world is. There is need for all to recognize the weakness of the present Christian movement in organization, concepts, and methods for giving a full Christian witness in "this present evil age."

At the same time, no man who shares in any adequate measure the passion of Christ can overlook the need of the world in every way for the witness of the Christian gospel.

The demand for unity of spirit and aim within organized Christianity, and the ever-increasing demands for institutional and organizational union of Protestantism make the matter of the true nature of the church of Jesus Christ a matter of primary concern to all who take their Christianity seriously. Within the last sixty years interest in the subject of "divided Christendom" has been growing gradually until "the ecumenical movement" now holds the center of attention for many Christian leaders.

The urgent efforts of evangelical leadership in the last quarter century to organize institutional Christianity around some common center have brought awareness of the key importance of "the church." But while this is true, discussions have made clear that there is confusion as to the nature of the church. The connotation of the term is obscure among those who are eager to work toward unification of the evangelical witness of this age.

THE NEW TESTAMENT FOUNDATION

By no means is there general agreement among leaders of various denominations that the New Testament provides an authoritative norm for the nature and functions of the church, but it is coming to be recognized that there is no other starting point for exploring the possibilities of union or even of unity. All Christians bring to New Testament study conceptions and misconceptions which have developed in the course of their varied and divergent denominational histories. Specific forms, traditions, and dogmatic formulas have not only become dear but also have conditioned thinking until they may be regarded as absolute truths.

An objective, inductive study of the New Testament will yield no explicit, detailed description of the church. Basic principles underlie all the New Testament writings; for details and uniformity, students seek in vain. The apostles and prophets and pastors and teachers in the New Testament era did not think in the terms of twentieth-century problems about the church. Many today demand detailed authority, but the inspired writers seem to have lacked any sense of this need. Apart from embryonic movements, the New Testament leaders knew no denominational-type divisions. Tendencies in that direction were opposed with great earnestness, dealt with in the spirit of love and fellowship, and checked short of any actual division throughout the apostolic period.

Since the New Testament nowhere has an explicit definition or description of the church, basic and determinative criteria must be reached by inductive study of the New Testament books. Dogmatic affirmations based on modern ideas and forms cannot be accepted as determinative. They are the result of developments in the course of history under influences narrowing the significance of Christ's incarnation and the divine nature of the true Christian movement. Multiple lines of historical development have given rise to the conflicting ecclesiological theories and ecclesiastical forms of present-day organized Christianity.

The teachings of Jesus in the Gospels contain nothing explicit about the church. Only one of the four evangelists recalled that Jesus used the term "church," and he recorded its use on only two occasions. In the first of these (Matt. 16), the concept is wholly spiritual and its origin attributed definitely to divine revelation. The second instance (Matt. 18) implies, without any explanation, a brotherhood having social and organizational aspects. There also is implied very definitely a supersocial, divinely induced quality. Without using the term "church" or offering a definition of any equivalent, the other Gospels assume the spiritual reality that constitutes the church.

Acts, "the Gospel of the Holy Spirit," is the first chapter in the history of the expansion of the gospel and the Christian movement under the guidance and by the power of the Spirit. Again no attention is devoted to the nature of the church as such. Rather, there are simple records of facts, acts, and incidental information as to organization, leaders (never officials) and functional activities of the apostles, prophets, evangelists, and the experiences and witness of other believers.

In the Epistles the churches have organizations, and the forms of their organizations are taken for granted. They are never defined or described in any detail. Bishops and deacons as such are recognized only in Philippians and the pastoral epistles. It is going quite beyond recorded facts to find anything approaching the idea of "orders of the ministry" in any part of the New Testament. "Elders" are named in Acts 11 as recipients of the relief funds brought from Antioch. There is no previous mention of them and no description of their function.

Deacons had been chosen earlier, and their qualities and qualifications are described in Acts 6. Even there they are not so named, but the name is implied in the use of the verb. Their duties arose out of an emergency situation. There is no indication that they were considered officers or that their role was continued after the emergency. The function of these, enlarged under a later emergency, was vested in the "elders" mentioned in Acts 11. In both cases, and as a principle in all similar cases, these were not officials. Rather, they were servants of the brotherhood. There are lists of offices and functions within the brotherhood in Romans 12, I Corinthians 12, and Ephesians 4. These differ widely, and the study of the differences leads to two conclusions: first, that there was no standard form, imposed or recognized, for the details of church organization; second, that there was no emphasis on official status or standing. The emphasis is in every case on service in the interest of the unity, the harmony, and the effectiveness of the church as the witness of the redeeming gospel.

All four classes of leadership mentioned in Ephesians are "gifts" of the risen, ascended, and administering Christ in order to develop a devoted, redeemed humanity. The functions of these four groups all tend primarily to the extension and the establishment of Christian centers in various geographical divisions. The first three have to do with bringing the gospel to new regions and helping those who receive it to begin Christian living. The work of "apostles, prophets, evangelists" prepares for, and culminates in, the work of "pastors and teachers" (two functions of the same group). These latter lead in the developing of the converts in their duties, their function, their organization, their Christian living "worthy of the gospel." Paul said that the function of each group looks to the equipment of all the saints for the work of ministering. The ultimate end is a continuous, harmonious, effective progress of the entire body, ever increasing in love as it becomes the "body of the Christ."

Although it provides no definition or detailed description of the church, the New Testament does use various terms which, by direct implication and by rich and varied symbolism, provide materials for understanding the nature of the church, universal and local. Most of the information available, of course, deals with details of the function and of the conduct of churches as local organizations. These are "the churches of God," as in Corinthians and Revelation. They are the "churches of Christ" and often simply "the church" or "the churches." While never called churches of the Holy Spirit, their relation to the Spirit is abundantly implied and declared. He works in them and through them as the power of God, the interpreter of Christ, the guide, the purifier, and developer of the church bodies.

The universal church and its local manifestations as congregations are distinctly divine in origin and in meaning. They are God's creation, the people of God, and of his Christ. They constitute a new humanity produced, preserved, and empowered as God's representative in the midst of "all the families of the earth." The church is the congregation of the true Israel of God, continuing, interpreting, and supplanting the Old Testament Israel in terms of "God's saints in Christ Jesus."

The description of Israel in the plan of God in Exodus 19:4-6 is appropriated almost word for word in I Peter 2:8-10 as the description of the body of Christian believers. In the Old Testament God's people are frequently called "God's heritage," and Paul used the same term for the Christian Church in Ephesians. Recent emphasis is sound in recognizing the historical and spiritual unity of the people of God in the Old Testament and in the New Testament. Yet it is not always clearly seen that Jesus at the close of his ministry (Matt. 21-22), with two powerful parables to illustrate his point, explicitly repudiated Israel—as understood by Jewish leaders of his day. Jewish people as such were no longer to be the husbandmen of God's vineyard. This new Israel was the new creation of God in Christ Jesus. It was to be the church of God in Christ Jesus.

This "new humanity" consists of those who have accepted God's grace and have committed themselves to it. Because of their dedication, they are designated throughout the New Testament by the term "saints." These sanctified individuals voluntarily unite—as a church in the local sense—to give expression to their common experience of redemption, through worship, fellowship, and witnessing to the gospel of the Lord Jesus Christ.

Fellowship or brotherhood is the outstanding characteristic of New Testament Christians and of all Christians of succeeding ages to the degree that they are truly Christian.

Each group of believers becomes in its own location the body of Christ. Each is "distinctly a temple of God in the Holy Spirit" and is so sacred that whoever destroys it will himself be destroyed (I Cor. 3:17). Its unity, its fellowship, its representative character is such that factions and divisions in that body divide Christ and bring his condemnation (I Cor. 10:14). Each member of each church is "baptized into the fellowship" and repudiates or neglects that fellowship to his own sickness and even spiritual death. Paul emphasized this by teaching that participation in the Lord's Supper is "fellowship in the body of Christ," whose unity is symbolized and enforced by the one loaf and the one cup.

The congregation, a local manifestation of the church, begins in, and follows from the fact that the total body of the redeemed constitutes the continuing, growing body of Christ. While the exact expression is never used, this comprehensive spiritual church is the continuation of the incarnation. In the book of Ephesians Christ and the church are so intimately related as to constitute one entity, neither being complete except in relation to the other. It is "in the church and in Christ Jesus" that God is to be glorified throughout all generations of the age of the ages. By the fact of his salvation the believer becomes a member of the church, "a member of the body of Christ." Under the impulse of the Spirit, this member of the spiritual church voluntarily takes his place in the local fellowship and assumes his responsibility as a Christian in that church, for that local church is a concrete, organized expression of the one spiritual church. This conception of the one church as the body of the Christ is more than a figure of speech. It is a spiritual reality apart from which there is no salvation and no true Christianity.

This total fellowship of the saints, this new humanity, is God's "household," his "family," his "commonwealth," of which all believers are alike members, whatever their social or religious background. All of these children of God created in Christ Jesus constitute the temple of God in the earth for his indwelling (Eph. 2). In the measure of its genuineness and integration and unity and love and its loyalty to its Head, each congregation is, in its situation, God's local humanity, Christ's local body, God's temple. Each local congregation is for its community "the pillar and ground of the truth." It is an association of evangelistic witnesses; it is the guardian of the "true gospel."

The unity and glory of the spiritual church as the body of Christ is emphasized in Ephesians 5, where the relation between Christ and his church is set out as the ideal for that between husband and wife. In view of the Biblical figure of the church as Christ's bride, the insistence of some that all uses of the term "church" in the New Testament refer only to local organizations becomes absurd almost to the point of sacrilege, attributing to Christ a bride in every locality where a church is found. Likewise the term "body of Christ" in Ephesians 1 and 2 cannot be restricted to local organized bodies. How can one conceive of any one local church as being "the full expression of him who is fulfilling all things in all respects"? How can one conceive of independent local bodies as growing into "one holy temple of God in the Holy Spirit," especially when the whole context of the paragraph emphasizes the unity of all members of the new human race produced by the cross of Christ? How can the concept of the church in the development of Chapter 3 be limited to the independent local body which is to attain "unto all the fullness of God"? How can this limited group be the medium of God's glory forever "in the church and in Christ Jesus"? How can the "one body" as presented in the transcendent concepts of Ephesians 4:1-16 be restricted at any point to a local church?

HISTORIC MISINTERPRETATIONS

The church as it has developed through history and as it stands "in the present divided state of Christendom" has experienced radical misinterpretations, and these misinterpretations now dominate the scene and hinder progress toward "the unity of the Spirit in the bond of peace," which more and more clamors for recognition and expression.

The first and most persistent and damaging is the theory of

treating the church as an institution. Some of the more radical evils of this misconception I have discussed in my book, *The Glory of God in the Christian Calling*. Emil Brunner has, in his recent work, *The Misunderstanding of the Church*, radically exposed the same error. He shows how this mistaken conception works as the inciting factor in the search for unity and especially in all schemes for ecclesiastical union.

Akin to this is the view of the church as primarily an organization. Never in the New Testament is the matter of organization primary, never is it stressed nor even clearly defined in any instance. There are certain dominant principles and ideas which must be preserved if the integrity of the gospel is preserved. Yet these principles and ideas do not find uniform expression in any detailed pattern of organization.

In addition to these misinterpretations of the church as such, certain mistaken emphases within historic Christianity have diverted and corrupted the church. The first of these is authoritative creed. All creeds and all confessions of faith are formulated and adopted in a contemporary context. They well serve their purposes of defining experience and conviction provided they are not taken as timeless, authoritative norms for creating experience and controlling new experience and Christian duty under all conditions and circumstances.

Emphasis on ritual likewise has curbed freedom of spirit and expression of worship and tends to become a hindrance to the Holy Spirit in his direct redemptive activity in individual lives. Creed and ritual too often contribute to lifting the worshipers beyond the obligations, constraints, and restraints of ethical Christianity, and of creative thinking. Ritualism is the great enemy to vital Christianity.

At the heart of the evils of ritual is the concept of the "sacrament." In itself the sacramental conception of the usefulness of material symbols for spiritual meditation and for the development of spiritual insight is not bad—and may be very helpful. This is especially true of the two symbols, baptism and the Lord's Supper, which were practiced in the early churches and which come directly from the teachings of Jesus. However, the tendency to attach magical significance to physical objects results in an interpretation of the "sacraments" that is deceitful, corrupting, and destructive of genuine experience of God.

There also are misconceptions about membership in the Christian church and in the churches. The different views and the variant practices in this matter attest the inherent evils of the departure from the basic individualism of Christian experience and responsibility, without which there can be no vital Christians nor genuine Christianity.

Finally there are misconceptions about the relation of the church and churches to the "kingdom of God" and also to "the people of the covenant of Israel." These latter concepts are distinct from each other, and both have largely been either overlooked or vaguely dealt with by many Christian leaders. They have become items of much study and concern by leaders of the ecumenical movement. Especially are these leaders disturbed and confused over practical questions of fellowship in the Eucharist; and about the relationship of Israel in the Old Testament of the church of the New Testament.

PRESENT IMPLICATIONS

The holy people of God, the Old Testament Israel, reconstituted but continued in the New Testament, are a special creation of God in the midst of, and out of, the human material found in empirical world history. They are an elect race in the body of humanity. In a unique sense the church is the creation and the continuation of the redeeming Christ, Son of the living God. On the rock of this regenerating experience and its relation of men to God in himself as its foundation, Jesus said, "I will build my congregation."

Just as the seed of Abraham were claimed by God from among all the sons of men, the remnant was chosen out of the generally unfaithful people of Israel to be God's heritage. When Christ came to press his claim to his people and his kingdom, he found the descendants of the remnant unfit and unwilling to be his people. Thus he rejected the old remnant and lifted the calling of God above the racial and institutional understanding of the Jews by showing its true meaning, a renewal experience in which man and God are united in Christ. This union of God and believing man, with all its consequences, has for its basic principle "faith working through love." To the old remnant, which had failed to accept and fulfil the purpose of God in history, Jesus declared, "The kingdom of God will be taken away from you and given to a nation producing the fruits of it" (Matt. 21:43, R.S.V.). The new people who would become Christ's "elect race" were the people of his choice, a dedicated people who would exhibit Christ's own excellencies. It was to this new spiritual reality that Christ referred when he spoke of "my church." Here is the primary base for all understanding of the one Christian church and of the local churches in which the one church realizes itself in objective experience and manifestation.

Our Baptist forebears had the right approach in defining the church. They began with the spiritually regenerate church and proceeded to define its individual "societies" as its functional agencies. See, for example, the London Confession of 1689 and its American counterpart, the Philadelphia Confession.

No church in the New Testament is an institution. Nor is any church in the New Testament ever primarily or essentially an organization. The organizations are functional expressions of the underlying reality. Certain kinds of activities grow out of the church's nature and are required for effectiveness under any conditions. Various other activities are required under special conditions: hence the variety in the lists of offices, duties, and gifts in Romans 12:3-8; I Corinthians 12:27-30; and Ephesians 4:11. Only in Philippians 1 and I Timothy 3 are the two officer groups, bishops and deacons, so named. In light of the whole New Testament it cannot be asserted that these two classes of leaders are thought of as officials in the church or even as essential to the reality of a church.

Any true church is primarily a creation of the Spirit of God. God's redemptive act is its starting point, followed by each man's response to God's work. After these events comes the corporate human-divine fellowship. Each church thus has three aspects:

God, the redeemed individual, and the fellowship. And in all these aspects each church should be consciously related to the whole body of Christ, through which God is functioning in redemption.

The church, therefore, is God's "new creation," a new humanity in the midst of unredeemed humanity; a local church is a concrete embodiment of this church.

The church is the extension of the incarnation. A local church is the manifestation of Christ in its community.

The church is the body of Christ, who is himself the fullness of God in redemption; a local church is the functioning of the redeemed body in a fellowship of redeemed men.

The church is the core of God's kingdom as being realized in human history. Local churches are the agencies of that kingdom and of its gospel; thus they are "colonies" of the kingdom of heaven on earth, located in the midst of the world which is to be won through the gospel. They are not only emigration centers for heaven but are also recruiting agencies and training instruments and supervising bodies for the recruits as they become active workers in the gospel.

The wide differences of denominations in organized Christianity—the misplaced emphases which each, in some way, embodies—confront everyone who is conscious of his membership in the body of the Christ with incompatible challenges to loyalty. No one can give unquestioning loyalty to his own denomination and at the same time devote himself fully to the fellowship of the spiritual church. Denominations have within themselves distinctive divisions which cultivate special loyalties. We Baptists are far from recognizing that thoroughgoing loyalty to Christ ought to sanctify and give deeper meaning to our loyalties to our denominational organizations. All Christians are apt to justify their separateness and even isolationism on the ground that they have to be loyal to the truth, claiming that, after all, it is the truth that divides.

Christians are faced constantly with a dilemma. Is it possible for them to be loyal to the truth in the deepest sense without being even more fundamentally loyal to the purpose, the passion, and the person of him who is the Saviour of their souls and the Lord of their lives, the Head of every group that names his name as a church of Jesus Christ? Either there is a living tension or else contentment with lesser loyalty is achieved by some narrowing dogmatism that repudiates full loyalty to Christ as Head of the entire spiritual body.

Here is a problem for all organizations within the Christian movement, one which demands rethinking in the larger light of God's purpose for the world. No local church and no denomination can come into the fullness of Christ's fellowship and experience without relating itself in its thoughts, its prayers, and its plans to all the saints who see the kingdom of God as the realm into which men are brought through the second birth by the working of the Holy Spirit. If any denomination or church shall say, "I am not of the body," is it, therefore, not of the body? If it shall say of any other church or denomination, "You are not of the body," is that other group, therefore, not of the body? If any denomination shall say, "We are alone the body," is that denomination the entire body? Must we not all come to grips with these questions, seeking the guidance of the Word and Spirit of God to strengthen the very imperfect expression the "Christian" world is giving to the meaning and mission of Christ Jesus?

The church in the New Testament never appears as an organized body, nor do the churches ever combine in territorial organizations. From that basic fact Baptists proceed in accepting and developing their call to membership in the spiritual fellowship with all who are in Christ.

BENJAMIN E. MAYS (1895-   )

PRESIDENT MAYS *was graduated with honors from Bates College, Lewiston, Maine, in 1920 and received his Ph.D. degree from the University of Chicago in 1935. He holds also many honorary degrees. Since 1940 he has been president of Morehouse College, Atlanta, one of the outstanding Negro colleges in America. Before that he was dean (1934-40) of the School of Religion of Howard University in Washington. He directed a study of Negro churches in the United States in 1932-34. He is author of eight books and more than fifty scholarly articles. Named "Alumnus of the Year" by the Divinity School of the University of Chicago in 1950. Our selection is the address delivered before the Eighth Congress of the Baptist World Alliance in 1950.*

"Christian Light on Human Relationships"

For nineteen long centuries Christian light has been shining on human relationships. As Goodspeed translates John 1:5, "The Light is still shining in the darkness, for the darkness has never been put out." This statement is applicable to our situation in 1950. War, economic injustice, political corruption, racial bigotry, chaos, confusion, fear, tragedy. "The Light is still shining in the darkness" in 1950 "for the darkness has never been put out." . . .

Christian light reveals a spiritual and ethical order which governs human relationship. Hatred between the two leads to estrangement and unhappiness. The fact that love binds two people together and hatred tears them apart is a discovery one may make but not create.

Whether we like it or not, Christian light reveals that we cannot build the world as we please. God and not man has created the ethical and moral laws that will bring peace between nations —between the United States and Russia. God and not man has created the ethical laws that will guarantee the continued existence of an economic system. God and not man has created the ethical and moral laws that will guarantee the stability of a political order. God and not man has created the kind of justice that will enable one race to live in peace, love, and harmony with another race. Our task is to discover these laws and live by them.

Strangely enough, Hebrew prophecy was born as a result of the sins and injustices in human relationships. Amos began crying out against the exploitation of the poor; Micah began declaring that God requires three things: to do justly, to love mercy, and to walk humbly with God; Jesus began by declaring that he was sent to preach the good news to the poor, to release prisoners, to restore sight to the blind, and to set at liberty the downtrodden.

Throughout the centuries, Christian light has declared that righteousness and not armaments, justice and not economic power, love and not hate, will sustain a people. Embrace these and live, says Christian light; reject them and perish. In the words of the prophet: "Let justice roll down as waters and righteousness as a mighty stream."

We get further light on human relationships when we consider the fact that with Jesus and in Christian experience a man's nationality or race, his occupation, or profession, his class or caste has never been a prerequisite for discipleship. Jesus took ordinary men—fishermen and tax collectors—and made them his disciples. He declared that they were the salt of the earth, the light of the world, and just as it was the function of light to dispel darkness and of salt to preserve and keep things from decay, they were to bring light to a dark world and keep it from corruption and death. It was a fisherman, a man of ordinary work, of whom Jesus declared "Thou art Peter and upon this rock I will build my church and the gates of hell shall not prevail against it." Jesus took ordinary people steeped in the inferiority complex and said to them in essence, "Son of Man, stand on your feet, throw your shoulders back, stand erect, stick your chin out and walk the earth with dignity and pride; for you, too, are sons of the living God."

God has called men from all walks of life to do his work: Abraham, a man of wealth; Moses, the keeper of the flock; Amos, the herdsman from Tekoa; Peter, the fisherman; Paul, the tentmaker; Jesus, the carpenter; Lincoln, the rail splitter; Booker Washington, the slave; and Albert Schweitzer, the learned physician—all have been called to do the mighty works of God.

This light broke upon Peter in his experience with Cornelius when he exclaimed—"of a truth I perceive that God is no respecter of persons, but in every nation he that heareth him, and worketh righteousness, is accepted with him." That God is no respecter of persons is validated in history. When H. G. Wells listed the six great men of history he went to Asia and named Buddha and Asoka. He moved on to Greece and picked up Aristotle. He stepped across to Palestine and named Jesus, a Jew. He traveled on to England and got Roger Bacon and then crossed the Atlantic and named Abraham Lincoln.

It is true that God reached up and took John Milton, somewhat of an aristocrat, and made him a great poet. But it is also true that God reached down and took Shakespeare, the son of a woman who couldn't write her name, and made him the greatest poet of them all. It is true that God reached up and got Cicero and made him a great orator. But it is also true that God reached down and got Horace, the son of a former slave, and made him perhaps the greatest of Roman writers. 'Tis true that God reached up and took wealthy George Washington and made him the father of his country. But it is also true that God reached down in a Kentucky log cabin and made Lincoln a great emancipator. It is true that God reached up and made Winston Churchill one of the world's great; but he also reached down in a two-room log cabin in Scotland and made Ramsay MacDonald one of England's great premiers. He made Schumann-Heink one of the great singers of the world, but he also gave Marian Anderson the voice of the century.

This light broke upon Paul when he smashed the bonds of the law and discovered that God is a God for all the peoples, and said:

"There is neither Jew nor Greek, there is neither bond nor

free, there is neither male nor female, for ye are all one in Christ Jesus."

It is demonstrated further by Jesus himself in the story of the Good Samaritan. The neighbor was not the priest and not the Levite, both of whom were Jews, but rather a Samaritan whom the Jews despised.

This passage throws a brilliant light on human relationships. It proves conclusively that neighborliness is not necessarily defined in terms of nationality or race. But a neighbor is one who responds helpfully and sympathetically to human needs.

The Christian light leads to the inevitable conclusion that God is the father of all and that all men are brothers. If God is a common father and if all men are brothers, then it follows that the human family is one. It belongs together. Even those who hold that God is father of believers only and that only believers are brothers must also hold that nationality and race are not prerequisites for brotherhood.

Christian light penetrates deeper. It is all too easy to preach that all men are brothers and then act as if only some men are brothers. Christian light says: either all men are brothers, or no men are brothers. Either God is the father of all men, or he is the father of no men. Either the lives of all children are sacred, or the life of no child is sacred. If the Americans and the English are brothers, then the Americans and the Germans are brothers. If God is the father of the Italians, he is the father of the Ethiopians. If the life of the richest child is precious, then the life of the poorest child is precious. Either all or none.

In other words, the destiny of each individual wherever he resides on the earth is tied up with the destiny of all men that inhabit the globe. Whether we like it or not we cannot do anything about it. The English poet and cleric, John Donne, has set the idea in language that is immortal:

"No man is an Island, entire of it Selfe;
  Every man is a peece of the Continent,
  A part of the maine;
  If a Clod bee washed away by the Sea,

Europe is the lesse, as well as if a promontorie were,
As well as if a mannor of thy friends or thine owne were:
Any man's death diminishes me, because I am involved in
    mankinde; and therefore never send to know for whom
    the bell tolls;
It tolls for thee."

Everything I have said up to now proves only one thing. It proves that we know pretty well what Christian light is. It has been shining brilliantly across nineteen centuries. It is clear in our minds what kind of human relations should exist among nations. It is also clear that Christian light condemns the inhumanity of man to man in our economic life. It is equally clear that the corruption in political life is condemned by Christian light. We know what Christianity has to say about war and racial discrimination.

Yes, we have light! Christian light and scientific light! We are the most educated people known to history. We have more colleges and universities, more schools of theology, more technical and professional schools than any age in history. We are the most degreed people in the annals of time: D.D.'s, LL.D.'s, M.D.'s, Litt.D.'s, Ph.D.'s—all kinds of D.'s. We know more science than ever before, more physics, chemistry, mathematics, biology than any previous age. We know more philosophy, literature, and religion, and yet we are nearer destruction today than at any previous time. We have plenty of light, but like Pilate, we have more light than faith. Pilate had light—so much light that he admitted that he found no fault in Jesus, but Pilate could not stand up to the light he saw. And herein lies the tragedy of our time!

We know the horrors and tragedies of war. We know that wars are seldom if ever won, that one war sows the seeds for another war, and another and another. We know that World War I laid the foundation of World War II and that World War II laid the foundation of what may be World War III.

We have Christian light on war. And yet we go on fighting and preparing for it. If there is anything we learn from history, it's nothing. Twenty-five or thirty centuries ago when the Egyptians and the Babylonians couldn't settle their difference through peaceful means they fought it out on the battlefield. In 1914 and in 1917 when we could not get together, we fought out our differences on the battlefields of Europe. Twenty centuries ago when the Romans and the Greeks couldn't get together, they went to war. In 1939 and 1941 when we couldn't settle our differences through peaceful means we fought it out on the battlefields of the world.

In 1950 the United Nations, Russia and the United States cannot settle their differences around the conference table, so we are shooting it out on the battlefields of Korea. We have nineteen centuries of Christian light on the subject of war, but the light still shines in darkness, for the darkness has never been put out.

We need more than light. And when war comes, we all become immoral. There is only one issue confronting a nation at war, and that is to win it. If it takes deception to win the war, we deceive. If it takes lying to win it, we lie. If it takes the starving of innocent women and children to win it, we starve them. If it takes the raping of women and girls in order to keep up the morale of the soldiers, we wink at it. If it takes the dropping of atomic bombs to win it, we drop atomic bombs. We all become immoral including the ministers of God. We need more than Christian light.

We have Christian light on cultural and race relations. And yet one of the most enlightened nations in history was responsible for the murder of 6,000,000 Jews. Despite Christian light we have a Christian church in South Africa which justifies its brutal Fascist, Nazi policy by an appeal to Scripture and theology. In Christian United States one of the most segregated institutions in America is God's church—segregated in the North, segregated in the South. Many of our so-called Christian statesmen will fight to the death any move to equalize opportunities for all peoples. It is clear that Christian light is not enough.

When it comes to business in human relations, we have plenty of light; and yet if a man can get ahead of his fellows by exploiting them, we Christians call it "good business." If a man can turn a business deal that will net him a hundred thousand dollars without working for it, we call him a good businessman. A politician running for office is concerned primarily with getting votes. He may appeal to religious or racial prejudice. But if he gets elected, we Christians say, "He is a good politician!" In all these areas, we seldom begin with what is Christian or just, what is right or honorable. We begin by asking what is expedient and how much will the traffic bear.

Christian light is not enough. We need the power of God unto salvation. "Except a man be born again, he cannot see the kingdom of God." Without redemption a man can see the Christian light in human relations and keep on hating his brother. Without redemption, we can know the truth and deliberately lie. Without redemption, we can see the high road beckoning us on and we can deliberately choose the low road. Every honest man knows from experience what Paul meant when he said in essence, I find myself doing that which I know I ought not to do. I find myself failing to do that which I know I ought to do. What is Paul saying? Paul is saying that light is not enough.

What then can we do to be saved? It is the responsibility of the church of Christ to launch an evangelistic campaign to convert men to God. We should begin first with ourselves, the ministers of Christ. Ask God, and mean it, to create within us a clean heart and renew a right Spirit within us. Ask him to purge our souls of sin and corruption. Let us submit our wills to God. We are not ready for an evangelistic campaign until the ministers themselves repent and are purified. . . .

The early Christians had what I have in mind. Their faith and belief in God were not theoretical. They lived them and many died for their beliefs. And in so doing they changed the character of the world. We Christians of 1950 can do the same for our day if we repent of our sins, change our ways, take the offensive for righteousness, and trust God for results.

You may well ask what will happen to us if we do this. I do not know. I cannot tell you what will happen to our positions, nor to our social prestige if we insist that Christian people be thoroughly changed. What will happen to our economic security? I cannot tell you. I cannot even predict what will happen to our lives. But I don't believe that Jesus and Paul, Peter and

John, Amos and Hosea, Luther and Knox, Ridley and Latimer, ever debated the question as to what would happen to them if they did God's will. These questions are beside the point. But if we have faith in Jesus Christ and believe in the Lord God, we will act, seek to do his will, and leave the consequences to him. God will take care of us. We do not follow the light we see because we trust ourselves and things rather than God. Nations trust their armies and navies, their airplanes and submarines and their atomic and hydrogen bombs and not God. If we cannot trust God, if we cannot convert men and women to God, our civilization is doomed. We need faith—the faith of Browning who said: "One who never turned his back, but marched breast forward, never doubted clouds would break, never dreamed though right were worsted wrong would triumph—held, we fail to rise, are baffled to fight better, sleep to wake."

The light is still shining in the darkness, for the darkness has never been put out."

CULBERT G. RUTENBER (1909-   )

PROFESSOR RUTENBER *has taught philosophy of religion at Eastern Baptist Theological Seminary in Philadelphia since 1939. He was a pastor in Camden, New Jersey, for eight years. The address we include was very widely acclaimed by the messengers to the Eighth Baptist World Congress. He is in wide demand as a lecturer in colleges all over the United States.*

"The Totalitarian State and the Individual Conscience" (1950)

. . . The world is going to hell as fast as it can get there. But it absolutely refuses to go there quietly. World disaster is cast in a setting of Wagnerian proportions. Apocalyptic fires light the horizon and thunder and lightning tear the heavens. We are spectators of catastrophe on a global scale. It is not only a civilization that sinks before our eyes. Human history itself is in question. Man with his culture, his pride, his failures and achievements is weighed in the balance. Indeed, to the eye of the secular prophet it must seem that God himself is at stake. Perhaps we have arrived at the last scene of William Vaughn Moody's play, *The Mask of Judgment*. At the rear of an empty stage there rises from the abyss a monster of evil. Waxing larger and larger the evil monster grows until he fills the whole stage. Dethroning God, he reigns supreme.

Eras merge into one another without any exact and sharp dividing line. But if we had to pick an exact date for the real end of the nineteenth century and the real beginning of the twentieth, we could do worse than pitch upon 1917. It was in this year that a sealed train, passing through Germany from Switzerland, hurried Lenin to Russia and revolution. The twentieth century was under way. The totalitarian revolt against modern history had begun.

The totalitarian state is a new factor in human history. Only the twentieth century could have spawned it, because only the twentieth century had the means to produce it. Our modern streamlined tyrannies had to await the rise of modern science before they could be born. It is science that has made possible a dictatorship so all-embracing as to make all previous dictatorships amateurish. For the first time in history, life can be effectively organized from a controlling center. . . .

Emil Brunner says that the totalitarian state is the most urgent problem of our civilization. And so it is. But we must be clear as to why this is so. It is not merely because the totalitarian state challenges the political and military structures of the West. To see the threat at that level is to miss the point. Nor is the menace of totalitarianism found in its challenge to the capitalistic system of free enterprise. To see the threat at this level is also to miss the point. The deadly peril which the Christian church detects in totalitarianism is neither economic, nor political and military.

It is moral. It is the judgment of the omnicompetent state that it robs a man of his God-given humanity and debases him into a mere repeater of slogans, a parrot of the party line with no will nor manhood of his own. The totalitarian state is a plunderer of the mind, a saboteur of the soul.

The following poem which appeared in a 1939 Berlin newspaper indicates what I mean.

"We have captured all the positions
And on the heights we have planted
The banners
Of our revolution.

You had imagined
That was all
That we wanted.

We want more.
We want *all!*
Your hearts are our goal,
It is your souls we want!"

It's your souls we want! Here is the authentic mark of the police state. The struggle between the Christian faith and the totalitarian state is a struggle for the soul and conscience of man. In the words of John Middleton Murry, "Man is called to decide which is indeed God: the God who declares himself in the human conscience, or the God who is incarnate in the State . . . which emancipates by eradicating conscience." For the totalitarian state must arrogate to itself the role of God in the modern world or it cannot survive. "Thou shalt have no other gods before me," commands the police state. And it has the power to be a jealous God, visiting the iniquities of the father upon the children unto the third and fourth generation. Are the attributes of deity omnipotence, omniscience, and omnipresence? These are the attributes of the deified state. It claims an absolute power over its subjects; it is the infallible guide of conduct; and its eyes and ears are everywhere. Like the true God, the new God effects a rebirth in the hearts of its worshipers, reconditioning the reflexes of the masses until they want no more. Moreover, it is the giver of every good and perfect gift. The state giveth and the state taketh away, blessed be the name of the state.

A human institution that makes pretensions of deity can brook no opposition. That is why the real enemy which must be liquidated is individual conscience. A conscience that dares to say No to the state because it has said Yes to God is intolerable. In the very nature of the case, the totalitarian state must itself be the definer of justice, the creator of right and wrong. Hence totalitarianism is a systematic effort to exterminate the human conscience. A man's soul must be eviscerated; his humanity stamped out of him. The image of God in man must be erased and for it must be substituted the faceless image of the mass man. Like a trained animal the creature must be made to respond in determinate ways to certain stimuli. He must be taught when to cheer and when to boo; when to shout and when to keep silent. He must have no will of his own, only a sense of identity and participation. The terrifying truth about totalitarian man, the truth without which we cannot understand him, is that he has no conscience. His personal integrity has been eaten away. Like the Cheshire cat, his substantial reality has vanished, leaving only certain functions remaining. The totalitarian man can flipflop with the changes of the party line, embrace evil as good, call falsehood his truth—and without batting an eye. The soul has fled, leaving only a depraved organism.

Against the terrifying power of suppression and torture which the police state commands, the individual conscience seems pathetically weak. But let us not sell it short. For God hath chosen the foolish things of the world to confound the wise. And God hath chosen the weak things of the world to confound the things that are mighty. Allan Hunter speaks of noting a tiny weed flourishing exultantly in a crack in the well-worn pavement of busy Los Angeles. His comment upon the sight is illuminating: "Defenseless, unsupported by high-powered promotion, the undaunted weed was quietly exhibiting a commodity which our frightened world craves but neither Hollywood nor Wall Street, neither the Kremlin nor Rome, is able to produce, conscript or impose; and that is the radical audacity of faith." The radical audacity of faith! As long as conscience has *that* dictators can never quite trample it into nothingness. For it is by faith that the Christian and his ever-insistent conscience lives.

To the totalitarian claims of the State the Christian opposes the totalitarian claims of Christ—absolute and all-embracing, gathering into one surrendered focus every area and energy of life. The Christian knows a secret—Jesus Christ is Lord. And the kingdoms of this world will yet become the kingdoms of our God and of his Christ; and He shall reign forever and ever. The power of the beast that wars against the saints and puts his mark of slavery and degradation upon the foreheads of men is a limited and finite power that will come to an end. The lamb that was slain shall yet be enthroned. He shall take his great power and reign over the hearts of men as the king of love and truth.

But we are living in the day of battle and not the day of triumph. And to us who bear the heat of the day comes the call to strengthen those things that remain. This will not be easy. The substance of the church has been wasted in worldly living; and the weapons of its warfare are rusty with neglect. But there is yet hope if the church everywhere will address itself to the defense of the individual conscience against those forces that seek to destroy it. We must rebuild the moral foundation of modern life, without which civilization cannot survive. Such an effort will take us into at least three areas: the political, the moral, and the spiritual.

On the political front, we must guard at all cost our political freedom. Surely one thing that recent history has demonstrated clearly is the primacy of the political. Political man has supplanted economic man. Where the government can define right and wrong in economic matters, the advantage rests with the power of the political. It should be now clear everywhere that political liberty is the source and guarantor, under God, of all of our other liberties. I do not think that democracy is the only kind of government in which Christianity can live. After all, the church was born in a dictatorship. But for the last four hundred years the power of the state has been steadily growing. And today the power of the state has become so great, that wherever political freedom is imperiled, the freedom of the church and freedom of conscience itself is threatened.

It is one of the terrifying facts of the police state that it can effectually block every avenue of moral protest. This is a new fact in history. As Bertrand Russell has pointed out, in the totalitarian state the moral reformer could not acquire any influence even by martyrdom. His doctrine would never become known, for every channel for its proclamation would be denied him and he himself would be liquidated. In such a state, Christianity could never have been born, for it would have had no means of coming to birth. This is the measure of the importance of the political in our time. Therefore let no Christian say any more, "I'm interested in spiritual things; I'm not interested in politics." No Christian can today evade his political responsibility. To do so is to deny his Lord. Political freedom is the foundation for all other freedoms, including the freedom of conscience.

Knowing this, the Christian in society will be sensitive to trends which might presage future trouble. He will guard jealously existing civil rights. He will resist efforts to establish guilt by association. He will protest all efforts, however subtle, to make people think alike and believe alike. Nor will he ever admit that the state has the power to define moral right and wrong.

If he takes up arms to fight in wars, he will not justify his position by saying, "The state commanded it," for he will know that no state can be the God of his conscience. He will seriously question whether war is not the breeder of the totalitarian spirit rather than its Nemesis. At all events, he will refuse to divide life into two parts, allocating one part to God and another to Caesar as though these were equals. He will know that the claims of God are totalitarian and absolute and that every right of Caesar is limited and defined by the righteous will of God. The divine origin of the state is also its divine limitation. By such precautions Christians will see the totalitarian man arising afar off, and will run to meet him and undo him before he gathers strength.

But political freedom is not an end in itself, it is only an opportunity. Political freedom merely secures the flanks of the Christian movement while the church itself grapples with the problems of justice and order. Justice and order are as important to society as freedom is. All three are necessary, synthesized in proper proportions. But if we are to be concerned with these, we must rebuild the sense of moral responsibility in the hearts of our citizens. And this leads us to the second area which the church must strengthen—the area of personal moral responsibility.

Our modern world has a wonderful solution for the problem of individual responsibility; it denies its existence. No one is ever at fault; the blame lies elsewhere. The guilt is society's and therefore nobody's. Blame can be traced to our economic system, or to bad plumbing, or to a defective school system, or to an inadequate home situation, but never to individuals. Individuals are more to be pitied than to be blamed. They are victims of poverty, or bad companions, or of a traumatic experience at birth, or the sinister powers of the unconscious, over which they have no control. And we sum it all up by saying, To know all is to forgive all. This is to say, if we really knew *all* the factors that enter into a man's life, no one would ever be blamable. A man is tumbling tumbleweed, blown helplessly about by every wind of influence. Whatever other failures may be his, modern theories of human behavior have been startlingly successful in undermining the sense of personal responsibility and in giving to modern man an easy conscience. Moral buck-passing is our favorite sport. In the words of Archibald MacLeish, we are refugees from consequences, exiles from the responsibilities of moral choice. And the result is just what may be expected.

Listen to Martin Niemöller as he comments upon the situation in his own country: "Nobody," writes Niemöller, "wants to take the responsibility of the guilt, no one of our German people is guilty, everybody shoves the guilt over to his neighbor. The local official says: I am only a little man, the whole guilt lies with you, Herr local commander; and he in turn says: I did not wrong anybody; I only obeyed orders. The whole guilt lies with you, you of the Gestapo, but the latter doesn't want it either and finally everything lands on Himmler and Hitler."

Let no one think that this problem is peculiar to Germany. This attitude is the prevailing one everywhere. Negatively, there is no guilt; positively there is no responsibility for improvement. Let others assume responsibility—the state, the rich, my neighbor. It is nothing to me. Pilate's hand-washing is repeated on a global scale.

But Christians know that the effort to dodge personal responsibility is illusory. Before God every man is guilty; and before God every man is responsible both for doing those things that he should not have done and for neglecting those things that he should have done. Indeed, guilt and responsibility can only be individual, ultimately. It is the man who is personally addressed by God who must personally answer for the sins done in the body. The Christian gospel is a highly individualized and individualistic thing. Committees cannot be convicted of sin; nations cannot repent. The "whosoever" of the gospel is a single person.

It is because the Christian church understands all this that it and it alone can reawaken in the hearts of men the sense of personal moral responsibility. We are not the puppets of fate or the victims of vast impersonal forces beyond human control. Man is endowed with the creative freedom of his Maker. He is free to take a hand in determining his own destiny, either for good or evil. And whether saint or sinner, he remains accountable.

Political freedom is necessary, but not sufficient. To it must be added the sense of moral responsibility. But even this is not enough. The freedom of man is not secure until he is free in the liberty of the sons of God. Until the conscience of man is washed and renewed in the mercies of Christ, it is not safe, saved. This is the church's supreme privilege in this as in every age: to point the way to spiritual freedom, to lay the foundations of that liberty which is found in Christ. The modern world is in revolt against a doctrine of liberty which has dominated the western mind since the Renaissance. The revolt was not surprising for the Renaissance view of freedom was false and misleading. We are now forced to rethink the true meaning of personal freedom.

There are two kinds of freedom. The one is the freedom of uprootedness, the freedom of a tree which, pulled up from the confining soil, lies proudly emancipated upon the surface of the ground. It is free all right—free to die. The other kind of freedom might be called the freedom of proper functioning. It is the freedom of the tree which, securely planted in the soil, lets down its roots and lifts its leaves to the sunshine that it might grow and express itself in the liberty of its nature. In our confusion of terms, both trees are called free; but their freedoms are exact opposites. The uprooted tree is free in the freedom of death; the planted tree is free in the freedom of life.

For human beings, too, there is a freedom of uprootedness and a freedom of proper functioning. And if a man mistakes the one for the other only disaster can result. The freedom of uprootedness is the freedom of the man who, emancipated from God and the good, is at liberty to run his own life anyway he wants to. This is the freedom which the western world has most prized. It is the false freedom of sin and it can only issue in death. For man, in being emancipated from God is also emancipated from his true self. Cut off from the elemental energies of life, the uprooted man is fated to wander through deserts of frustration, loneliness, insecurity and meaninglessness. His freedom becomes an intolerable burden to him of which he would be gladly rid. He becomes an easy prey to the dictator who promises him meaning and security if he will but submerge himself in the group and submit to the discipline of the party. The liberty of uprootedness ends in the bondage of the totalitarian state.

But there is another freedom, the freedom of proper functioning. The man that knows this freedom is like a tree planted by the rivers of water, which bringeth forth his fruit in his season. This is the freedom which Jesus Christ died to give; and if the Son shall make you free ye shall be free indeed. Those who possess this freedom are rooted deeply in the love of God and, drawing sustenance from that love, grow and fulfill themselves to the full measure of their nature. This is the freedom of life and not death; the gift of God to every man who believeth. Planted in the love of God, he finds both the meaning and the security of life.

Here is the urgency for the preaching of the gospel. Only when the conscience of man is under the Lordship of Christ is it safe against the pressures of evil. It is a fact worth pondering that the main resistance to the totalitarian evil has come not from the universities and not from the corporations and not from the trade unions, but from the churches. Those who have been bought with a price can never be servants of men.

The Niemöllers, the Berggravs, the Verniers, and all the nameless heroes that follow in their train, cannot prostrate themselves before the dictator because they have already kneeled before the Crucified. They cannot be broken by men because they have already been broken by God. These are they, who in their day and generation, exemplify the spirit of Samuel Davies, the simple preacher of the gospel who rebuked a king. Seeing King George the Second of England whisper, the young man, still in his twenties, paused and addressed himself to the monarch in these words: "When the lion roars the beasts of the field keep silence, for he is king. When King Jesus speaks the kings of the earth keep silence."

Berdyaev once wrote, ". . . the time is coming, indeed it has already come, when freedom will be found only in Christianity, when the Church of Christ will defend the freedom of man against the violence of the kingdom of this world." This is the calling to which God has called us in our day. Let us not falter. "There is a foe! There is a fight." But, thank God, there is more. "There is a victory!"

VI
HYMNS AND PRAYERS

———◦❦◦———

JOHN BUNYAN (1628-1688)

This seventeenth-century Baptist preacher, while confined in Bedford Gaol, wrote verses which had such lyrical qualities as to become hymns for general worship. In addition to the hymn below, John Bunyan wrote "The Shepherd Boy's Song in the Valley of Humiliation."

"He Who Would Valiant Be"

He who would valiant be
'Gainst all disaster,
Let him in constancy
Follow the Master.
There's no discouragement
Shall make him once relent
His first avowed intent
To be a pilgrim.

Who so beset him round
With dismal stories,
Do but themselves confound—
His strength the more is.

No foes shall stay his might;
Though he with giants fight,
He will make good his right
To be a pilgrim.

Since, Lord, thou dost defend
Us with thy Spirit,
We know we at the end
Shall life inherit.
Then, fancies, flee away!
I'll fear not what men say,
I'll labor night and day
To be a pilgrim.

ROBERT ROBINSON (1735-1790)

Robert Robinson was converted while listening to a sermon by Whitefield in 1755. From 1761 until his death he served as minister at Cambridge. He was eccentric but was broad in his sympathies.

"Come Thou Fount"

Come, thou fount of every blessing,
Tune my heart to sing thy grace;
Streams of mercy never ceasing,
Call for sounds of loudest praise:
Teach me some melodious sonnet,
Sung by flaming tongues above;
Praise the mount, O fix me on it,
Mount of God's unchanging love.

Here I raise my Ebenezer;
Hither by thy help I'm come
And I hope, by thy good pleasure,
Safely to arrive at home.
Jesus sought me when a stranger,
Wandering from the fold of God;
He to save my soul from danger,
Interposed his precious blood.

O to grace how great a debtor
Daily I'm constrained to be!
Let that grace, Lord, like a fetter,
Bind my wandering heart to thee.
Prone to wander, Lord, I feel it;
Prone to leave the God I love;
Here's my heart; Lord, take and seal it;
Seal it from thy courts above.

O that day when freed from sinning,
I shall see thy lovely face!
Richly cloth'd in blood-wash'd linen,
How I'll sing thy sov'reign grace!
Come, dear Lord, no longer tarry,
Take my raptur'd soul away;
Send the angels down to carry
Me to realms of endless day.

SAMUEL MEDLEY (1738-1799)

*Born of a tutor and schoolmaster, Samuel Medley received a
sound education. Later he responded to a call to the ministry*

*and to serve in Liverpool. Here he had his own hymns printed
and distributed as leaflets to the congregation. His two best
known hymns are the one below and "Awake, My Soul, in Joyful Lays."*

"O Could I Speak the Matchless Worth"

O could I speak the matchless worth,
O could I sound the glories forth
Which in my Saviour shine!
I'd soar and touch the heavenly strings,
And view with Gabriel while he sings
In notes almost divine.

I'd sing the precious blood he spilt,
My ransom from the dreadful guilt
Of sin and wrath divine!
I'd sing his glorious righteousness,
In which all-perfect, heavenly dress
My soul shall ever shine.

I'd sing the characters he bears,
And all the forms of love he wears,
Exalted on his throne:
In loftiest songs of sweetest praise,
I would to everlasting days,
Make all his glories known.

Well, the delightful day will come
When my dear Lord will bring me home,
And I shall see his face;
Then with my Saviour, Brother, Friend,
A blest eternity I'll spend,
Triumphant in his grace.

JOHN FAWCETT (1739-1817)

At the age of sixteen John Fawcett was converted upon hearing a sermon by Whitefield. His church at Bradford, Yorkshire, sent him forth to preach at Wainsgate and Hebden Bridge. Renowned for his character and learning, he was invited to be principal of Bristol College but he declined. His desire to promote efficient training for ministers, however, later led him to establish the Northern Education Society, known now as Rawdon College. He is best known by the verses below.

"Blest Be the Tie that Binds"

Blest be the tie that binds
Our hearts in Christian love;
The fellowship of kindred minds
Is like to that above.

Before our Father's throne
We pour our ardent prayers;
Our fears, our hopes, our aims are one,
Our comforts and our cares.

We share our mutual woes;
Our mutual burdens bear;
And often for each other flows
The sympathizing tear.

When we asunder part,
It gives us inward pain;
But we shall still be joined in heart,
And hope to meet again.

This glorious hope revives
Our courage by the way;
While each in expectation lives,
And longs to see the day.

From sorrow, toil and pain,
And sin, we shall be free;
And perfect love and friendship reign
Through all eternity.

ROBERT KEEN (eighteenth century)

In 1886, H. L. Hastings settled the question of the authorship of this hymn, pointing out that George Keith did not write it. The author, Robert Keen, was precentor at Carter Lane Chapel from 1776 to 1793. He was also manager of the Particular Baptist Fund, and he was a friend of Whitefield who appointed him as trustee of his tabernacles on Moorfields.

"How Firm a Foundation"

How firm a foundation, ye saints of the Lord,
Is laid for your faith in his excellent word;
What more can he say than to you he hath said?
You, who unto Jesus for refuge have fled.

In every condition, in sickness, in health,
In poverty's vale, or abounding in wealth;
At home and abroad, on the land, on the sea,
"As thy days may demand, shall thy strength ever be.

"Fear not, I am with thee, O be not dismayed,
I, I am thy God, and will still give thee aid;
I'll strengthen thee, help thee, and cause thee to stand,
Upheld by my righteous, omnipotent hand.

"When thro' the deep waters I call thee to go,
The rivers of woe shall not thee overflow;
For I will be with thee, thy troubles to bless,
And sanctify to thee thy deepest distress.

"When thro' fiery trials thy pathway shall lie,
My grace all sufficient shall be thy supply;
This flame shall not hurt thee, I only design
Thy dross to consume, and thy gold to refine.

"Even down to old age, all my people shall prove
My sovereign, eternal, unchangeable love;
And when hoary hairs shall their temples adorn,
Like lambs they shall still in my bosom be borne.

"The soul that on Jesus hath leaned for repose,
I will not, I will not, desert to his foes;
That soul, though all hell should endeavor to shake,
I'll never—no never—no never forsake."

SAMUEL F. SMITH (1808-1895)

Samuel F. Smith's fame rests chiefly upon his authorship of the patriotic hymn which is said to have been written in less than a half hour on February 2, 1832, and first sung on July 4, 1832, at Park Street Church, Boston. He is also known for his missionary hymn "The Morning Light Is Breaking," written in 1832 while he was a student in Phillips Andover Academy. He was a class-

mate of Oliver Wendell Holmes. In addition to being a Baptist pastor in Massachusetts, he became professor of modern languages at Colby College, and he edited several magazines.

"My Country, 'Tis of Thee"

My country, 'tis of thee,
Sweet land of liberty,
Of thee I sing:
Land where my fathers died!
Land of the Pilgrim's pride!
From every mountain side
Let freedom ring!

My native country, thee,
Land of the noble free,
Thy name I love;
I love thy rocks and rills,
Thy woods and templed hills;
My heart with rapture thrills,
Like that above.

Let music swell the breeze,
And ring from all the trees
Sweet freedom's song:
Let mortal tongues awake;
Let all that breathe partake;
Let rocks their silence break,—
The sound prolong.

Our Fathers' God, to thee,
Author of liberty,
To thee we sing;
Long may our land be bright
With freedom's holy light;
Protect us by thy might,
Great God, our King.

BASIL MANLY (1825-1892)

Attending Newton Theological Institution and Princeton Theological Seminary, Basil Manly later held pastorates in Alabama and Mississippi and at the First Baptist Church of Richmond, Virginia. He established the Richmond Female Institute and became principal. He was twice professor in the Southern Baptist Theological Seminary (Greenville and Louisville), and served as president of Georgetown College in Kentucky. Being the author of approximately forty hymns, he was requested to write the hymn below for the first commencement of the Southern Baptist Theological Seminary at Greenville in 1860, and this hymn has been sung at every commencement since, as the seminary hymn.

"Soldiers of Christ"

Soldiers of Christ, in truth arrayed,
A world in ruins needs your aid,
A world by sin destroyed and dead,
A world for which the Saviour bled.

His gospel to the lost proclaim,
Good news to all in Jesus' name;
Let light upon the darkness break,
That sinners from their death may wake.

Morning and evening sow the seed,
God's grace the effort shall succeed.
Seedtimes of tears have oft been found
With sheaves of joy and plenty crowned.

We meet to part, but part to meet,
When earthly labors are complete,
To join in yet more blest employ
In an eternal world of joy.

BAYLUS BENJAMIN MC KINNEY (1886-1952)

A man of the people, B. B. McKinney rose from the logging camps of Louisiana to become professor of music at Southwestern Baptist Theological Seminary and later the first secretary of the Department of Church Music of the Southern Baptist Sunday School Board. He never lost the common touch and throughout his career found his highest joy in evangelistic singing and gospel hymn-writing. He was involved in the composition of over 250 songs. Among the 149 for which he composed both words and music is the one that follows. McKinney was pleased that it came to be one of the favorites of George W. Truett, for whom he led the singing many times.

"Have Faith in God"

Have faith in God when your pathway is lonely,
He sees and knows all the way you have trod;
Never alone are the least of His children:
Have faith in God, have faith in God.

Have faith in God when your prayers are unanswered,
Your earnest plea He will never forget;
Wait on the Lord, trust His Word and be patient,
Have faith in God, He'll answer yet.

Have faith in God in your pain and your sorrow,
His heart is touched with your grief and despair;
Cast all your cares and your burdens upon Him,
And leave them there, oh, leave them there.

Have faith in God though all else fail about you;
Have faith in God, He provides for His own;
He cannot fail though all kingdoms shall perish,
He rules, He reigns upon His throne.

(Refrain):

Have faith in God, He's on His throne;
Have faith in God, He watches o'er His own;
He cannot fail, He must prevail;
Have faith in God, have faith in God.

PHILIP PAUL BLISS (1838-1876)

Though born to Methodist parents, Philip P. Bliss joined a Baptist church in Pennsylvania when only twelve years of age. His tragically short life was devoted to gospel music. As an evangelistic singer and song writer, he became widely known. When he was only thirty-eight years of age, he and his wife lost their lives in a train wreck.

"Man of Sorrows"

"Man of sorrows," what a name
For the Son of God who came
Ruined sinners to reclaim!
Hallelujah! what a Saviour!

Bearing shame and scoffing rude,
In my place condemned He stood,
Seal'd my pardon with His blood;
Hallelujah! what a Saviour!

Lifted up was He to die,
"It is finished," was His cry,
Now in heav'n exalted high,
Hallelujah! what a Saviour!

When He comes, our glorious King,
All His ransomed home to bring,
Then anew this song we'll sing,
Hallelujah! what a Saviour!

SAMUEL H. MILLER (1900-   )

More and more Baptists are finding deep satisfaction in public and private worship through prayer helps. Samuel H. Miller's book is recent and helpful. He is minister of Old Cambridge Baptist Church in Cambridge, Massachusetts, adjunct professor of philosophy of religion at Andover-Newton Theological School and lecturer in pastoral theology at Harvard Divinity School.

Two Prayers

O God of ancient prophets and holy martyrs, pour out thy spirit upon us in this new day, that once again in the hour of our need we may dream dreams and see visions. Drop the plumbline of thy justice beside every wall we have built; weigh in the balances of thy truth all the accomplishments of our skill and science; test with thy consuming fire the permanent worth of our industry and art. If the earth be shaken, and the foundations tremble, grant us courage to look beyond the ruins to that which has not fallen. If judgment falls, and the hollow vanity of much that passed for the substance of life is revealed as nothing, steady us until we lift up our eyes unto thee, and know that our hope is in thee, both now and forever. In the name of him who was steadfast against death and sin, we pray for our own perseverance in all good works. Amen.

. . . . .

Eternal Father, when we think of all who counted it not unwise to labor and love beyond all that was asked or expected of them, we grow conscious of the shamefulness of our own meager, careful way of doing good. We are humbled by the memory of men and women whose work made the world in which we live; of those whose tired hands and wearied hearts have carried on in faithfulness; of those handicapped but courageous, desperate but undaunted, mistreated but magnanimous; of all who have cast aside the cautious bookkeeping by which benevolence is scrimped to a profitable venture, and out of their generous faith created wide margins of confidence and freedom for the lives of others. Keep alive in us the faith of those who trusted us and grant us grace so to exercise it that it may be the liberation of souls now held in bondage of fear and embarrassment. Amen.

THE BAPTIST TRADITION

An Arno Press Collection

Lambert, Byron C., **The Rise of the Anti-Mission Baptists** (Doctoral Dissertation, University of Chicago, 1957). 1980

Lewis, James K, **Religious Life of Fugitive Slaves and Rise of the Coloured Baptist Churches, 1820-1865, in what is now Ontario** (Bachelor of Divinity Thesis, McMaster Divinity College, 1965). 1980

McBeth, H. Leon, **English Baptist Literature on Religious Liberty to 1689** (Doctoral Dissertation, Southwestern Baptist Theological Seminary, 1961). 1980

Macintosh, Douglas C., **Theology as an Empirical Science.** 1919

McKibbens, Thomas R., Jr., and Kenneth L. Smith, **The Life and Works of Morgan Edwards.** 1980

Morris, Elias Camp, **Sermons, Addresses and Reminiscences and Important Correspondence, with a Picture Gallery of Eminent Ministers and Scholars.** 1901

Olson, Adolf, **A Centenary History as Related to the Baptist General Conference of America.** 1952

Pitman, Walter G., **The Baptists and Public Affairs in the Province of Canada, 1840-1867** (M.A. Thesis, University of Toronto, 1957). 1980

Powell, Adam Clayton, Sr., **Against the Tide.** 1938

Purefoy, George W., **A History of the Sandy Creek Baptist Association, from Its Organization in A.D. 1758, to A.D. 1858.** 1859

Seventh Day Baptist General Conference, **Seventh Day Baptists in Europe and America.** Two volumes. 1910

Shurden, Walter B., **Associationalism Among Baptists in America, 1707-1814** (Doctoral Dissertation, New Orleans Baptist Theological Seminary, 1967). 1980

Smith, Elias, **The Life, Conversion, Preaching, Travels, and Sufferings of Elias Smith.** 1816

Stealey, Sydnor L., ed., **A Baptist Treasury.** 1958

Stiansen, P., **History of the Norwegian Baptists in America.** 1939

Taylor, John, **A History of Ten Baptist Churches.** 1827

Tull, James E., **A History of Southern Baptist Landmarkism in the Light of Historical Baptist Ecclesiology** (Doctoral Dissertation, Columbia University, 1960). 1980

Valentine, Foy D., **A Historical Study of Southern Baptists and Race Relations 1917-1947** (Doctoral Dissertation, Southwestern Baptist Tehological Seminary, 1949). 1980

Wayland, Francis, **Notes on the Principles and Practices of Baptist Churches.** 1857

Whitsitt, William H., **A Question in Baptist History.** 1896

Wood, Nathan E., **History of the First Baptist Church of Boston (1665-1899).** 1899